PARENTING *with* PRIDE
Latino Style

also by CARMEN INOA VAZQUEZ

The Maria Paradox: How Latinas Can Merge Old World Traditions
with New World Self-Esteem
(with Rosa Maria Gil)

PARENTING with PRIDE

Latino Style

How to Help Your Child Cherish Your Cultural Values and Succeed in Today's World

CARMEN INOA VAZQUEZ, PH.D.

rayo

An Imprint of HarperCollinsPublishers

This book is written as a source of information only. The information contained in this book should by no means be considered a substitute for the advice, decisions, or judgment of the reader's physician or other professional advisor.

All efforts have been made to ensure the accuracy of the information contained in this book as of the date published. The author and the publisher expressly disclaim responsibility for any adverse effects arising from the use or application of the information contained herein.

The names and identifying characteristics of parents and children featured throughout this book have been changed to protect their privacy.

PARENTING WITH PRIDE—LATINO STYLE. Copyright © 2004 by Carmen Inoa Vazquez, Ph.D. All rights reserved. Printed in the United States of America. No part of this book may be used or reproduced in any manner whatsoever without written permission except in the case of brief quotations embodied in critical articles and reviews. For information, address HarperCollins Publishers Inc., 10 East 53rd Street, New York, NY 10022.

HarperCollins books may be purchased for educational, business, or sales promotional use. For information, please write: Special Markets Department, Harper-Collins Publishers Inc., 10 East 53rd Street, New York, NY 10022.

FIRST EDITION

Designed by Fearn Cutler de Vicq

Printed on acid-free paper

Library of Congress Cataloging-in-Publication Data
Vazquez, Carmen Inoa.
Parenting with pride—Latino style / Carmen Inoa Vazquez.
p.   cm.
Includes bibliographical references and index.
ISBN 0-06-054301-9
1. Child rearing—United States.   2. Hispanic American children.
3. Hispanic American parents.   4. Parenting—United States.   I. Title.
HQ769.V37   2004
649'.1—dc22   2003067575

04 05 06 07 08 DIX/QW 10 9 8 7 6 5 4 3 2 1

To all the Latino parents who taught me by sharing their own experiences.
To my husband, Martin, who gave me love and support throughout this project and always.
To my children, Jaime, Miguel, and Oriana, the best teachers of all.

Acknowledgments

Help came from many sources in writing this book. I thank all the Latino parents who have trusted me to help them to raise their children in a balanced cultural manner in the course of my work with them as a clinician.

I feel privileged to have been able to interview Latino parents who are also psychologists and who have a firsthand understanding of the intricacies, strengths, and struggles of parenting a Latino child in the United States. I thank these parents and colleagues for being so generous with their time and for their willingness to be interviewed.

A very special mention to Carolyn Fireside, who again became a full-fledged Latina to support this project with sensitivity and wisdom. Carolyn, your enthusiasm throughout preparation of this book will always be appreciated. Thank you for your dedication, ideas, and advice, and for believing in me. I feel so lucky to count you among my supporters.

I am deeply appreciative of the interest and support of the following friends and colleagues who offered ideas and resources and shared their very rich personal experience:

Yvette Caro, Ph.D., my dearest friend and colleague, you gave so much to this book in your generous and always supportive way; thank you. I am also very grateful to Josie Diaz, Ph.D., Alejandra Morales, Psy.D., Ilena Rodriguez, Ph.D., Joan Bello, Ph.D., Eduvijis Cruz-Arrieta, Ph.D., Dinelia Rosa, Ph.D., Myriam Velez, Ph.D., Cynthia de Jesus, Nereyda Brenner, Ph.D., Fran Melendez, Eugenia Mejias,

Consuelo Melendez, Hepsy Caban, Marjorie Silverman, Elena Avila, Ema Genijovich, and Rosa Gil, D.S.W.

I am very thankful for the love and support of my nuclear and extended family for tolerating the long hours of work required by this project, which took me away from sharing their love.

I also had the fortune to be supported, advised, guided, and nurtured by many friends—too many to mention, but you know who you are. Among these is my literary agent, Barbara Lowenstein, who believes in me and my work and who has guided me with her marvelous experience. Thank you also to her work partner, Madeleine Morel. Thank you, Jim Freund, for your helpful technical support and for being there whenever I called.

Finally, a very heartfelt thank-you to Toni Sciarra, my editor, who not only believed in this book but dedicated an enormous number of hours to its thorough review. She has guided me not only with superb editing skills but with so much grace, always being pleasant while helping this book to become a reality. Toni, thank you for being there; your help was invaluable. It has been a pleasure working with you.

Contents

I Understand What You're Going Through—I've Been There

Let me introduce myself. I'm a Latina psychologist who for the past twenty years has been helping Latino families, children, and adults with their problems of daily living in North America. I am also the founder of a clinic at Manhattan's Bellevue Hospital where our mission is to help Latinos and to train those clinicians working with them to understand the effects that immigration and acculturation can have on us. Gaining this understanding translates into respect and sensitivity to cultural differences. I am also a first-generation Latina who is the mother of two fine, bilingual/bicultural young men.

When I was only sixteen, I came to this country from the Dominican Republic with my mother, who espoused traditional Latino values. My father and brother were not allowed to leave (in those days, the rules of the dictator Trujillo were that landowners and doctors were needed in the country). In the course of adjusting to my new country, I went through the acculturation process and gained a first-hand understanding of its challenges. Not only did I have to learn English, but I had to grow up fast and master the North American social and cultural system.

When I was twenty-three years old I fell in love with and married a wonderful Puerto Rican man in New York City, where I have lived ever since. I became a devoted Latina wife and mother while working, attending college, and earning a graduate degree in philosophy, specializing in clinical psychology. I can honestly tell you that during this time neither my family nor my career suffered; admittedly, performing successfully in two spheres was a constant challenge, requiring a great deal of cultural prioritizing, flexibility, and ability to handle the many doubts an acculturating Latina-American mother faces. I raised my two sons in the hope that they would grow up bicultural. I'm proud to say they have.

I also became a widow, and instantaneously a single mom and a professional woman. Years later, I met and fell in love with a caring and lovely North American man who is now my husband. This also presented new challenges for my traditional Latino side, catapulting my family into an unfamiliar situation that required adjustments for all of us and an integration of new and old values.

Of course, I am not unique. I am only one of the many of us who have had to adjust to a new world that included different values and language. I love my two countries and my two cultures. Just like many of you, I am living proof that balancing cultures and languages not only is possible but can be a wonderfully rich experience.

My own story provided me with an understanding of what it takes to be able to function in two cultures with two different sets of values that at times may collide with each other. My experience as a mother and as a professional continues to give me an understanding of how it feels to walk in those shoes and what can be done to make the process easier.

I would be the last person to tell you that finding a balance between Old World values and New World standards is easy. But I strongly feel that it is possible, because I understand what you are feeling—I've been there.

I hope that *Parenting with Pride—Latino Style,* written from my experience as a psychologist, a mother, and a Latina, will serve as a bridge between the world of our grandparents and that of our grandchildren.

New Traditions for New Life

There's never been a better time to be Latino in North America. We are now the largest minority in North America, comprising 13.4 percent of the population. Not only are we growing in numbers, we are also growing in status. From the world of entertainment (think of crossover pop music icons such as Marc Anthony and multimedia megastars such as Jennifer Lopez) to the front offices of major corporations (the Spanish-language media conglomerate Univision, for example, and Goya, the Latino food mega-corporation), we're here! Now that the tortilla chip has replaced the potato chip as North America's favorite snack food and advertisers have actively begun to target us, North American culture is telling us we have a lot to be proud of. Not that pride is a new concept for us—quite the contrary.

Pride—*orgullo*—is one of the most treasured of all traditional Latino values. *Orgullo* does not connote pride in the sense of arrogance, but as personal dignity and self-respect—achieved and maintained by behaving according to social rules validated by centuries of tradition. *Orgullo* is the means by which we pay homage to our birthright.

Since passing these rules to the next generation is all-important to us, *orgullo* plays an especially crucial role in child rearing: for many Latinos, their *orgullo* is affirmed by raising children who are *bien educados* (well educated), *simpaticos* (respectful of others), *amable* and *trabajadores* (polite, gentle, kind, and diligent), reflecting what a good parenting job they have done by ensuring that their ancestors' values will live on in their descendants.

On the other hand, when a Latino child does not seem to be well educated, respectful of others, or hardworking, parents are frequently forced to ask themselves: "Where did *I* go wrong?" Being considered "a bad parent" by others or by yourself carries with it an enormous amount of guilt, even shame, which of course erodes *orgullo*. Still, North American parents, too, spend sleepless nights agonizing over whether or not they're doing an adequate job with their kids. So what's so unique about us?

The Heart of the Dilemma

A colleague recently asked me that very question, although he phrased it differently: he wanted to know, "What is the difference between raising a Latino child and a non-Latino child in the United States *today?*"

My answer is that strains in Latino parent-child relations, which are considered manageable in the native country because of the parents' absolute authority, become magnified and can get out of control in a different, North American context. In short, given the two radically different cultures to which Latino children are exposed here and with which mothers and fathers must cope, the chances of being "a bad parent"—one who isn't getting the traditional cultural message across—increase dramatically.

Being a Latino parent in this country is one tough job: if you are too permissive with your child, for instance, letting him go out for pizza after school with his friends, even though you aren't comfortable with his choice of companions, you're allowing *him* to dictate the rules. And giving the child power over the parent is, according to traditional wisdom, an invitation to disaster. If you err in the other direction and insist on governing by the old rules of complete authority, your child will be receiving conflicting cultural signals—one sent in the home, the other in school—which can cause problems with self-esteem, communication, and discipline. Caught between a rock and a hard place, what are you as a Latino parent to do?

First and foremost, it is essential for Latino parents in the United States—and for their relatives and children—to understand and accept the fact that the rules have changed. If you want "a piece of the American pie" for you and your sons and daughters, you *must* adjust.

Balancing Act

Cultural adjustment—what we professionals call *acculturation*—is similar in significance to the loss of a significant person in one's life and is experienced as a form of mourning. In fact, most research on the relationship between acculturation and child rearing indicates an "urgency" or an "immediacy" in parent-child communication during this transitional time. This is often due to a perception on the part of parents and family elders that acculturation signifies surrender of traditional authority, which will tear asunder the social fabric of their lives and lead to moral chaos. Faced with that unthinkable possibility, many mothers, fathers, and grandparents revert to the autocratic dictates of "the old school": attacks on the new culture and an emphasis on proving "our superiority" at all costs. It is the children who pay the price.

Raising modern Latino children in North America is not a simple matter of enforcing absolute, inflexible rules from the past. Despite the pressures to preserve the past, can we do what it takes to make our children culturally flexible? Absolutely! That is the goal of this book, and it has been the essence of my work as a psychotherapist with Latino families for the past twenty years. What I have come to see is that acculturation is a matter of balancing the demands and desires of different generations within the family and among the children.

Satisfying several generations is a challenging task. As an experienced therapist, I know that for a family to function smoothly, cultural currents and crosscurrents must be dealt with in a communal context. In my practice, I am always careful to be sensitive to the necessity of including the voices of *all* family members—the parents, the extended family, and of course the children—in establishing child-rearing guidelines.

I have always loved being a therapist and am devoted to every one of my clients, while appreciating that the number of people I can help is limited to the number of hours in the day. I am writing this book because I want to reach out to you Latino parents who can't come to see me in my office. I want to share with you that we can strike a balance between cultures, helping our children thrive in North American society without becoming totally assimilated and discarding their Latino heritage. But we can only do this if we are not unconsciously dominated by the past.

My own upbringing, as I mentioned, was according to the old ways: when we visited friends and I was offered a *refresco,* a sweet drink, *my mother* would decide whether or not I wanted it. She did so with the best of intentions, and I never doubted her love. Still, that was not the way I wanted to bring up my own children, Jaime and Miguel, in North America. I felt strongly that enforcing absolute *obediencia*—in which children cede their individuality to their parents and grandparents—simply would not work here. Not for a minute did I feel that my boys should be given free rein to do whatever they wanted. If their actions were unconstructive, I saw it as my duty to act. But I was—and still am—convinced that in today's world, demanding absolute *obediencia* may well produce the opposite of its desired effect: rebelliousness.

Parenting with Pride: *El Nuevo Tradicionalismo*

Children will do what you want only if their own thoughts and feelings are taken seriously; that way, they'll learn to feel responsible for their actions and know that if they really step out of line, they're going to have to face the consequences. We can raise well-adjusted Latino-American children if we revise the ways we relate to them following what I call *El Nuevo Tradicionalismo* of *Parenting With Pride,* my intercultural approach to child rearing.

The gist of parenting with pride is simply this: applying a fresh, more open, and relaxed child-rearing system or *El Nuevo Tradicionalismo* to the process of teaching children our cultural values. Following its precepts will help you instill traditional values such as *respeto, familismo, simpatia, obediencia,* and being *bien educados* through an updated method of open communication between parent and child.

Here are some "trouble spots" parents may confront in the course of a typical day, and how my intercultural approach to child rearing helps to make you aware that they are *intercultural* problems—which is the first step in resolving them:

Your eleven-year-old daughter wants to go to school wearing a particular sweater that you do not feel is appropriate. Rather than simply forbid her to wear it, try to grasp why she wants to do so. This will foster the habit of good communication, always useful to practice when the issue at hand is not a matter of life and death. Without it, you will risk having constant battles and a very unhappy child. It is important to know when it is worthwhile to demand obedience and when to let go.

On the first day of school, your five-year-old sees you plastered to the school window, unable to go home—even when all the other mothers have left and the teacher says, "It is okay to go, Señora." Seeing your anxiety fosters unrealistic fears in your child. She will sense your anguish, know something is wrong, and feel responsible for it.

If you feel that you have to solve all of your son's problems without letting him try to do so on his own, your child may get the message not that you love and want to protect him but that he is incompetent or that you don't trust his common sense.

Bridging the Past and the Future—with *Orgullo*

I hope that reading *Parenting with Pride—Latino Style* will feel like having a chat between friends who feel secure enough with each other to bare their souls. It will help parents and caregivers involved in the teaching of Latino children to feel the satisfaction that they are doing what's best for their children by integrating two cultures. And it will help them to become better, more effective caregivers, secure in their *orgullo* as well as their rightful place in North American life.

Through self-awareness quizzes, step-by-step crisis-management exercises, and illustrative case studies, I'll help you create a harmonious balance between the seemingly conflicting cultural messages you face daily as you bring up your children. These techniques will give the perspective to select those aspects of Latino culture you will always honor—such as *respeto, orgullo, familismo,* and *simpatía*—and dispense with those that have become counterproductive.

Parenting with Pride—Latino Style doesn't guarantee instant parenting success. What it does promise is that you will discover what worked in my own experience as a parent and as a professional who counsels many Latino parents. Mothers and fathers will learn that there is not one single way to parent; there are, in fact, always a number of positive options from which to select, all of which will be thoroughly covered in this book.

Parenting with Pride: The Roadmap

I have divided this book into two sections:

In Part One, I will guide you through the process of redefining those aspects of parenting within the Latino culture that we want to retain in a modern form—starting with *orgullo,* then moving on to the primary cultural practices that comprise it: *respeto, familismo, simpatia,* and *obediencia.* You will be able to see differences between the old and the new way of raising your child. Understanding these differences will help you to choose what works in bringing up your child Latino style.

Part Two takes a developmental approach, dealing with specific problems that may be expected to appear as the child progresses from infancy through adolescence, including the child's world at home, at school, and in the community, with friends, relatives, neighbors, teammates, and others in the child's life. Issues range from bilingualism to dating, from corporal punishment to peer pressure.

Part Two ends with a look at those problems your child and your family may be experiencing that are intertwined with adjustment to a new culture. You will see the relationship between culture and some of these problems, and I'll provide some guidelines for knowing when you may need to seek professional help. These safeguards will inform you by developmental stages on what to look for in your child's behavior that may be cause for concern—as well as when a family crisis mandates professional guidance. I'll also describe exactly how to choose the most effective counseling to resolve your dilemma.

Each of the first five chapters begins with a series of relevant questions to help you discover your level of traditionalism, as well as problem areas you may need to work on. At the conclusion of each of these chapters, you will be offered a series of contemplations called *las reflexiones.* You may find it valuable to write down your responses and use them as the basis for a journal or diary: by self-testing every so often, you will gain a clearer sense of personal change and progress.

Taken as a whole, *Parenting with Pride—Latino Style* is your road map to the superhighway of child rearing within *El Nuevo Tradicionalismo*—because it offers the first and only bicultural child-rearing system designed to ensure that pride in *tradicion Latina* will be passed on to our children and our children's children—in a time-honored yet thoroughly modern way.

You will note that I alternately use "he" and "she" throughout the book. This is intentional in order not to give priority to one gender over the other.

The New Traditionalism
(El Nuevo Tradicionalismo)

In Part One, I will guide you through the process of re-defining those aspects of parenting within the Latino culture that we want to retain in a modern form—starting with *orgullo,* then moving on to the primary cultural practices that comprise it: *respeto, familismo, simpatia,* and *obediencia.* You will be able to see differences between the old and the new way of raising your child. Understanding these differences will help you to choose what works in bringing up your child Latino style.

CHAPTER 1

Parenting with Pride—Latino Style: The New O.R.G.U.L.L.O.

Select the number for each question below that best describes your personal attitude; then add all the numbers to calculate your total score.

5=Always 4=Frequently 3=Sometimes 2=Rarely 1=Never

1. Do you find yourself at odds with the way your child is communicating with you? _____

2. Do you find yourself saying to your daughter, "You are not going to do that because I say so"? _____

3. Do you feel trapped between your parents or in-laws and your children in a no-win situation? _____

4. Do you find yourself doing things for your children that non-Latino parents do not do and feeling bad about it? For example, chaperoning *every* party your daughter attends. _____

5. Do you find yourself automatically saying and doing things your parents and grandparents did, although you feel you now know a better way? _____

6. Do your children keep telling you, "You don't understand! You're too old-fashioned!" _____

7. Do you feel it is your child who must understand your point of view, not the other way around? _____

8. Are you often told by others that you demand too much obedience from your children? _____

Use the following scoring format for self-assessment, in this and the chapters that follow: if your total score is 30–40, you are a true *tradicionalista* who could face significant problems with your children; you need to increase your *Nuevo Tradicionalismo* skills.

If you score 20–30, you show signs of potential problems and could benefit greatly from learning the Parenting with Pride techniques.

If you score 10–20, you are already in great shape, but go ahead and read on to hone your skills even more.

~

Mercedes has just delivered her first baby, a boy whom she named Julio. Her mother-in-law, Juana, has come from their country to help out. But Mercedes, instead of being relieved, is feeling extra stressed since the older woman arrived. She does not want to be disrespectful, but Juana is trying her patience severely, believing, as do most women of her generation, that the baby must always wear socks and T-shirts, even in the middle of August. Juana also feels that Mercedes is acting unwisely by taking Julio outside after sunset, which will expose the baby to the *rocio,* the evening dew, which is an invitation to catching a *resfrio,* a cold.

Mercedes and Juana also disagree about whether or not to follow a feeding schedule, as the pediatrician advised. Juana insists that she saw eight healthy children through infancy without following any schedule other than the one dictated by the baby: that is, when the baby cries, he knows he is hungry. Following a regimented schedule is not what Juana sees as being best for the baby, regardless of what the doctor indicated.

The only action that Mercedes can take to avert a family crisis is count the hours until her mother-in-law goes home.

~

How can you take the bottle away from him?" demands Nina's mother, referring to one-and-a-half-year-old Pedrito. Even worse, the *abuela* (grandmother) thinks she is putting one over on her daughter by continuing to give Pedrito the bottle behind Nina's back. Nina feels torn between what her mother considers the right thing to do and what her friends are doing with their babies. When confronted, the *abuela* defends her position by claiming that she brought up five children, including Nina, and never weaned any of them from their bottle at such an early age. In the *abuela*'s world, a Latina mother who takes the bottle away from her child at eighteen months is being unkind to the child.

Old Ways versus New Ways

These examples illustrate how all Latino groups in the United States have brought with them traditions stemming from their country of origin. A Latino child's development often tends to be interpreted in terms of a particular history and culture that dates back many generations. These traditional values must be understood and respected—but so must the contemporary settings in which Latino children are growing up today. Being Latino or Latina is really a state of mind, not necessarily based on the length of time a person or his or her family has lived in the United States. It includes membership in one's group, but also experiences associated with that membership. From this vantage point, to be a Latino or a Latina is a conscious (and at times unconscious) determination of who we want to be, what we esteem, and the importance we place on passing these values on to our children.

Many Latino parents and grandparents have expressed having difficulty letting go of the "way things were." But when we are living in North America, clinging rigidly to these "time-honored" beliefs can cause friction between you and your child. Lack of cultural balance can stir up problems with discipline, communication, and the proper channeling of anger and sadness, all of which may affect your child's self-esteem. Latinos are very clear that they do not want to abandon the many wonderful aspects of traditional values, nor do they want their children to. But given modern times and the need to adapt to the culture of the United States, the best way to ensure that these values are accepted by our children is to make some adjustments in how we translate them in our daily lives.

How do we move beyond the ironclad authority of traditional rules and steer our children toward a more flexible meshing of old and new—so that they can enjoy the best of what both worlds have to offer them? What follows is my redefinition of an Old World tradition—*los consejos,* or words of wisdom. Through them, I share with you techniques I've used successfully with clients to broaden their cultural horizons and raise well-balanced kids. Providing insight on how to change with the times, *los consejos* not only give precise instructions for offering your children the guidance they need but also demonstrate *El Nuevo Tradicionalismo* in action: keeping your values, but recognizing when there must be an adjustment.

Consejos to Develop Your Parental Problem-Solving Skills

Los consejos are a highly prized Latino mode of teaching. With them, our *abuelas* taught our parents how to be respectful, to have pride in our culture, to be always mindful of the importance of the family, and to be considerate to others—to be good *machos* and *marianistas*—which connotes following specific behaviors that determine what it means to be a good man or a good woman, such as bravery in the first case and obedience in the second. But that was then. Now is now. In fact, the one question parents most frequently ask me is, "How do we know which traditional values are good to keep?"

We want our children to be proud to be Latinos, which involves maintaining our traditions, but at the same time, we want them to be successful and resilient—to be citizens of today's world. The most effective approach to this dilemma is accepting that our children, whether or not we choose it for them, are a hybrid of both Latino and North American cultures.

My first technique for helping your sons and daughters achieve cultural balance involves mastering seven steps that correspond to the acronym O.R.G.U.L.L.O. The word *orgullo* has long meant "pride" to Latinos, but I will redefine it according to the precepts of *El Nuevo Tradicionalismo.* The sooner we begin to practice these *consejos,* the sooner our children will learn to function comfortably in their two worlds. When you parent your children with O.R.G.U.L.L.O. cross-cultural problems can be resolved within the climate of family values.

Here then are the seven steps, or golden rules, of the *consejos*:

1. O Organize your feelings
2. R Respect your child's feelings
3. G Guide and teach your child; do not dictate
4. U Update your media awareness often
5. L Love your child for who she or he is
6. L Listen to your child
7. O Open the communication channels—and keep them open

Consejo *No. 1: Organize Your Feelings*

The first *consejo* deals with sorting out and confronting emotions you may not even know you are feeling. In order to understand something, you first must identify what that something is. Identify your feelings. This process is actually very simple. For instance: if you forbid your six-year-old to go to her best friend's house for a play date simply because you cannot be there, have you honestly assessed your rationale for saying no? Be frank and ask yourself whether you are overreacting. After all, a play date is radically different from your child's crossing the street without checking for traffic. In the latter case, you say, "Don't do that. Look both ways first," and then explain the consequences. This is a survival skill you need to instill in your child, and you must be there personally to monitor her until you are satisfied that this habit has been instilled. A play date, on the other hand, is not a life-or-death issue and may not demand your personal supervision, once you determine that there is going to be appropriate supervision by a trustworthy adult.

If your child asks you for an explanation of your behavior, you must be clear on the reasons. Here are questions that will facilitate your ability to face your deepest feelings, always bearing in mind the enormous influence of traditional values on your actions:

- Is there a real safety reason for my concern?
- Is my definition of being a good parent based largely on what my parents or grandparents taught me?
- Am I trying to hold on to the past—sometimes irrationally?
- Why am I so afraid to embrace North American culture?
- Do I feel conflicted at times about my own Latino identity?
- Do I need to feel in control of everything at all times?
- Am I passing my fears to my child?
- What is more important—doing what is good for my child or pleasing my parents?
- Am I afraid of facing my parents' rage or disapproval?
- Am I communicating with my parents or in-laws as an adult, explaining assertively, not angrily?

After you have answered these questions, you will appreciate that there are two very distinct paths for dealing with child-rearing issues, as illustrated below:

The Old Way

Bertilia's eight-year-old daughter, Margarita, refuses to ask her *abuelita's bendiciones. Bendiciones,* which literally means blessings in North American parlance, is a beautiful *costumbre,* an old way of sending a family member out of the house protected by the family's love. It is like saying "May God be with you," but it also conveys reverence and *respeto,* since it gives the elderly members of your family a sense of power to protect you through God. But Margarita refused to ask for blessings in front of her friends. Grandma complains to Bertilia about Margarita's behavior. Bertilia explains to Grandma that Margarita is dealing with a number of adjustments since the family moved to their new house and that she doesn't want to put too many pressures on her. But Grandma, set in the old ways, will not tolerate what she sees as Margarita's disrespectful behavior. Bowing to her mother's will, Bertilia *demands* that Margarita ask for the blessings.

The New Way

Before you act on instinct—without thinking—like Bertilia did, step back and consider why Margarita is refusing to ask for her *abuelita's* blessings. It will not take long for you to realize that asking for blessings is a remnant of the old *tradicionalismo.* There is nothing wrong about it, but with an eight-year-old who may be asked by her friends, "Why are you doing that?" it is wise to explain what a special thing it is to ask for blessings—and how good it makes Grandma feel. Bertilia explains this custom to her daughter, and Margarita decides to explain to her friends how important asking for blessings is to her family. Bertilia is amused and proud when Margarita's North American friends' mothers inform her that their children have begun asking for blessings at home!

Your sons and daughters do not wish to lose touch with their Latino heritage. But always remember that the passing on of traditional values is best instilled when conveyed with a positive slant and in a collaborative way.

For instance, I asked a sixth-generation Mexican-American man, "How are you able to maintain so many traditional aspects of the Mexican culture, even though you and your family have 'graduated' from acculturation?" "We did it by *orgullo de raza,* pride of race," he answered. "Through special events like family celebrations, and through *positive* identification with my people."

I knew exactly what he meant. Staying connected to who we are in terms of culture and heritage has been scientifically proven to be a powerful source of support. Studies of Puerto Rican boys and girls in the United States demonstrate that resilient, fully functioning young children and adolescents almost always display a solid appreciation of their identity, which reflects respect for Latino culture and family values as well as biculturalism and, often, bilingualism.

Consejo *No. 2: Respect Your Child's Feelings*

Youngsters, like adults, have to cope with insecurity, anger, envy, anxiety—the whole gamut of distressing emotions. So when your child tells you "I do not want to do that," her refusal to obey you may not be capricious, but it could be sending a message that goes deeper than the situation would suggest. Let me illustrate what I mean:

Four-year-old Marcos: There is a monster behind the closet and it scares me. I want to sleep with you and Dad.

Mother: Marcos, you know monsters are not real. You must be thinking about some really scary things. How about if we play a game where we imagine only very pretty and pleasant things? What do you want to start with?"

After the game is over, Mother can say: "You cannot sleep with us tonight, darling, you must sleep in your bed. Mami and Papi must sleep alone and you must sleep alone—but I will stay with you until you get sleepy, and I will leave the light on." She gives Marcos a kiss and says with a smile, "I love you."

Many parents ask, "Is it a problem to have our child sleep with us?" I will be discussing this topic in detail in chapter 6, "The World of the Preschooler," but for now, my answer would be "It depends." Like everything in life, there are situations where you may want to consider allowing it once in a while for one night (if a child is very upset or sick), but it is not a good custom. Setting these kinds of limits is the beginning of teaching boundaries—of having your own space and communicating that your child must do certain things on his or her own as part of the process of growing up. You and your partner may not agree on whether to allow your child to sleep with you, and this might be a source of friction between you and your partner.

~

Twelve-year-old Melania: I do not want to go to school tomorrow. I hate it. Nobody wants to play with me.

FATHER: You sound awfully unhappy, honey. Did something happen in school today?

MELANIA: They say I talk and look funny.

FATHER: Funny? What do you mean by "funny"?

MELANIA (crying): I don't know . . . they are mean and laugh at me. They keep asking me what I am.

FATHER: Oh, I understand. You must be really angry that the other children can't understand that you are both Dominican like me and American like your mother and that you are part white and part black. Do you realize that the most beautiful roses in the garden are the ones called hybrids?

MELANIA: What is a hybrids?

FATHER: A hybrid is a mixture, a combination of things. In your case, it is a combination of the most beautiful things. Remember I told you that in my country, we had the very first cathedral and university on this side of the world, even before the United States. Remember what I told you about the wonderful African rhythms in merengue music. Remember how much our family loves each other. Tomorrow we will talk about the many other wonderful things about our family and our heritage that both your mother and I have passed on to you. But now you must go to sleep so you will be fresh and bright for school tomorrow.

MELANIA: I love you, Papi. You are the best.

In this case, Melania was encouraged to air her feelings. Then she was reminded of special aspects of her father's culture of origin and to think equally positively about her mother's. Imagine how much more effective a parenting style this is than cutting off communication by saying, "Oh, come on, that is silly. Nobody dislikes you. You are going to school tomorrow, period." Such an approach can put unhealthy distance between you and your child and reinforce her negative emotions.

Consejo *No. 3: Guide and Teach Your Child; Do Not Dictate*

The third *consejo* entails gently steering your child in the right direction, rather than commanding him to do as you wish. It deals with what is called reciprocal communication.

Obedience is important and goes hand in hand with discipline. But discipline cannot be taught by forcing blind obedience. It must convey strong messages that establish in your child a sense of morality, empathy, and common sense. What you definitely do not want is a child who is obedient and compliant to your face but a *diablito,* a little devil, behind your back. In fact, if you *do* demand absolute obedience, you will end up with a child who probably will not want to go to places with you or confide in you when he is struggling with life problems. Here are examples showing this *consejo* in action:

The Old Way

Three-year-old Alfredo demands to wear a suit and tie to the park to play.

MOTHER: Alfredo, you cannot wear a tie and suit to the park.

ALFREDO (starting to cry): I want to! I want to!

MOTHER: Alfredo, you are not going to wear a tie and suit to the park; it is not right.

ALFREDO (sobbing): Why not?

MOTHER: Because *I say so!*

The New Way

MOTHER: Alfredo, wearing a suit and a tie to the park when you are playing will get your good clothes dirty.

ALFREDO (starting to cry): I don't care, I want to . . . I want to!

MOTHER: I know you want to, but I wonder, why is it so important for you to wear a suit to the park?

ALFREDO (momentarily stopping sobbing): I want to be like Daddy. He wears a suit to work.

MOTHER (tenderly giving Alfredo a kiss): Oh! I understand. Sweetie, there are different clothes for different places. On Sunday when we go to church, you can wear your suit and tie, like Daddy.

ALFREDO (beginning to smile): Okay, Mami.

~

Eleven-year-old Rosa tells her mother about an upcoming school dance. Rosa is transferring schools at the end of the term, so this is her farewell dance. Marta, Rosa's mother, asks her for details so that they can make plans. Rosa responds but seems disinterested in going to the dance. After a long conversation, Marta is under the impression that Rosa does not want to go to the dance and that she should forget about it. The next week, half an hour before the dance is scheduled to begin, Rosa tells her mother she really wants to go.

The Old Way

Marta tells her daughter, "Rosa, I asked you last week about the dance and you told me you were not interested in attending; therefore, young lady, it is now too late." Rosa bursts into tears, tells Marta she is a bad mother, and accuses, "You never listen to me; you never understand me. That is not what I told you." Marta shouts back: "That's it. You're grounded. I am your mother. How dare you talk to me like that! Go to your room at once!"

The New Way

Marta tells Rosa, in an emphatic tone: "It's too late, sweetheart. I'm really sorry, but you cannot go." Marta goes to some lengths to explain to Rosa the importance of time management and proper planning. When Rosa becomes extremely angry and agitated, Marta says she understands her feelings, but she cannot go to the dance tonight. She calmly tells Rosa that the next time an event comes up, plans will have to be made in advance.

This "new way" anecdote illustrates how you can set limits while acknowledging your child's feelings and helping her understand the consequences of her actions. Marta knows her own mother would feel Rosa was being spoiled and, instead of encouraging discussion, would simply state, "You asked for it! I told you to let me know about the dance. It is now too late, and I don't want to hear any more about it!" or, "Your problem is you can never make up your mind." Marta also knows that such a tactic would only make Rosa angrier and more rebellious.

Consejo *No. 4: Update Your Media Awareness Often*

The fourth *consejo* deals with your need as a parent to be up-to-date on such influential cultural media as TV, music, and the Internet. You should be familiar with what is being presented in the two cultural worlds, not only in Spanish. If you are going to talk to your child about drugs and sex—and you should—you need to have the proper data in order to communicate effectively. But you need to have information on different types of sports, games, TV shows, publications, and even Internet pornography. Be aware that these media feature provocative themes of which your child is well aware—including drug use, underage drinking, suicide as the ultimate form of problem solving, violence, and the glorification of sexuality. You can play a strong role in teaching your child fun activities that embrace two cultures, but you have to know "where they're coming from" before you attempt to keep your children on the right track.

Being technologically aware can also help you to teach your child about different cultural values and to respect other cultures. Many communities offer wonderful programs designed specifically for children, such as museum puppet shows, theater, art and science fairs, and many other events—some of special interest to Latinos—that are listed in newspapers and on the Internet.

Some parents pride themselves on exposing their kids exclusively to Latino culture, yet the nature of today's North American society in the United States is the promulgation of diversity—starting as early as day care or nursery school.

My younger son Miguel's first preschool experience was at a nursery program held at a synagogue, where he observed Chanukah; but, at the same time, Miguel attended religious instruction in our faith, and we celebrated Christmas with our non-Latino and non-Christian neighbors. Miguel also celebrated Easter and the Greek holidays at the homes of his friends. He later attended the United Nations nursery school, public school in Queens, and then Brooklyn Tech High School, where he mixed with many different cultures. This broad-based exposure only served to strengthen his identification with

Latino culture while also making him feel very much a North American. As a result of his cosmopolitan education, Miguel is both very Latino and very international. My older son Jaime's first language was Spanish, yet he is open to and feels very comfortable with different cultural values; he, too, is very proud to call himself both a Latino and a North American.

Flexibility is essential not only in terms of exposure to different cultural values but also in learning through the media about new understanding and accordingly modifying cultural parenting practices that may no longer be applicable or useful. For example, you need to accept the fact that your toddler will naturally be exposed to some amount of germs. It is considered unrealistic scientifically to maintain a totally antiseptic environment for a child. In the old days, particularly in the tropics, parents had to be very cautious about exposing their children to parasites and germs; children were not allowed outdoors without shoes. Today, total germ avoidance is a mission impossible, as we can see in the following anecdote:

Alicia's babysitter, Gladys, feels that at the age of fifty-two she is an expert in child rearing: she has raised six kids of her own and feels this gives her the right to tell Julia how to parent eighteen-month-old Alicia. Gladys scolds Julia for not being a good mother when she lets Alicia walk outdoors barefoot, saying that the baby will be exposed to germs. But Julia knows through her reading that exposure to a moderate amount of germs boosts a child's immune system and that it is easier for babies to learn to walk if they are barefoot. She also realizes that it is very important to communicate this information very gently to Gladys in order for Gladys to adhere to Julia's wishes when Julia is at the office. So, with great deference, Julia begins by conveying her appreciation of Gladys care and concern for Alicia, and then says that she wants to share some written useful information she has gotten from Alicia's pediatrician. She reads aloud and they discuss the articles on contemporary child-rearing practices. Finally, Gladys begins to see things Julia's way.

Consejo *No. 5: Love Your Child for Who She or He Is*

The fifth *consejo* advocates loving your child just the way he or she is and working to parent within the context of the child's individuality. Here's an example of how an overly aggressive child's behavior can be contained:

Three-year-old Juanito gets furious when his mother, Lilia, scolds and spanks him because he broke a vase. Juanito smacks Lilia back. This is not an isolated incident. In fact, Lilia consults me because Juanito is generally *insoportable,* unmanageable. She will not even risk taking him with her on errands because he is impossible to control. As I explore with Lilia the specifics of her dilemma, I come to realize that, although she is not aware of it, she has a habit of comparing Juanito unfavorably to her older child, Anita, who is obedient by nature and *bien educada.* Lilia is also not expressing love to Juanito verbally or physically and is not accepting him as a unique individual; she has already labeled Juanito as "trouble," although he is only three years old.

I'm happy to report that, in the course of our working together, Lilia learned how to put a stop to her parenting misstep by honestly asking herself whether or not she was expecting too much from a child Juanito's age. The answer, of course, was yes. She faced the fact that she was not infallible and that her stock response to the boy— "Juanito, no!"—was counterproductive. First she learned not to leave valuable objects in Juanito's reach and to guide him by saying, "This is not to be touched; you can look at it, but if you touch it, it will break and you can get hurt." In other words, she taught him by explaining. She found age-appropriate pastimes for Juanito, such as doing puzzles together, where she could teach, guide, and communicate with him. Lilia was now able to exert control over her son's behavior by dealing with him as the person he is, not as the perfect little man she wanted him to be.

You, like Lilia, may sometimes be unaware of the intensity of the verbal and body language you use to express disapproval to your daughter or son. Too often what we parents desire for our children translates into trying to make them replicas of who *we* are. If your child happens to have inherited many of your positive traits, you are ahead of the game. Even so, you may still harbor traditional expectations based on age or gender that may not be possible for your child to meet.

Children, due to their inborn temperament, may be shy, anxious, or strong-willed to the point where your patience is sorely taxed. We all know that siblings in the same family may have very different personalities and that some of these differences are based on whether the child is *congenitally* anxious, angry, fearful, detached, clinging, or rebellious. So you must always keep in mind that the notion of parental impartiality is a myth—a carryover from the old values when mothers took pride in saying, "I love all my children exactly the same." The truth of the matter is that although you do love them all, you still relate to each one differently, according to his or her temperament and personality, and you probably relate to some better than others.

You may convey to your little one in a thousand ways that she is special—by the music in your voice or the tenderness of your touch. No matter how it is conveyed, communicating your love to your child will lay the groundwork for your relationship later on—because babies begin to comprehend at an earlier age than most people realize. An eight-month-old might not grasp an idea intellectually but will react viscerally to your soft voice and find it soothing, or might withdraw or fuss in reaction to your anxiety, fear, or anger.

At about a year and a half, the child begins to develop the ability to express herself verbally and begins to progressively learn how to articulate complex emotions such as pride, shame, envy, empathy, and anger. For example, she may clap her hands with joy when she has pleased Mami by using the potty; he might laugh when told "You are a good boy" or express anger by refusing to wear a certain shirt or share a toy. It is to be expected that you may find some of these emotions unpleasant, particularly if your standard of judgment is based on your own childhood experience or on what is "normal" for your other children.

Always remember that productive parenting cannot begin until you have confronted your own feelings about a child's actions. Keeping this in mind, I urge you to do the following exercises and to consider the results carefully:

- List any aspect of your child that you consider a problem

  _____

- My child acts that way when

  _____

- How do you feel about this aspect of your child?

  _____

- My child is that way because

  _____

Then ask yourself:

- How do I respond to what I consider a problem?

  _____

- What is my responsibility in this situation?

  _____

- List five positive attributes of your child
  1 _____
  2 _____
  3 _____
  4 _____
  5 _____

Apply these suggestions when the appropriate occasion arises:

- Take a deep breath before you react to something your child is doing that seems designed to provoke you—unless, of course, it is an emergency.
- Help your child develop a clear and organized routine, including when to go to bed, when to start homework, when to play. Do not forget that some children may need more reminding and structure than others; it's a matter of individual nature.

- Never compare your children. Your second child could behave completely differently from your first one—people are different by nature!
- Never compare your children with your friends' children.
- Teach an excitable child to stay calm by your own example. If he sees you excited, he will imitate.
- Use age-appropriate assignments and exercises, such as creating posters and writing on the blackboard. These are activities that can be fun, teach concentration, and promote a sense of competence in your child.
- Suggest to your child that he make a poster setting goals for completing homework, rather than attempt to force him to study by calling him lazy or slow.
- Leave your child notes by the refrigerator or in his lunch box reminding him how much you love him, without any strings attached. Hug and praise him every chance you get; frequent displays of affection work wonders in establishing trust.
- Devise with your child a common definition of what it means to be respectful.
- Embrace your child when he makes a mistake, then discuss with him how to do the task better—without resorting to accusations or insults.
- Facilitate your child's ability to express emotions, whether happiness, anger, pride, envy, anxiety, disappointment, or fear, by allowing their expression and then discussing them. Do not be afraid that your nine-year-old will be damaged for life if she is permitted to say, "Mommy, I am so angry with you," as long as it occurs without a tantrum. You can then ask: "Why?" and go on to suggest that she should consider what you have to say—not because "I say so!" but because you are older and more experienced at living.
- You can only help your child identify the source of a problem if you communicate directly with her, so always make time to talk. Before you establish a dialogue, make sure that you are calm and your anger is under control. You can always wait until the next

day, when you are feeling better, to talk to your child. The results will be just as good and everyone will be better able to have a productive talk.

Consejo *No. 6: Listen to Your Child*

The sixth *consejo* stresses the importance of really hearing what your child is telling you. The ability to listen is one of the greatest gifts we can give others, and children need the security of knowing you are emotionally "there" for them.

Remember that the ideal child as portrayed on television and in books is only that, an ideal. Children will differ and every developmental stage has its own implicit behavior, but for all children, no matter what their age, obedience is not achieved *al pie de la letra,* according to the rule. Very few children (or adults, for that matter) conform to all the rules. Many boys and girls "go to pieces" over what appears to parents a very simple issue; if you listen closely, you will see that it might not be so simple to the child. Armed with this knowledge, you will be prepared to work through problems effectively with your child.

Listening to feelings should begin the moment a baby is born. Children do not become competent managers of their feelings on their own; they need their parents to guide, to structure, to teach. The best way to do this is by listening. Sometimes parents feel it is their own fault if a child becomes distressed or does not behave properly. Nothing could be further from the truth, because our children are individuals separate from us. Similarly, some parents feel that it is not appropriate to be tender with boys lest they become "soft." Children, regardless of their sex, need understanding and tenderness in an age-appropriate manner. Look at how different it is to communicate with four-year-old Maximo than with fourteen-year-old Roberto:

Maximo runs in from the garden screaming because a butterfly has flown into his face. Grandfather says, "Oh, come on, you are a boy, be brave! Go back and play in the garden." Maximo's mother, on the other hand, focuses on what it will take to soothe her son. She realizes that what Maximo needs is a big hug and for her to reassure him by saying, "That butterfly really frightened you, didn't it? Would you rather play inside with your puzzles?" Maximo nods yes, Mommy dries his tears and kisses him, and soon he is happily playing with his puzzles. By listening to her son, his mother is able to validate first that he is frightened and eventually that he is fine.

~

Fourteen-year-old Roberto storms into the house, slamming the door behind him, and heads directly for his room. Grandpa calls to him, "Why don't you come here, son, so we can talk?" Roberto responds by shouting, "Just leave me alone!" Grandpa says nothing, waits a while, and then goes to Roberto's room.

GRANDPA: It seems that today was not a good one.

ROBERTO: Oh, Grandpa, please leave me alone!

GRANDPA: Okay, I will. But before I do, I want you to remember that if you ever do feel like talking, I am always here for you.

Different ages, different needs, different approaches. Here are some more examples of different ways to listen to your child:

Four-year-old Tatiana and her seven-year-old sister, Carmen, are taken by their father to the church fair. Tatiana is having a ball on the Ferris wheel when Carmen announces that she feels sick. When father tells Tatiana, "Your sister does not feel well; we have to go," she begs him for one more ride. When he insists on going home, Tatiana throws a tantrum. Father feels torn, since it disturbs him to see his four-year-old this upset; after all, she is too young to be expected to empathize with her sister. He identifies with Tatiana's frustration, yet he is confident he is acting in her best interest, because he is beginning to teach her to feel for others. He doesn't call her a bad girl or spoiled brat. Instead, he assures her that he understands how upset she is, but that right now getting Carmen home is the top priority. He also offers the youngster an alternative: "We have to go, but before we do, I will get you the ice cream you wanted," and Tatiana is pacified.

~

Six-year-old Martita comes home from her first day at her new school feeling very distraught because her family has just relocated and she does not know any of the other students, who are not the least bit welcoming. Her mother, Emilia, calls from her new job at a bank to find out from Grandma how Martita's first day of school went and to share her guilt for not taking her daughter to school herself, although there was no way she could afford to be absent from her new position, and her husband, Juan, is traveling and also wouldn't do it in any case. Grandma Matilde reassures Emilia that Martita will be fine as soon as she adjusts to her new environment and repeats to Emilia the conversation she and her granddaughter shared. Emilia feels blessed that Martita has such an understanding and loving *abuelita*. This is the dialogue that Grandma Matilde shares with her granddaughter:

MATILDE: My lovely *nieta*, let's have milk and cookies while you tell me about your first day of school.

MARTITA: I feel very bad, *abuelita;* nobody played with me. I don't want to go back to that school. I want to be with my friends Juanita and Alicia.

MATILDE: Come here and let me give you a hug and a big kiss. You are a beautiful *princesita,* Grandma's *orgullo.* You are truly my princess and my pride. How could you think that nobody wanted to play with you? Sometimes this happens on the first day of school. Maybe all the other children feel more comfortable with their old classmates. I know I would, but I also know it will pass.

MARTITA: But I don't know anybody, *abuelita.*

MATILDE: I know, *preciosa,* but I assure you that by tomorrow you will know your classmates a little bit better, and the next day better still. I have an idea. Tomorrow when you go to class, bring the beautiful kaleidoscope you received for the Three Kings Feast and show it to the other children. You will see how much fun you will all have. Besides, do you remember how lonely you felt when I took you to your first days of kindergarten?

MARTITA: Yes, *abuelita,* I remember, but that went away.

MATILDE: Exactly. It went away, and this feeling will go away too. You will see.

MARTITA (hugging Matilde): *Abuelita, abuelita,* I love you! Can I please have more milk and cookies?

~

Ten-year-old Victor—who is half Hispanic and half Chinese—comes home from school very upset because his friends are pressuring him to declare himself a Latino; they threaten to beat him up if he doesn't. Victor's mother insists that he is both Latino and Asian and should be proud of being both. She tells him she has decided that tomorrow she is going to speak with those kids as well as their parents to make sure they leave him alone. Victor objects. When his mother proceeds anyway, he feels as if he's lost even more face with his peers. The end result is that Victor stops confiding in his mother—who neither listened to him nor made him feel that his conflict made sense to her—about what transpires at school. Victor's mother should have listened and seen if together she and Victor could have come up with an acceptable solution for everyone.

To enhance your listening skills, follow this advice:

- Avoid power struggles by acknowledging your child's feelings.
- Do not solve every problem your child is faced with as a sign of love.
- If your child is very upset, wait to talk until your child has calmed down; otherwise you may simply end up arguing.
- If a child *has* violated rules, never threaten by saying: "I am going to ground you for months." Instead, apply an appropriate punishment that fits the violation and explain the consequences if he does not obey. For example: he will not be trusted to do what he had been given permission to do, since he did not comply with the rules.
- Establish a routine of daily quality time with your child, whether he is a toddler or an adolescent. When he is younger, you can read

books together, listen to music, have puppet shows, or play at the computer. Later on, your shared time will include talking and listening. Remember that listening equals being empathetic to what your child is feeling.

Consejo *No. 7:*
Open the Communication Channels—and Keep Them Open

Seven-year-old Leticia comes home from school in tears. Her mother, Zarela, is caring and concerned.

ZARELA: What is wrong, *cariño?*

LETICIA: Umm . . . well . . . my friend Rudy asked me to let him touch me.

ZARELA (staying calm and collected): And what did you say to him?

LETICIA: I said that it is not right to do.

MOTHER: Yes, sweetie. Rudy was wrong to do that. When you are a grown-up, you will decide about these things by yourself. I am so glad you talked to me. But why were you crying?

LETICIA: I was confused and frightened. I didn't know what to do.

MOTHER: Well, coming to me shows that you knew exactly what to do. I want you to know you can always talk to me about anything because I love you and I will always be there for you.

~

Nine-year-old Luis comes home from school obviously upset and asks his mother if he can talk with her. Mother is on the computer, trying to meet a deadline for her job as a translator. She tries to continue working and listen to Luis at the same time. At some point, Luis realizes his mother isn't really paying attention to him and goes to his room, feeling even worse. Mother complains that Luis never confides in her. She could have explained to him how important it was for her to hear what was upsetting him, but that she wanted to be able to give him quality time, and that she would come to talk with him as soon as she finished her job.

This last but very crucial *consejo* mandates that you and your child maintain an ongoing dialogue. By doing so, you can achieve a double purpose: first, you will increase the likelihood that your child will turn to you when faced with problems—from being afraid of a butterfly to telling you about inappropriate touching. Second, by your own example of communication, you will be doing your child a marvelous favor—since experts agree that few skills enhance a person's autonomy and self-esteem in adulthood more than being good communicators.

Through good communication, you will also be reinforcing the importance of *familismo,* one of the most beautiful traditions in Latino culture. *Familismo* signifies that the family is there to help its members *en las buenas y en las malas,* in good and bad times.

In order for true open communication to exist, there are a few skills you need to master. Over the years, I have found that the following recommendations are the tickets to productive parenting:

- Establish trust with your child. Do not judge or criticize her harshly. Use logic, not emotion, when you communicate.
- Allow your child to make mistakes; then ask for her interpretation of what occurred and why. Be patient and listen.
- Show your child that you understand her feelings by listening attentively without blaming her and by helping her label what she is feeling: that she is angry, sad, unsure, or happy about something.
- Never overreact, no matter what she tells you. Reserve your judgment and don't interrupt her until she has finished speaking.
- Avoid critical phrases, such as "I told you," "You never pay attention," or "You don't listen."
- Maintain eye contact with your child during your dialogue.
- Monitor your nonverbal communication, such as gestures and facial expressions.
- Find specific times for initiating communication, always taking your child's developmental level into account so that you will know how much of what you're trying to say can be absorbed.
- Use the example of a movie or a story to corroborate your own opinion.

Las Reflexiones

Below are a series of questions, *las reflexiones,* to be used as the basis for contemplation on how you regard yourself as a parent. After you've written down your responses, review, ponder, and compare them to the results of the quiz you took at the beginning of this chapter. Take your time. Ask yourself: What have you learned? How far have you come on the cultural adjustment continuum?

- How good a mother or father are you to yourself? In other words, do you give yourself time to fulfill your own needs? How essential do you feel this is to your parenting skills?
- Do you blame yourself for mistakes you made when you did not know better? How important is it to you to remember that we all make mistakes, and that they can actually offer us opportunity to grow?
- How would you describe the way you feel when you get terribly angry? Do you believe anger is *una emocion humana,* a very normal emotion, and that how we process it is of great importance—or do you feel you should suppress all strong and threatening emotions?
- Are you afraid of making your loved ones angry, *especially* when you are doing what feels right to you as a parent?
- What would you like to change about your parenting style and what do you treasure and want to retain? You might want to write down your answers in list form and keep them so that you can refer to them later and see how much *El Nuevo Tradicionalismo* has altered your outlook and behavior.

Leaving You with O.R.G.U.L.L.O

I want to leave you with *orgullo,* that is, pride in your parenting skills, which will help you relax and not be overly vigilant about your child's well-being. Trust yourself to do a good job and keep in mind that children are considerably more resilient than adults. Just love them as you follow the *consejos* of O.R.G.U.L.L.O., and you'll find that their growing up will be a much more delightful and positive experience for all of you.

Imagine that you hear the voice of your wise and wonderful *abuelita* or other beloved family member saying to you: "I am so proud of you. I love you. Love yourself, love your child, love your culture, but maintain your values balanced with those of the new culture you and your child are now living in."

CHAPTER 2

Raising Children Is a Two-Way Street: The New *Respeto*

Take the following self-assessment quiz to help you become better attuned to your level of traditionalism in terms of *respeto*.

5=Always 4=Frequently 3=Sometimes 2=Rarely 1=Never

1. Do you believe that explaining your actions to your child undermines your authority? _____

2. Do you feel you are spoiling your son if you explain your actions to him? _____

3. Do you and your spouse consult each other on important parenting decisions, but only one of you always has the final say? _____

4. Do you disregard your child's feelings and if necessary scold her in front of her friends? _____

5. Is your child not allowed to choose the clothes she wishes to wear to school or to a party? _____

6. If your child differs with you, do you ask him to tell you his reasons for his opinion? _____

7. Do you ever avoid discussing the meaning of *respeto* in your household? _____

8. Do you demand *respeto* for others from your child, regardless of how they have treated her? _____

Sandra is celebrating her fifth birthday when her cousin Blanca, also five, grabs a balloon from her and keeps it for herself. Sandra grabs it back—a very normal reaction for a child this age—and her cousin starts sobbing, "My balloon! My balloon!" At that moment Sandra's father walks into the room and observes the scene. Without asking Sandra what provoked the incident, Papa orders her to give the balloon back to Blanca. Sandra tries to explain, but she is not allowed to speak.

Unfortunately, by his actions, Sandra's father is failing to teach both his daughter and her cousin that property must be respected. Even more important, he is not giving Sandra the opportunity to explain her side of things—that Blanca took without asking something that was Sandra's. He is not respecting his daughter's property, actions, or feelings. Papa resolved the dispute according to the tenets of the old *respeto,* where children are permitted neither to defend themselves nor to question parental judgment; they must simply obey.

If Papa's main concerns were to teach Sandra *respeto* and how to be *simpatica,* or agreeable, he meant well, but his methods were counterproductive. What he did manage to instill in the two girls was the knowledge that life isn't always fair—a lesson they'll have plenty of time to learn later on. He would have accomplished a lot more if he had followed the *consejos* of O.R.G.U.L.L.O. described in chapter 1 and practiced the new *respeto.*

Many Latino parents who grew up having experiences similar to Sandra's find their parenting methods in conflict with what I call the new *respeto.* The new *respeto* is founded on the belief that fostering submission, absolute obedience, and gender inequalities will not teach your child to navigate successfully in the culture she faces every day. It's more like being expected to steer a vessel through rough waters without ever having been near a boat.

The Old *Respeto* versus The New *Respeto:* When Worlds Collide

The best way to understand the conflicts around *respeto* faced by many Latinos raising children in the United States is to appreciate the distinctly different definitions of the Spanish word and its English equivalent.

Within North American culture, respect implies a fairly detached, self-assured egalitarianism. For Latinos, *respeto* refers to a relationship involving a highly emotionalized dependence and dutifulness, within a fairly authoritarian framework. In other words, while in English respect means having a high opinion of and recognizing the importance of others, it does not convey the deference and approval-seeking that have been internalized in Latinos—especially in determining how children should relate to adults, in which *respeto* is most assuredly a one-way street.

The Old Respeto: A One-Way Street

As we've seen in the previous anecdote, Latino children traditionally are expected to offer absolute *respeto* to parents and adults, but adults are not expected to respect the children in return. There is a belief that including children's feelings in conflict resolution will harm or spoil them. In this way, *respeto* is very close to traditional notions of obedience, but it also includes other considerations, such as expecting the child to validate the feelings of others, whereas violation of children's feelings is not part of the equation. Period.

However, the old *respeto* also has beautiful and dignified connotations worth keeping. One wonderful way of teaching our children to respect others is through the teaching of empathy, or the understanding of other people's sacrifices and dedication. Be careful not to do this in a guilt-inducing way, though. You want to teach children to understand others' feelings by telling them stories about their ancestors' struggles, sacrifices, and accomplishments. Doing so gives them powerful role models of responsibility and validation of the family. Rather than instill guilt by comparing them unfavorably to others, help them to see that they are part of this wonderful, good-hearted family.

The New Respeto—A Wider Highway

The beauty of the new *respeto* is that it incorporates those aspects of the old values which we hold dear, including but not limited to valuing others' worth, recognizing their merits, deference to age, and maintenance of self-discipline, with the addition of one component: the inclusion of our children's feelings in every interaction we have with them.

Let's see how this is illustrated in the following examples contrasting the old *respeto* and the new *respeto*. We will also see how these parents could have handled the situations differently by following the *consejos* of O.R.G.U.L.L.O.

The Old Way

The parents of nine-year-old Peter order him to straighten his room, which could win an Olympic medal for messiness. Peter manages to do everything except straighten his room until his friend Mark arrives to play. Since his mom was in another part of the house when the doorbell rang, it is only later that she discovers them in Peter's unkempt room blissfully playing computer games among the clutter. Mom promptly calls Peter a pig in front of his friend, asks Mark to go home, and demands that Peter straighten his room immediately. After Mark leaves, Peter gets furious with Mom:

PETER (sobbing): You're a bad mom! You never let me have any fun! I hate it that you're my mom.

MOM (trying to ignore his words): Peter, your room is a mess. Pick up your toys, clothes, and books at once!

PETER (screaming): Why did you make Mark go home? Why did you call me a pig in front of him? Dad isn't ever so mean! I hate you!

MOM: That's it! No TV for one month. I have really had it with you! You are driving me crazy! You are so disrespectful. You'd better respect me, do you hear me?

This type of scenario occurs more often than Mom can handle. Mom calls her friend Elena to find some solace and tell her how Peter is driving her crazy. She says he is a terror, disobedient and disrespectful, and that she frankly does not know how to handle this situation. Her husband comes home too late to help her with Peter and is usually very tired, making it exclusively her job to discipline Peter—which has begun to seem like the Impossible Dream.

Having exhausted all means of getting through to her son, Mom feels that she has no alternative other than to clean up his room herself. She does this out of desperation and to avoid open warfare, so it is at best a temporary solution, guaranteeing that the problem will only continue unresolved.

Now let's see how this situation could be resolved differently if Mom applied some of the *consejos* of O.R.G.U.L.L.O.—specifically, organizing her own emotions, respecting Peter's feelings, and offering consistent guidance rather than dictating.

The first thing Mom must do is discuss the situation with an ally—in this case, Papa. Together they can assess the problem and the options for solving it. The second thing to do is to establish an open channel of communication with Peter. Here is how Peter's parents applied the new *respeto* techniques to the situation.

The New Way

PARENTS: Peter, we want you to put your toys away in this bag when you finish playing with them. This is a small apartment and we need to put things in their place once we have finished using them so that everyone can enjoy our home. Would you like to be reminded when it is time to do that? (The parents have provided an explanation and offered a plan that helps Peter while also sustaining their authority.)

PETER: But this is my room. Your room is messy too!

PARENTS: Our room has papers neatly stacked on the floor because we use our bedroom as an office. It is different from having things all over the floor. We really want you to put your toys away in this bag when you finish playing. How can we help you to do that? (The parents do not call him sassy or disrespectful for protesting, but they continue explaining their reasons, employing a consistent and straightforward approach.)

PETER: You can let me play with Mark! (manipulation)

PARENTS: No, Peter, that is not what we asked. The question was, how can we help you remember to put the toys in the bag and how can you maintain your room neat after playing? We have a rule that works for us and helps us to put our papers in order after we have finished our work: we don't leave the room until we have straightened the room. That is a good rule for you: put your toys in the bag before you leave your room after you are finished playing. Would you like to write yourself a note and put it on your cork board that says—Peter (interrupts, very excited): PUT TOYS IN BAG BEFORE LEAVING ROOM!!

PARENTS: That is great! You are terrific! This rule will work well.

PETER: Okay, Mom, okay, Dad. I promise to put my toys in the bag.

The next day, when Peter puts his toys away, both Mom and Dad comment on what a nice job he has done.

Consistency Is Key

Peter has had a few lapses since the family's conversation, but both parents maintained a firm position, explained their thinking when necessary, clarified Peter's questions, and did not let him get away with manipulations such as "Let me play with Mark." Still, their most essential action was including all three of them, not just Mom, in solving the problem. Since Mom and Dad presented a very strong and united front, they were able *without a loss of authority* to ask Peter to come up with a feasible way that was agreeable to them and that helped to resolve the problem. Note that Mom and Dad accomplished this without dictating, but also without permitting Peter to continue manipulating them.

The old pattern of discipline hadn't worked because Mom was reinforcing Peter's behavior by being inconsistent: Peter knew that if he managed not to clean his room long enough, Mom would either do it for him or, through her screaming, tell him when it was time to really take her seriously. But the whole game was as frustrating to Peter as it was to Mom because eight-year-olds crave the structure adults provide, even if they consciously fight it.

Undoing old unproductive habits and working toward obtaining more positive results requires patience, tolerance, and work. In this situation a patient, clear, structured approach was rewarded when the parents in unison said: "Peter, we want you to put your toys away in this bag when you finish playing." There was no negotiation here: they clearly stated the importance of keeping his room in order. The crucial element was involving Peter in the decision and firmly structuring him when necessary—both strategies are bound to work better than dictating or saying "Do it because I say so."

If Kids Were Perfect, They'd Be Life-Sized Dolls

It is not realistic to expect that your child will be perfectly behaved, the child you might have been in the past, or the way you might have fantasized a child should be. Many Latino parents have told me that deep inside they want their children to be obedient and dependent on their parents and elders. This is indeed a fantasy, a wish stemming from the desire to have your perfect child be yours forever.

Private Property! Trespassers Will Be Disrespected!

In the course of writing this chapter, I consulted with parents, both Latino and non-Latino, about aspects of *respeto*. I asked a North American parent: "Did you ever go through your daughter's drawers or open her mail?"

Obviously offended, she responded emphatically, "Of course not! Why would I ever do such a thing?"

One of the Latina mothers said, "My mother always did." (Mind you, her mother is a second-generation, educated, professional woman!)

Another Latina parent confessed that as a result of her own therapy, she recently stopped looking into her daughter's drawers and telling her she was not allowed to do things Mom disapproved on the grounds that "Latinas do not do that. Maybe North Americans do that, but we do not." But here is the punch line: one of the Latina parents announced, "That is why I don't want to have much to do with that culture"—meaning her own Latino culture. She said this with anger and disdain, indicating how alienated she felt from her own group. But if you hate your roots, which are part of you, aren't you rejecting part of yourself?

Research shows that the further away Latina girls drift from their culture, the more personality problems they experience. Acculturation involves combining two different views of life, not adopting one at the expense of the other. Therefore:

- Parents must be involved in their children's affairs
- Privacy *does* have limits

A degree of privacy can and should be respected, particularly when you have developed a strong basis of *confianza* (trust) in your child through open communication. The bottom line is that when behaviors need modification, the best way to accomplish the task is through communication with your child, which should always include strategic planning—rather than going behind your child's back or waiting until a crisis occurs and any suggestion becomes an order.

For Adults Only—
Strategic Planning for Respectful Exclusion

We now know that it is not respectful and definitely not helpful to children's self-esteem to have parents or adults "talk over their heads," as if children cannot understand the adults' conversation. This is not to say that a child should equate herself with an adult and monopolize a conversation being held by adults, but she should be given opportunity to participate for a limited period of time so that she learns how to converse gracefully with others.

Such behavior cannot be instilled in a child by saying, after the guests arrive, "Juanita, leave us alone. This is for adults," but by strategic planning—that is, by telling your child ahead of time that this is a situation in which the adults will want to discuss private things. You begin by teaching Juanita that adults talk about things that are not appropriate for children to hear, and that you will expect her to leave you and your company alone when you indicate so to her by saying "Okay, dear, you can go now, thank you." Then, if nine-year-old Juanita breaks the rules, she will be reminded after the company leaves of what was expected of her. You are teaching Juanita the importance of respecting boundaries. The older she gets, the more you'll need to apply these boundaries to her, as well. It might not be easy for you to break the old *costumbres* or habit of doing things, but you will be in a winning situation if you do.

Strategic planning should be applied, for example, when Juanita brings home her girlfriends and wants to listen to music or watch TV with them in privacy. There is no magic formula for determining the appropriate level of privacy to be accorded your child. You need to consider your child's age, maturity, and self-discipline. I know from talking to many Latino parents and from my own experience as a Latina mother that leaving a child unsupervised is not good practice. But closing the door of the room is not leaving a child unsupervised. I also know that neither is it good practice to set such strict privacy limits that your child feels not trusted—simply because this is what you grew up with. Here again, the approach that best respects your child's wishes as well as your own is strategic planning, including a clearly stated explanation of the "house rules," and space for your daughter to express her point of view, for example, about wanting to be with her girlfriend alone in her room watching TV. The best and most reassuring way of protecting your child while honoring her autonomy is not being present 100 percent of the time but making your values clear to her and emphasizing the house rules that you feel need to be followed. If this process is not instituted in childhood, it could lead to trouble in later life. For instance, traditional parents often forget the need to respect their adult children and how these adults raise their own children.

Respeto **and the Adult Child**

Witnessing Anita's behavior with her twenty-six-year-old daughter, Melanie, reminded me how often children's feelings are not respected by parents, even after children become adults. Anita and

Melanie are always bickering: Anita feels that Melanie does not respect her, while Anita makes decisions that affect Melanie—such as using her credit card without letting her know until Melanie gets the bill, wearing her clothes, taking money out of her purse, and making household decisions—all without consulting her. When Melanie complains, Anita ignores her because she feels that the way she was brought up—not questioning *her* mother—should be the way Melanie should act.

One day Anita asks Melanie and her boyfriend, Michael, to accompany her and *abuelita* Zulema on an outing in her car. Michael wanted to drive his own car, which was more comfortable, but Anita insisted on bringing hers. Knowing that Zulema prefers to sit in the front and without consulting anyone, Anita shepherds her to the front seat next to Michael, who is driving, and sends Melanie to the backseat.

I asked Anita why she didn't check with Melanie first as to whether this arrangement was okay with her. Anita looked surprised at my question because she felt that since this was her car, she should not feel obligated to consult Melanie about the seating. It was obvious to me that Anita was missing the whole point, which was to be sensitive to the fact that Melanie might want to sit next to her boyfriend so that they could talk to each other and not be relegated, as if she were a child, to sitting in the back with her mother. If Anita were respecting Melanie's needs, she would have at least asked her, "Is this okay with you?" Alternatively, Anita could have driven the car herself and Melanie and her boyfriend could have sat together in the back. In the old times, it was the mother who sat with the boyfriend, not the daughter—Anita was unwittingly imposing old ways that reinforced *respeto* between mother and daughter.

Borders and Boundaries

It is very interesting to note that Anita often complains Melanie does not respect her and cites boundary problems as evidence. It should come as no surprise that *abuelita* Zulema behaves in a similar way with Anita. Here is a modern solution:

Anita could still respect her mother's preference for sitting in the front seat, if this is more comfortable for her, but Melanie should be consulted, or, at the very least, informed beforehand. Anita should recognize that Melanie is an adult and has every right to want to sit next to her boyfriend. Given the circumstances, it would be very normal for Melanie to expect and want to sit in the front, and Anita should respect that expectation. But in a household where Latino values are esteemed, it is very likely that Melanie would have given the seat to her *abuelita.* Still, she should have been given the opportunity to decide for herself.

The best solution is maintaining a balance between old and new cultural practice. In my work with families, I have seen this inclusiveness help prevent what I call Cultural Pendulum Syndrome. Let's examine it in terms of *respeto.*

The Cultural Pendulum Syndrome: How Not to Change with the Times

The Cultural Pendulum Syndrome occurs when parents totally distance themselves from the child-rearing practices they grew up with—which they consciously or unconsciously hated—simply because they do not know that now they have the option to balance old and new. They allow their children to do anything they want in the name of freedom, boosting their self-esteem, and love. But permitting a child to be disrespectful to parents and elders sets the child on the road to big problems, as in Mariana's case.

Five-year-old Mariana is the apple of her mother Regina's eye. Regina is a second-generation Latina, married to a North American man, who defines herself as acculturated. She is determined to give Mariana only the best upbringing—definitely different from hers, which demanded absolute *respeto, obediencia,* and what she calls "those super Latino values."

Mariana and Regina were visiting some friends, and Mariana was vying to be the center of attention. This, of course, disrupted the hostess's plans. When Regina did not take charge of her daughter, the hostess asked Mariana to visit with the other children in the next room. Mariana responded by telling her, "You are saying something real silly." Regina did not intervene or reprimand Mariana, nor did she apologize to the hostess.

This is not an isolated incident. Regina's letting the pendulum swing to the extreme and refusing to discipline Mariana is what we call "transference behavior": Regina is rejecting having been ordered around in her own childhood and is "acting out" that rejection by letting Mariana be disrespectful—thereby retarding her daughter's development as a person in a way that can take a heavy toll later.

The New Respeto Is Very Serious Business

As I've said, there is an old *respeto* and a new *respeto*. Both are useful, but some aspects of the old *respeto* do not work any longer. Practicing the new *respeto* can help parents avoid anger, frustration, even heartbreak.

A therapist providing services in a clinic in the Southwest reports in *Womensnews,* an Internet magazine, that she feels overwhelmed by the number of Latina adolescents who are attempting suicide. This therapist is surprised by this data because Latino families practice closeness and are supportive, two components listed in the professional literature as discouraging suicide. Still, this grim statistic has been corroborated by the National Alliance for Hispanic Health. Only this past July 2003, *JAMA,* the *Journal of the American Medical Association,* suggested that suicide attempts by Latina teenagers are significantly more likely than by white or black adolescents.

The reason may have to do with alienation from Latino culture. Dr. Glenn Flores, a pediatric epidemiologist who has studied this behavior, writes: "We discovered in our research . . . that the more Americanized or acculturated Latino kids become, the worse it is for their health." These studies clearly indicate that the best way to bring up a child from a different cultural background is to have that child be functional in both cultures. We know that many adolescents feel confused when they are confronted with different sets of expectations from the two cultures. Here is where kids need full support from their parents and help in learning to function in a bilingual/bicultural way.

Parents: The Best Teachers

Many mental health researchers corroborate that adolescents by nature want to do things their way and in the manner of their peers. When they do not get the support of the family unit, they may begin to lie, grow detached, or become frustrated. The list of risks that such Latino children are faced with includes depression, suicide, drug abuse, delinquency, drinking, pregnancy, low self-esteem, and dropping out of school. These risks can be minimized by the closeness of the family and by instilling *respeto,* but never forget that *respeto* must be a two-way street in order for children to feel comfortable admitting to the inevitable mistakes we all make.

What must be done is to help the child learn to express and channel anger *constructively* in a respectful and empathetic manner. Parents can teach their children that and much more; they are the best teachers. They can be the facilitators for their children to learn to function in North American culture by achieving a balance that allows children to retain the best of the two worlds.

R.E.S.P.E.T.O.: The Seven Points of Light

Attaining a balance is an essential part of the new *respeto.* To be a balanced bicultural/bilingual individual, valuing both the Latino and North American cultures, can be a source of pride and well-being for our children. They should not have to feel that any part of who they are is inferior or undesirable. In order to model or demonstrate this balance, look at yourself and those around you and reflect on how you relate to your mother, in-laws, and other family members and how they relate to you. Keeping and adapting the best of Latino and the North American cultures can be done with what I call the Seven Points of Light, or the Essence of the new *respeto.*

The Seven Points of Light have been quite useful for Latino parents I have worked with who were struggling with the old ways that were not working. When they applied these new ways, they felt they were instilling a powerful new *respeto,* raising a child who obeyed but who also communicated with them and was able to express his feelings. The result was a happier, better adjusted, more obedient, more lovely Latino child.

The Essence of the New Respeto: *The Seven Points of Light*

1. R Repeat often to your child the things you like most about him
2. E Explain the meaning of new experiences through dialogue
3. S State your desires and demands clearly and simply
4. P Provide opportunities for your child to develop skills and assets
5. E Express your feelings as feelings, not as labels
6. T Take the time to listen when your child has a problem
7. O Open your child's eyes to understanding other people's feelings

Point of Light No. 1:
Repeat Often to Your Child the Things You Like Most About Him

Focus on the positive aspects of your child. Decide on the qualities you like most about him and write them down. Think about whether these are traits you also like about yourself, or whether you may be lacking them to some degree. Make it a point to share with your child just what those positive things are.

Some Latino parents adhere to an unwritten belief that by telling their child he is great, they will spoil him. They feel it is better to foster humility by avoiding positive reinforcement. In my view, nothing could be further from the truth. In my practice, I have seen time after time the great benefits of validating a child's *orgullo.* Let's see how the old way can be modified to include *respeto* in the new way.

The Old Way

Margarita, who is twelve years old, has changed seemingly overnight. Her mother, Petra, notices she has started keeping a diary, acting secretive when talking on the phone, and closing the door when she is in her room. Petra tells Margarita that she must keep the door open when she is talking with her friend Romilda. When Margarita finds that Petra has been eavesdropping and reading her diary, she complains to her. Petra tells Margarita that she is her mother, is only acting out of love, and that she must watch out for her welfare. Margarita, on the other hand, feels very resentful that Petra does not trust or respect her.

The New Way

Rather than acting suspicious, eavesdropping, or reading Margarita's diary secretly, Petra asks Margarita to sit down for a talk. She begins by acknowledging that Margarita is entitled to her privacy (by doing so, she is showing her daughter respect) but that she is concerned that something could be wrong, and she assures her daughter that she loves her too much to let her do things that could be harmful. She tells Margarita that mothers of preteens naturally worry about drugs, relationships, and bad company. Margarita in turn explains to Petra that she now feels more grown up and has begun wanting to have privacy, as Petra has taught her to, but that she is not interested in drugs or even boys. Petra then tells Margarita how much she trusts her and not to forget she will always be there for her.

Point of Light No. 2:
Explain the Meaning of New Experiences Through Dialogue

Consider the importance of new experiences in your child's life and initiate discussion about them. Whether these experiences deal with death, divorce, the loss of a friend or grandparent, the birth of a sibling, changing schools, or moving to a new apartment, house, country, or neighborhood, they affect your child's feelings about herself and everything around her. You may even share her feelings. Still, the best person to tell you about the extent of the impact on your child is your child herself.

I cannot stress enough the importance of finding the time—on a daily basis, if possible, but definitely once a week—to sit down with your child and ask what is new in her life and how she feels about the changes. This will give you valuable insights you need and want as a parent, and allow you to become a buffer against the stressors that can seriously affect a child's self-esteem and may endanger her well-being. Mental health professionals have found that a child's alienation can lead to secrecy, depression, drugs, bad company, and more. Ask your child what is going on in her life. Is she fitting in? Is she feeling unpopular? Is she feeling ugly or inferior to her peers?

If your child finds it difficult to talk, you can begin by sharing what is new with you. Tell her how a new experience you are having is making *you* feel. Be honest, but do not use your child as a dumping ground for your own anxieties. Your goal is to model or demonstrate a realistic depiction of emotions for the child to follow.

Old Way

Seven-year-old Ramon asks his mother, Rosina: You and Dad are going to get a divorce, aren't you?

ROSINA: Don't worry. We will be fine.

RAMON: But Mom, I saw you crying and screaming at Dad that you want a divorce.

ROSINA: Don't you worry about a thing, I will be fine; everything is fine. Go and play.

The New Way

Rosina says to Ramon, "Papi and I are having some problems. We have tried to work things out, but sometimes people who loved each other fall out of love and do not get along well. But this only happens with couples, never between parents and their children. Papi and I will always be there for you. We have worked out things in such a way that we hope you will not be too hurt by this, but we both want to hear whatever and whenever something is bothering you. We will try to be there together for you, but most importantly we both love you very much."

The old way attempts to protect Ramon from becoming upset over his parents' imminent divorce, but it does not acknowledge he is already aware of what is happening and would benefit from a clear explanation appropriate to his age that validates his awareness and emotions. His feelings are not being respected.

The *consejos* of O.R.G.U.L.L.O. would have helped Rosina to understand that even though she feels guilty about making the decision to divorce, she needs to maintain an open dialogue with Ramon about what is happening, during which he can air his fears of being lonely and forgotten. Only then can she reassure him that some things will indeed change, but that he will always have a mother and father who love him and will always be there for him.

Point of Light No. 3:
State Your Desires and Demands Clearly and Simply

Point of Light no. 3 entails engaging each family member in healthy communication using simple and clear statements. You must tell your child why you do not want him to bring a particular friend home, for example, but you must also respect his feelings if he does not understand your reasons. Do not say "That's final" and refuse to explain why you feel as you do. Perhaps by talking to your child, you may change your mind about the friend's visits—but you will still state clearly that you want to know what is going on and that if you're not pleased with what transpires between the two boys, you're ready to take action. Your decision, of course, depends on the severity of the situation and your instincts about whether to be flexible in this particular conflict with your child.

Old Way

Magaly overhears a conversation between her thirteen-year-old daughter, Ana Maria, and her thirteen-year-old friend Evelyn in which Ana Maria is using obscene language. Magaly walks into the room and tells Ana Maria to stop talking like that and that the next time she hears her using such bad words she will wash her mouth with soap. Then she asks Evelyn to go home, claiming it is late when it is obviously early. Ana Maria gets very upset and demands to know why her mother did that. Magaly says, "Because you have been disrespectful in my house; this is not acceptable and I don't want to see Evelyn here again. I bet it is her fault that you talk that way."

New Way

Magaly waits until Evelyn goes home and asks Ana Maria to talk. She tells her she understands that nowadays many schoolchildren curse in order to feel grown up and sophisticated. She also knows that many children cannot help being exposed to foul language in movies and on television. Magaly, however, says that she feels very uncomfortable with this type of language because it goes against the values she grew up with, which she wants to pass on to her daughter. She also says that she wants to hear Ana Maria's position and respect her feelings, even if they are radically different from her way of seeing things:

ANA MARIA: Mom, it's nothing. All the kids talk like that, so what's the big deal?

MOTHER: I realize that such talk is common in some settings these days, but I want to be very clear that I feel uncomfortable with trash talk and do not want you using it. It is disrespectful to you, as well.

ANA MARIA: Mom, everybody talks like that. I'd feel like a dork if I didn't!

MOTHER: I don't think that people who have a good vocabulary and respect themselves talk like that. Granted, when we are angry we may curse, but not as a habit. I know that many teenagers use four-letter words to look cool, but it is really an immature thing to do. Most important, it is not acceptable to me.

ANA MARIA: Okay, Mom, I understand that this is very important to you and that this is the rule of the house and I will try to remember that.

MOTHER: Thanks, Ana Maria.

Mom's message is clear and to the point. Ana Maria was allowed to state her position, as long as she listened to her mother's point of view, as well. There was respect on both sides of the dialogue.

Don't Protest! Explain!

Sometimes, abandoning old ways that do not work is not an easy task. It becomes even more complicated when extenuating forces collude with changes, as is the case with Ramiro and Elena's family.

Ramiro and Elena have three children, ages three, six, and twelve. Elena tries to make all her telephone calls at times when the children are watching TV or doing their homework, in order to avoid being interrupted. However, it seems whenever she is on the telephone, everyone has a question for her—including Ramiro. Elena answers everyone's questions but feels furious. When she gets off the phone, she screams her dislike of being treated this way.

Upon exploration with the family, it becomes clear that in this household interruption and similar crossing of boundaries are the norm. It also becomes clear that Elena herself often interrupts the children when they are on the telephone or when they are with friends, demanding they do chores that could easily wait until later, and asking them questions that do not require immediate answers. She does this with Ramiro, as well. Everyone gets angry about being interrupted, and the family has so many problems, accusations, fights, name-calling, and sheer frustration that they have to seek professional help.

All the family members in this household had screamed, gotten very angry, and accused one another, but they had never really sat down and communicated in order to establish clear rules and find a solution to the constant interruptions, which did not bestow respect on anyone in the family. They needed to apply the O.R.G.U.L.L.O. *consejos* here. For example, they needed to explain to the younger children how to contain themselves when Mom was on the phone by using *consejo* no. 7: Open the communication channels—and keep them open. Mom and Dad needed to show by example to the oldest child that everyone's boundaries needed to be respected. This meant not interrupting their time with friends—With some respectful co-operation and after applying O.R.G.U.L.L.O. *consejos* nos. 2 and 3, respectively: Respect your child's feelings, guide and teach your child; do not dictate, the problem was resolved.

The "old way" here was a result of Ramona and Ramiro's own childhood experiences. They each grew up in households where boundaries were not respected, where everyone entered everyone's bedroom; their *mami* and *papi* felt free to look through their children's drawers, and children were forbidden to close the doors to their rooms. Ramona and Ramiro were not even aware that in order to establish boundaries, they had to listen to their children, clarify their own expectations, and respect everyone's boundaries.

Point of Light No. 4:
Provide Opportunities for Your Child to Develop Skills and Assets

Identify your child's unique skills and abilities—not yours, your mate's, your parents', or your in-laws'. This is usually achieved by allowing the child to try a variety of things, such as studying different musical instruments and participating in several sports. If she shows particular promise in something, tell her so. If she is enthusiastic about an activity but shows no aptitude for it, try to steer her gently toward activities at which she has a better chance of succeeding. Share your own strengths with her, but remind her that we are all unique, like fingerprints, and must experiment before we find what we are good at. What follows is a case in point.

Old Way

Ten-year-old Julia is keenly aware that her stage performance in the Christmas play is being judged by her parents, who are in the audience and would prefer that she study piano, in which she has no interest. Julia gets so anxious that she forgets her lines. On the way home, her parents tell their sobbing daughter to stop crying; it is not that important; it is only a play; they don't understand why she was so nervous. Following is an old and a new way dialogue:

Old Way

> FATHER: We don't know why you don't study the piano instead, just like Aunt Betina. She would gladly teach you, and it is more within our family tradition. Your mother has always dreamed of playing the piano. Since she never did, she would be delighted if you would learn to play. Being an actress is so difficult, and you have to be extremely good because the competition is so tough. Are you sure that is what you want? Are you sure that is what you are really good at?

> JULIA: But I don't like playing the piano. That is what *you* want from me. I feel you are forcing your wishes on me and that you are saying that I am no good at acting. How do you know that? You are not being supportive.

> Julia's weeping begins to distress her parents, who are trying their best to soothe her but are not succeeding. Julia is inconsolable and finds it very difficult to stop crying even when her father orders her to. The parents do not see that they are imposing their wishes on Julia and not really encouraging her to explore what she likes. They also do not see that Julia is only ten and could easily change her mind about becoming an actress, but their opposition could only make her be more adamant about it. She needs to be given an opportunity to explore her true talents, not coerced to comply with her parents' wishes.

New Way

> JULIA: I am upset. Acting is very important to me; I really want to be an actress when I grow up.

> PARENTS: It hurts us to see you so upset. We are not concerned about you forgetting your lines, but we are really worried by how upset you are. We understand that this is very important to you. We wonder what you think happened up there on the stage. Can you tell us?

> JULIA: I was worried you would be disappointed and angry with me if I didn't do well, and I know that you prefer me playing the

piano. I got so nervous, I messed up my lines. I failed; I'm not good at acting.

PARENTS: Ah, now we understand. First of all, the answer is no, you didn't fail. You need to continue practicing and working on developing your skills as an actress. If this is what you think you want to be, just be good at what you like, not what we like. We thought that you might have talent for playing the piano, but you might also have talent for acting, and we believe that you should follow your goals and desires. We will support you 100 percent because we believe in you and love you very much.

Besides, we think you should feel good about the fact that in spite of everything you hung in there and finished the play. That tells us a lot about your courage and dedication, and we are very proud of you. It takes a lot of training and perseverance to do a good job at anything we want to be good at, and you are just starting to learn acting. Would you like to see a professional teacher to help you with your lines? Remember that we should never allow the mistakes we make to discourage us. We ourselves make mistakes. Do you see us as failures?

JULIA: Oh, no!! I love you! And thanks for making me feel much better and seeing my way. I know you would prefer me learning the piano, but I don't like the piano. I would love to take acting lessons and try to develop my talent.

Julia's parents are very concerned that acting might be too difficult and competitive for her. They are anxious to protect her and want Julia to consider other professions, with piano lessons as an enhancement. But understanding Julia's desires by communicating with her and listening to her reasons for wanting to be an actress helped them sort out their feelings and desires as well as Julia's, and to understand how their fears and concerns were preventing them from supporting Julia and what she thought were her future goals. They understood that Julia needed all the support they could offer to help her pursue her passion.

To that end, they offered her an opportunity to develop her acting skills, and to find out whether indeed she had the talent and drive needed to succeed. If in the course of her training she finds out that she does not have the talent or the drive, she will come to see that in her own time. Had Julia's parents insisted on her doing what they wanted, she might have pulled hard in the opposite direction, rejected their wishes about piano lessons altogether, or allowed her distress to impede her progress in acting. Julia's parents also remembered the importance of picking their battles. In this case, discouraging Julia from developing skills in what she felt she had talent for would not have been a practical choice and would not have been respectful of Julia's individuality. Here we can see the effective application of O.R.G.U.L.L.O. *consejos* nos. 1, 2, 3, 5, 6, and 7 respectively: Organize your feelings, Respect your child's feelings, Guide and teach your child; do not dictate, Love your child for who she or he is, Listen to your child, and Open the communication channels—and keep them open.

Point of Light No. 5:
Express Your Feelings as Feelings, Not as Labels

Point of Light no. 5 deals with clearly expressing your feelings without labeling your child. For example, you can say to your child, "When you do such and such a thing, I do not like it," rather than "You are so impossible. I cannot deal with you." You can also say, "I find it disrespectful when people talk to me the way you just did. Do not do it again," rather than telling the child he is fresh and nasty. You can also say, "This is simply not allowed. I do not like it. Don't do it again," rather than "Why is it you are always doing these things to annoy me?"

If you express your feelings calmly, the effect is soothing, often defusing a tense situation. If you are very angry, try to keep silent. Then, when you've calmed down, you tell your child, "We need to talk." If she becomes upset and starts yelling, remind her without yelling back that this behavior is not acceptable. If she sees you in control, she will gain control of herself, even if it takes a while. By example, show your child that strong feelings can be expressed calmly and respectfully. Never label your child by calling her careless, lazy, a crybaby, or any other denigrating names.

Old Way

Seven-year-old Samuel becomes furious every time his two-year-old sister, Lula, takes his toys to play. This morning he finds his favorite truck broken. He throws a tantrum, crying and screaming at Lula. His father tells him to stop carrying on and not to be a crybaby.

SAMUEL (sobbing): But she broke my truck! She broke my truck!

FATHER: You should not have left it on the floor. When you are careless and forget to put things away when we tell you, that is what happens. It is your fault. This will teach you to be more careful. (Think what it would feel like if someone told you it was your fault when you lost a precious object and were feeling awful about it.)

New Way

FATHER: Samuel, I understand how upset you are that Lula broke your truck, I would be upset, too, but she did not mean to break it; she is just a baby. Mami and I get very upset when you scream at Lula like that. Screaming is not allowed, no matter how upset you are. Let's you and I together find the best place to put your toys so that Lula will not get to them, okay?

SAMUEL: Papi, I have a great idea! I'll put them in my chest.

FATHER: Great! Mami and I will remind you in case you forget.

Here the father is sending the message that his son needs to be responsible for his possessions without calling him irresponsible or careless. Samuel's feelings are acknowledged and the father offers support both in finding a secure place for his private property and in reminding him to put his toys away without negatively labeling him. This is working within the principles of *consejo* no. 2 of O.R.G.U.L.L.O.: Respect your child's feelings.

Point of Light No. 6:
Take the Time to Listen When Your Child Has a Problem

Point of Light no. 6 helps you keep today's hectic lifestyle from affecting the quality of your parenting. It shows you how to cope with the daily pressures that may interfere with listening to your child in a way that fosters *respeto* for his feelings and circumstances. Often, our schedules are so demanding that we do not have the necessary time a child might need to learn a new task or to tell us he needs help. Many parents work, and children like to call their parents at the office when they need reassurance; however, there are occasions when this is not feasible.

Pedrito, a six-year-old, calls his mom at the office when she is in the middle of a deadline crisis.

PEDRITO: Hi, Mom! I am so excited! I danced all day today at the class party. I am a good dancer. Let me tell you all the things I did.

MOTHER: Hi, sweetie, that's nice, but I cannot talk to you now, I am busy. I will call you as soon as I can. (The problem is that Mom has no time and never calls—because her work is very demanding, and in spite of her best intentions she does not have time to call Pedrito during the day whenever she wishes. Pedrito calls again.)

PEDRITO: Mom, I am so excited! I danced with Mary and I had so much fun. They say I'm a good dancer.

MOTHER: Pedrito, I have to go, I am busy, okay? I have to go, please understand, sweetie. I will talk to you tonight.

PEDRITO: (crying and feeling rejected): You don't love me; you don't listen to me.

This is a very difficult situation for Pedrito's mom because she really wants to be there for him, but she has pressures at work and can't attend to his needs right then, or at many other times for that matter. She will have to explain tonight to Pedrito that Mom cannot interrupt him when he is in the middle of classes at school, and it is sometimes the same way when he wants to talk to her at work. She will tell him that tonight over dinner she wants to hear all about his day. It is important for mothers to remember that they cannot compare themselves with the old days and old ways, when many mothers did not face these tense business situations.

Pedrito's mother needs to explain in terms that he can understand—and without making him feel like a nuisance—why she could not talk to him. If there is no time to listen to him that night, a date in the near future should be set aside. Perhaps this is the kind of thing that needs to be prioritized: listening to her child should be more important than washing the dishes or making the bed or preparing a gourmet dinner. Pedrito will never be as affected by these things as by feeling his mother never has time to listen to his needs or to celebrate his successes. If there is no time to listen to him, he will not feel respected.

I understand that many Latino parents may not have the luxury of speaking with their child from their workplace due to their work demands, but children understand if you explain your work situation and make sure to set some time apart to talk every night. Most important, they will feel respected and appreciated by you, valuing both work and family. This is as significant as following through and helping them with their homework. This is what you can do:

- You can tell a very young child to tape his thoughts so that he will not forget what they are. This is a good exercise in learning self-discipline and to delay gratification.
- You can ask an older child to write her thoughts either on a writing board or on a pad, which you can then look at together and discuss.

I have recommended this technique to many Latino parents with good results. It follows the O.R.G.U.L.L.O. *consejo* nos. 1–7: Organize your feelings, Respect your child's feelings, Guide and teach your child, Update your media awareness often, Love your child for who she or he is, Listen to your child, and Open the communication channels—and keep them open.

Point of Light No. 7:
Open Your Child's Eyes to Understanding Other People's Feelings

Helping your children understand other people's feelings can be accomplished by role modeling and by having open discussions about friends, relatives, and adults in their lives. However, talking about feelings cannot be a one-way street. Children should be allowed to tell you their own feelings and express their likes and dislikes without being ridiculed or dismissed. Whenever there arises a need to think of others' feelings, regard it as an opportunity to inculcate *respeto*. These are good opportunities to help children understand why there are times when we choose to make a sacrifice.

Old Way

Nine-year-old Martha lives next door to her grandparents, who take care of her while her mom and dad are at work. The *abuelitos* find it easier for them if Martha would bathe in the evenings. Consequently, Martha is told that she has to do as she is told and bathe at night because bathing in the morning is a problem. However, she constantly complains about this, making the evenings a chore.

Martha prefers to take a bath in the mornings before going to school, rather than at night, but this arrangement creates problems for everyone because Martha is very sleepy in the morning and dawdles over her bath. This means she is late for breakfast, which is deemed essential by everyone in her household. Consequently, she is often late for school and everyone is upset.

New Way

Martha's parents ask her why it is so important to bathe in the morning rather than at night.

MARTHA: Because at night I have to do my homework, and then I like to watch TV, and you say I have to go to sleep by nine o'clock. There is no time to take a bath at night.

PARENTS: Well, the problem with bathing in the morning is that you do not get up in the morning on time, and you are making it very difficult for your grandparents to make you breakfast and walk you to the bus before they have their own breakfast. You have to think about how hard it is for them to do all these tasks in the morning.

MARTHA: If I can watch my favorite TV program after I finish my homework, I promise I will get up half an hour earlier to bathe.

PARENTS: No, this has not worked before—you still get up late and your grandparents are stressed. This is not acceptable; they are old and do not have the energy they used to have. You have to bathe in the evenings, but you can tape your programs and watch them during the weekend.

MARTHA: But my friends would have watched the programs before I have!

PARENTS: We have given you a choice; the solution is to bathe at night and either not watch TV or tape the programs.

The parents found a way to discuss these issues with Martha and help her come to an understanding that she was imposing on her grandparents and not being respectful of their needs. They agreed that she could tape her TV program, and if that worked everyone would be happy. Everyone's feelings were respected, valued, and understood. In fact, Martha's parents told her to explain to Grandma why she preferred to bathe in the morning, and that she understood their situation and would abide by their wishes. Here the O.R.G.U.L.L.O. *consejos* nos. 2, 3, 4, 6, and 7 were very useful: Respect your child's feelings, Guide and teach your child; do not dictate, Update your media awareness often, Listen to your child, and Open the communication channels—and keep them open.

LAS REFLEXIONES

It's time again to use *las reflexiones* as a basis for contemplation of how you regard yourself as a parent. Remember to write them down and compare them to the results of the quiz you took at the beginning of this chapter. Do this as often as needed. Ask yourself: What have I learned? How far have I come on the cultural adjustment continuum?

• How would you deal with your child's closing the door to her room when a friend comes to visit?

- When your child tells you angrily, "Mom, I hate you," how do you respond? Do you feel that, while this is behavior you don't like, you must respect your son's right to his feelings and try to understand them?
- What steps do you take when your four-year-old refuses to give Grandma his seat?
- How do you tell your five-year-old daughter that her exuberance has to be toned down?
- How do you handle your fifteen-year-old demanding that you justify your actions to him?
- Do you let your three-year-old cook with you and make a mess when you are pressed for time? What do you think is the best way to deal with your conflict?

Cruising Up and Down the Two-Way Street

If you want to travel smoothly in both directions along the two-way street of *respeto,* you must decide what parenting priorities need to be modified from those you grew up with.

Change is always fraught with feelings of anxiety, because we are more comfortable with what we know, but we are in the United States to stay, and we must balance the old and the new and pass that flexibility to our beloved children.

In order to achieve this new balance, continue looking into your mind and heart. Learning is a wonderful process, and learning about ourselves is even more wonderful because through *respeto* for ourselves and our children, we can convey our *orgullo* to the world.

CHAPTER 3

Keeping the Peace: The New *Familismo*

Before we begin discussing *familismo,* please rate yourself on how often the following questions apply to you.

5=ALWAYS 4=FREQUENTLY 3=SOMETIMES 2=RARELY 1=NEVER

1. Does the family come before anything else in your life? _____

2. Are you obliged to support family members who need your help—even if you don't necessarily approve of their actions? _____

3. Do you believe that having children is one of life's greatest rewards—and that one of its glories is giving your parents grandchildren? _____

4. When you have personal problems, do you turn first to your family? _____

5. Do you feel your mother is the best-qualified caregiver with whom to leave your child? _____

6. Do you believe children should be respectful of their elders, regardless of the inappropriateness of their demands? _____

7. Do you believe that blood is thicker than water, no matter what? _____

8. Do you overlook your relatives' flaws because they are family? _____

Three-year-old Eugenia is unwilling to go kiss and hug her grandmother today—because children her age are notorious for doing exclusively what they want and because Grandmother recently scolded her for acting too "wild." Fearing that her mother will be offended, Elsa said to Eugenia: "How could you not want to kiss and hug Grandma?" She then demands, "Kiss and hug her right now!" Eugenia refuses and is called *una niña mal criada,* a bad girl.

Your Struggles Are Real

You might be just like Elsa, struggling to keep harmony among all the members of your family who are so important to you. Making the family a priority has probably been instilled in you since childhood. But having to think constantly of the needs and wishes of your relatives, as well as those of your children, can be a struggle. Please remember and understand that your struggles are very real. As a Latino parent raising your children in modern times in the United States, you may feel at times as though you're caught in an emotional upheaval. This is a natural reaction to the stress of making cultural adjustments in your life and the conflict between those changes and *familismo,* or the power of loyalty to the family.

The Power of Loyalty

It has been said that for traditional Latinos, the family is the strongest link in the social chain to pass cultural knowledge from one generation to another. The family also serves as the supporting force: the entity that advises, and that only wants what is best for you. I remember when my family decided to leave the Dominican Republic, my mother and father had a family reunion, which included my aunts, uncles, and grandparents. At this reunion everyone was informed of our plans and everyone expressed their opinion and then gave us their blessing. This family support was very soothing for my parents as they faced this difficult decision.

Latino culture says that what parents have done for their children can never be repaid. This sense of loyalty prompts many adult children to care for their parents even when they don't really feel that their parents were "there" for them in the past. Traditionally and ideally, everyone is to be loved, respected, and revered. Children are highly valued and become the center of the parents' world, and the couple makes mutual sacrifices for the benefit of the children. In principle, it is a beautiful concept that assures support and protection to every family member in good times and bad.

However, acculturation brings conflict, resulting from differences in how Latino and North American cultures view the role of the individual in the family. This can create tension between older and younger family members if not understood correctly. Understanding how to negotiate solutions to these differences is essential. Notice that I say negotiate, not dictate. We will explore how to negotiate later on in this chapter.

The Dueling Definitions of *Familismo*

Familismo, or the centrality of the family, is a force for Latinos that permeates every aspect of life. It embraces not only the nuclear family but extended members and close friends, as well. *Familismo* requires that family secrets not be brought into the open. It places the safety and welfare of family members above all else. And it ensures that you can count on your family in difficult times.

Latinos would agree that this loyalty brings deep, warm feelings and is a powerful source of support. For example, when one of my children was in the process of moving and needed help caring for his dog, one of my cousins took care of the dog for three weeks with love and total dedication. In fact, my aunt, my cousin's mother, who is allergic to dogs, was loving and understanding simply because this was my son's dog and he is family; therefore, everything about him is loved and part of us.

Latino *familismo* is distinct from North American familism because Latinos are expected to be members of their family first and individuals second, while the concept of the primacy of the individual is a powerful basic tenet of North American culture. This duality challenges many modern Latino families in the United States who want to raise a culturally balanced child by maintaining their *familismo* while also helping their children function competently in their new culture. Although many parents see the importance of achieving this balance, they ask: How can I do it harmoniously?

The Transition from Conflict to Harmony

A smooth transition from conflict to harmony within *familismo* begins with the understanding that in spite of the beauty of *familismo,* there are times when it can cause misunderstandings and create discord between pediatricians and parents, teachers and parents, and even parents and children.

Conflicts can arise when parents or relatives take the position of knowing what is best without considering the entire situation, which includes the entire world of the child: school, friends, the community, and home. By no means am I proposing that you should let your child do what he wants when what he wants is not good for him. I am proposing that the child be given an opportunity to explain to you why he wants what he wants and that you proceed from there. You may decide that what he is asking is acceptable, or you may have to say, "I understand this is very upsetting to you, but I cannot allow it because . . ." The point is that you have given your child some space to express his views as an individual. He might not like your decision, but it is unlikely that he will accuse you of not listening to his feelings.

The truth is that nobody knows the best solution to a problem without evaluating all the options before making a decision. As a Latino parent, you might be faced with having to make choices for your child that might not have been available when you were growing up. You may feel as if you are breaking a rule or disrespecting a tradition. For example, I have many colleagues who opted not to pursue the opportunity to attend Harvard, Princeton, or similar Ivy League universities because their parents felt that making these choices would separate them from the family. The difficulty here is that, because they are now successful professionals, they might want to apply their own experience to their children, viewing it as the only option.

Although there may be good reasons for a son or daughter not to go away to college, if these reasons are based only on maintaining the closeness of the family, following in your footsteps, or being there to take care of your family, they really are not acceptable. Discouraging your child from availing herself of the best educational opportunities in order to keep her close to you might be depriving her of what she is entitled to and it can backfire: I have seen many Latinos who were forced to stay close to their family in the name of *familismo* who feel that this has hurt their professional prospects and now resent and avoid their families.

In addition, in the name of *familismo* many parents acquiesce to requests from relatives that they know in their heart are not in their children's best interest, but that they feel powerless to refuse. They say, "What can I do? He is family." (Or "She is my sister," "She is my mother.") The thing to do is to make a balanced evaluation of the issues in which you and your children's feelings are fully considered. Take a moment now to ask yourself the following:

- Should I prevent my child from going far away to an excellent school simply because I want her to be close to me?
- Should I allow my kid brother to move in with me in spite of his drug problem?
- Could there be a time when my father acts inappropriately toward my five-year-old?
- Should my fifteen-year-old not be angry with Grandma when she clearly embarrassed him in front of his friends?
- Should my responsible ten-year-old be forbidden to go out to play with his friends because his younger brother wants to go as well?
- Should my elderly mother-in-law live with our family because this is what she asked of me, even though her other children have a better situation at their home?
- Should I bring my mother with our family on a vacation when everyone might benefit from taking a break from one another?
- Should everyone in my family feel happy to go visit the grandparents every weekend?

- Should I feel angry with my spouse for not wanting to visit with my family every weekend?

How to Maintain the Balancing Act

Maintaining a balance between *familismo* and the surrounding culture is easier said than done. Even in large cities such as New York, where there is a certain level of diversity, many Latinos tell me that it is very difficult to achieve cultural balance, specifically when it comes to behaviors or values that are deemed superior by either culture or that conflict with either culture, such as being individualistic versus being family oriented.

It's important to be aware that your struggles are real and that you may at times find yourself in an emotional upheaval. This is a normal reaction to making cultural adjustments in your life. Culture gives us an understanding that is sometimes unconscious. We don't even think about it—it is simply there. It guides us and gives us very clear steps to follow in relating to our families, friends, and children. Our culture is in essence a script helping us to function in a certain way that makes a great deal of sense to us. This script might be lost when we have to adapt to a new culture, unless we are very conscious of wanting to keep it and then able to take specific steps to do so.

Keep in mind that individuality and loyalty to the family can coexist very harmoniously, as exemplified by a study conducted by a group of researchers in Brazil who compared Brazilian and U.S. students. They found that Brazilian college students, consistent with their Latin-American heritage, spent more time with their families, but they were also very self-reliant. Interdependence and support among family members need not compromise the individuality of a child. On the contrary, it gives children a very strong basis for handling situations in healthy ways. But, while children need parents' protection, they also have to learn to fend for themselves, within reason. This balance begins with the initial separation from the parents that the toddler must achieve. The toddler needs the security of knowing his parents are there, but parents need to know when to let the toddler venture into situations that could be challenging to the child but need to be mastered. It means knowing when to let go.

Letting Go: The Spirit of The New Familismo

The first thing to understand in considering the new *familismo* is that historically, many situations that involved the family's closeness were based on economic realities. For example, maintaining separate residences for aging parents or college students was not and still may not be within the means of many Latinos both in their old and in their new countries. Despite economic pressures, however, some accommodations must be made. The current demands of daily life may make seeing your family regularly, or always being available to take your mom shopping or your father to doctor's appointments, very difficult. The reality is that many Latino parents I have worked with feel so stressed having to be 100 percent supportive of and available to their relatives that at times they feel they are doing so at the expense of their own health. They often resent that their families do not understand their limitations and expect them to do their duty no matter what. Paradoxically, many of these parents also expect the same blind loyalty from their children and feel that to overprotect, or to blindly facilitate everyone's needs, is the only way to maintain *familismo.* These parents follow their earlier experiences, perhaps unconsciously, as the only way to be. You might need to be careful that your own childhood experiences do not cause you to overprotect your daughter or your son in the same way that your parents protected you. If you find yourself doing this, you may need to do some soul-searching.

Your Love and Support Will Always Be Needed

The importance of the family is always going to be instilled in a child who has grown up with parents providing emotional support to that child and to their own family. It will never go away because a child goes away to study or to an apartment of her own. In fact, your emotional support is a better indicator of closeness with your child later in life than the actual physical proximity. This support should be exemplified early in a child's life by both parents being there to help with homework, play with their daughter or son, and take the time to listen to what their child is facing out there in the world. When children leave home, they take your love with them. When they leave, you feel a void in your heart at first. I remember feeling that void when my younger son went away to college, and he was not even that far from home. But he was back soon enough on school breaks and he was as loving as ever. Letting him go was a compromise, but I know that this was the North American way, which is part of who he is.

¿Soy un Americano? *For Better or Worse?*

In my work with Latino parents I have seen their very strong desire to maintain their own and their children's ethnic identity. They want to keep their uniqueness and they feel threatened when their children act too "Americanized." In fact, what they say, mantra-style, is, "You are not an American, you are . . ." However, the term *Americano* has been defined as "a group of people bound together by their languages and traditions, as varied as America itself."

Many Latino parents and grandparents have indicated to me that what they really mean when they say to their children "You are not an American" is: "Don't you dare not be the way I think you should be," "Don't you dare not hold the values of my people," and "Don't you dare not cherish the loyalties I cherish." They feel terrified that they will lose their children's love and respect, and that there will be an irretrievable cultural and affective distance between them and their children. They feel that they have already sacrificed too much to the North American way of life by working long hours, struggling with a language that is not theirs, experiencing new climate conditions, and working in jobs that are beneath what they were doing at home. These parents often say, "I did not come this far and sacrifice so much to lose you." To see cultural changes in their children's attitude toward *familismo* is quite threatening. In fact, it poses a real double bind for many parents.

Familismo **and the Double Bind**

Pedro and Nelly came to me looking for help in resolving some problems with their eleven-year-old son, Arturo.

The Old Way

"We are having so many problems with our son, Arturo. He is dressing very weird, wearing very baggy pants that nearly fall off of him."

As we talked, it became clear that what was creating the biggest problem was that Nelly's parents, who lived upstairs, vehemently opposed the way their grandson dressed. The problem extended to Arturo's teacher, who called the parents because Arturo was looking very sad in the classroom and confessed what was going on at home when the teacher approached him. The teacher at this progressive school could not understand why Pedro and Nelly were so opposed to what he saw as a harmless thing. He was even more confused when the parents explained how the grandparents felt. He did not see why they were not making their own decisions as parents.

The teacher felt that Arturo should be allowed to decide whether he wanted to wear the stylish pants that everyone was wearing in school, and that the parents and grandparents were not allowing Arturo a level of safe individualism. Pedro and Nelly felt very misunderstood and condescended to by the teacher. However, when they came home they allowed Arturo to explain his point as to why wearing the fashionable baggy pants was important to him. Once they understood Arturo's point, which was to be like his peers, then they proceeded to talk to the *abuelitos*. But the *abuelitos* were still opposed.

I Hear What You're Saying, but This Is the Way I Feel

What was needed in Arturo's situation was an open dialogue among the grandparents, the parents, and Arturo. It is possible that someone in this group might not like the solution that they would eventually reach, but dialogue fosters a sense of *familismo* through O.R.G.U.L.L.O. by inclusion, valuing the input of the entire family. This is an important message to convey because it fosters good communication among everyone involved. When the input of those who mean well is respected, the message given to the child is one of teaching, which implies: I hear what you are saying, but this is the way we feel and these are the reasons why we feel as we do. In the case of Arturo, the same message is also given to the grandparents. Even though they might not be too happy with the solution, they can gain a further understanding, a good *entendimiento* of the situation. Another very important point is one I have mentioned: pick your battles. It's not harmful to a child to wear fashionable pants, even if they look weird to you. Giving in on smaller points will give you more *confianza* to discuss and forbid what is indeed harmful and not acceptable, such as drugs and alcohol, which are two issues your child is likely to face, and he or she will need to make the right decision of saying no. Here's how a healthy dialogue might sound:

The New Way

Pedro and Nelly: Mama, Papa, we know how upset you are that Arturo is wearing those weird pants. We think they are awful ourselves, but Arturo is such a good boy in every other way and he really likes these pants.

Abuelitos: We don't understand what has gotten into you. Mother and I can't believe you both allow Arturo to wear those things. He looks like a clown; people will think we don't care for him. You are spoiling him, and you will be sorry. I never brought you up to think you could do anything you wanted, and that is why you are a good person. Arturo is not like those American kids who do whatever they want. We are different. You have to tell Arturo.

Pedro and Nelly: Mama, Papa, Arturo is a good boy. He loves you very much and because of that he is facing a problem, because he wants you to support him. The teacher said he is very sad in school and this is going to affect his grades and the way he feels about himself. Remember he is a good student, he helps in the house, and he doesn't talk back. Everyone in his school is wearing those pants. He told us that if we force him to wear regular pants that are not fashionable he will feel very strange. That is not the way we would like him to feel, but that is the way he feels and we have to help him get through this. This is only a phase. We are helping him to be his own person. He is young and sometimes will make choices we think are a little odd, but this is a harmless decision.

ABUELITOS: *Ay Dios mio!* (Oh my God!) We don't understand things these days, but we never looked at it this way. Perhaps you are right. We will pray to St. Joseph for this to pass.

Negotiate, Don't Dictate

It is possible to keep valuable traditions such as *familismo* while assuring that your child will be able to function competently in two cultures. To achieve this balance you must negotiate, not dictate. Negotiation does not mean letting your child do whatever he wants. You have the power: you are the one who knows what values you feel are essential to keep.

Negotiating asks that parents and grandparents sometimes be flexible in order to achieve a harmonious balance in the family. But many Latino parents keep asking: How can we do that? The answer is by following the nine understandings or *entendimientos* of F.A.M.I.L.I.S.M.O.

The techniques below have worked for many families I have counseled. They have helped to maintain *familismo,* assuring peace among family members.

Entendimiento—the Bridge to Balance

Entendimiento means having an empathic understanding of everyone's feelings and position. It must include everyone significantly involved in bringing up your children: the *abuelitos* and other important relatives, such as *tias, tios, padrinos, madrinas,* yourselves (the parents), and, of course, the children. If we teach our children the importance of *familismo,* what we truly value and want to keep, if we include them by explaining through *entendimiento* the importance of loyalty to the family, they will follow our lead more harmoniously. The idea is to teach both our children and the older members of our family that change is needed, but that it's important to change without losing what we hold so dear.

1. F   Facilitate communication
2. A   Attuned Americanization
3. M   Maintain traditions—it is never too late to facilitate changes
4. I   Inclusion with distinction—avoiding enmeshment
5. L   Lessen the apathy—for you and your child
6. I   Insist on your own well-being
7. S   Sustain your power as a parent
8. M   Mañana is another day
9. O   Old is important, but . . .

Entendimiento *No. 1: Facilitate Communication*

Whether it involves issues with the *abuelitos,* your beloved aunt, uncle, cousins, *compadres, comadres,* or your child, communication is essential with every extended family member who interacts with your child.

It is not going to work to order your child: "You have to be nice to Grandma." That doesn't tell him *why* respect is important. You can force him to be respectful and polite, particularly when he is young, but you are not establishing an understanding of why he should do so that will endure. If you force, you are not instilling *confianza,* which is a basic trust that will enhance the child's inner adoption of your values and beliefs.

Take the example of Carlina, a grandmother who complains to her daughter, Maria, that her son Pedro's children do not come to see her as often as they visit their mother's mother. Carlina feels that they should want to come because she is their blood, she is their family. She accuses her son of not being supportive and loving. She feels rejected and neglected. Although it is known that maternal grandmothers are usually closer to their grandchildren than paternal ones, it is worth exploring why the children are not as attentive to Grandma as she would like. Carlina feels uneasy about discussing this with the children. When they do come to visit, she feels they are disruptive, ruin her neat home, and scream too much. She sees her grandchildren as *mal educados,* not well behaved.

Carlina is lucky that Malvina, her son's wife, believes that grandmothers are important in children's lives. Malvina suggests that Carlina call the children and ask them what they want her to cook for a special Sunday visit and meal. They say they want to eat *croquetas* and *empanadas,* which are Carlina's specialty. After the meal, Carlina decides to have a sing-along with the children. There is laughter and everyone has great fun. When the children leave, they ask, "Grandma, when can we come back again?"

Instilling these changes was not easy for Carlina. What made it possible was Malvina's communicating that she valued *familismo* and facilitating the necessary change. It required a great deal of patience and skill, but this is the nature of the new *familismo:* a lot of *entendimiento* from both women.

Entendimiento *No. 2: Attuned Americanization*

The second *entendimiento* deals with differences. It is not always easy to have someone we love be different from us. I have seen how difficult it is for some relatives to see the "Americanized" child put ketchup on *maduros,* sweet plantains, or on rice. It can seem like a violation of the old traditions.

Julio and Nereyda have Leila, an eight-year-old daughter, and Manuel, a seven-year-old son. The family visited Disney World with their uncle Fermin. In fact, this was a gift that he gave to the family. Everyone was having a great time in a Mexican restaurant until Manuel started putting ketchup on his rice and *maduros.* Uncle Fermin felt that this was not correct and demanded that this be stopped immediately. Manuel started crying and his dad called him a crybaby. Later on Manuel asked his mother why she didn't take his side. She said, "Fermin is your uncle and he loves you. He means well, so what is the big deal?"

Uncle Fermin grew up eating *maduros* in a certain way. But why should that become the only way? Nereyda would have been more helpful to everyone if she had said to Uncle Fermin, "Ah, don't worry. Manuel just loves ketchup." Manuel would have felt supported, which helps his sense of self and the way he views himself. Raising our children requires letting go of some behaviors and traditions that were very much part of our childhood, but that perhaps now may not be in the best interest of the children, may not be useful, or may not make much sense anymore.

Although acculturation requires letting go of some traditions and of some of the things that worked in the past, the beauty of it is that it does not require letting go of the things we truly value, at least not completely. In the situation with Uncle Fermin, Nereyda could have been sensitive to Manuel's feelings, which is really what this was all about: Uncle Fermin scolded Manuel in front of everyone. Mom also could have supported Uncle Fermin's feelings by saying to Uncle Fermin that she understands he means well and that he is doing these things because he loves Manuel. Children are very resilient and can survive many unpleasant experiences, but in my work with adolescents and adults it is obvious that many of these unpleasant experiences end in low self-esteem, shyness, resentment toward the parents, and feelings of anxiety and depression.

Entendimiento *No. 3:*
Maintain Traditions—It Is Never Too Late to Facilitate Changes

Family traditions such as the *Pascuas* and the Christmas holidays can be wonderfully meaningful and fun, but they also can put a great deal of stress on families. It is not always realistic to maintain every tradition. Sometimes adjustments must be made by everyone in the family. Trying to do the opposite can create a lot of grief, as in Irma's story.

Abuelita Irma, like many Latinos, has always felt that *Nochebuena* (Christmas Eve) is a very special time of the year, particularly for children. She describes this time as being magical and bringing her great happiness, particularly since she has little pleasure in her life other than her two children, Elsa and Victor, and her two grandchildren, Arturo, three, and Jose, four. Victor has no children and lives in another country, so Irma doesn't see him too often. For all practical purposes, Elsa, Arturo, and Jose are her only family. Because of these circumstances, Elsa pleases her mother in every way she can, even sometimes at the expense of the children. This is why every Christmas Eve, she puts the children to bed at nine o'clock, their regular bedtime, and then feels obligated to wake them up at midnight to open gifts, because this is what *abuelita* Irma wants.

Although most children will be very excited to open gifts at any time, Arturo and Jose were not too enthusiastic about this arrangement. They preferred to sleep. They fussed and cried, but *abuelita* Irma felt this tradition was good for them, since it had been good for her throughout her entire childhood. Elsa knew that her children would be happier and would enjoy their toys more in the morning. She herself would be less tired and could enjoy the opening of the gifts the next day, but she felt that pleasing her mother was the most important thing.

There was simply no distinction here between *abuelita* Irma, Elsa, and the children. *Abuelita* Irma found it hard to believe that the children would not be as excited as she was over such an important celebration, particularly the way she remembered it back in her country: the family gathering, the joy and happiness of having everyone together. Of course, back in her country the children did not go to sleep on *Nochebuena*.

Here again, we see an example of a rigid adherence to the old ways and the difficulty that a good daughter can face with a good and dedicated mother. When Elsa related this experience to me, she said she simply could not hurt her mother and did not know what else to do. It never occurred to her to talk to her mother and see if she could convince her to wait until the next day to open the gifts. As we talked, it became clear that Elsa was not actively looking for other solutions, since the only solution was to please her mom—she was the best mom in the world, mothers are sacrosanct, and Irma would do anything for the children and for Elsa, so what was the big deal of annoying the children once a year? The truth is that this particular incident occurred once a year, but others recurred on a regular basis in which *abuelita* Irma did not differentiate between her wishes and those of her family.

The bottom line was that Elsa ended up resenting her mother and then at times exploded in anger at Irma for no apparent reason, which understandably hurt and mystified Irma.

Communicating everyone's needs does not assure that everyone is going to be happy, but it can eliminate feelings of resentment and repressed anger that can contaminate loving relationships. In a later conversation with Irma, I explored her thoughts on the issue. It became obvious that Irma was finding it difficult to be objective about what she valued. She needed things to be the way she thought was right. The best solution to this dilemma had to come from Elsa. Elsa had to learn that the changes had to come from her and that she needed to take the initiative in deciding what she felt was good for her children. This is a component of parenting with O.R.G.U.L.L.O.: organization of your feelings. She told me sadly, "I regret that I made my children get up when they were so sleepy." I said to her, "It is never too late to do things differently."

Entendimiento *No. 4:*
Inclusion with Distinction—Avoiding Enmeshment

The example above leads us to the fourth *entendimiento,* which focuses on maintaining a balance between the individual needs of all the family members. Family closeness is essential, but there are times when you will be challenged by this closeness.

Enmeshment is a concept that has been widely discussed in family therapy literature. It refers to overprotection of children and a lack of differentiation between parents and children. I am not implying in any way that the closeness of the family is bad, but I am suggesting that you be open to the idea that there might be different ways of seeing this closeness now.

You could easily say, "I'll do it my way," but this is not only about you. It is also about the world out there that you and your child face on a daily basis. To fight that world can be very lonely, difficult, and debilitating. The best solution is to find a balance between not intruding on your child's personal boundaries and offering the guidance she needs.

Ask yourself what you really liked about your childhood regarding *familismo*. This might be a good compass to guide you while navigating the vast cultural oceans. But you must be very honest with yourself and try to differentiate when you are being overprotective. What is overprotection? Perhaps the best way to answer that question is to consult with others to glean their views on a particular situation. Seek out others whose views may not match yours. You must also look within yourself and assess which actions have truly helped your relationship with your family and which have not worked so well. This is well exemplified in the case of Betsy and her mother, Alina.

Seven-year-old Betsy goes shopping for school clothes with her mother, who asks her whether she likes the blue or the green blouse. When Betsy responds that she likes the green, her mother says, "No, you look better in the blue; green is not a good color for your skin." Although Betsy protests, Alina still buys the blue blouse. Alina's message was: "I ask your opinion, but I know what is best for you." Unless Alina takes a careful look at what she is doing, she might continue making these decisions for Betsy and either get a lot of grief when Betsy begins to challenge her on bigger issues, or discover that Betsy is unable to make decisions on her own.

One way for Alina to begin understanding her behavior is to recognize that some of her conflicts are based on bringing up her daughter in a culture different from the one in which she grew up. Alina feels that loving Betsy means doing the things for her that Alina's mother did for Alina. Alina feels that she must think for Betsy in order to help her avoid negative things in her life, even if they are as simple as choosing an unbecoming color—particularly since green is a color Alina dislikes.

Entendimiento *No. 5:*
Lessen the Apathy—for You and Your Child

The fifth *entendimiento* deals with teaching empathy to your child, rather than provoking empathy by making him see things your way. Teaching empathy to your child can be done by sharing your entendimiento of *agradecimiento* (gratitude). Sharing *agradecimiento* and empathy with your child can be a very effective and permanent way to instill those cultural values that you want him to keep. They will teach your child the importance of appreciating the love and support family members can offer one another, rather than teach him to comply with family demands out of guilt. Empathy and gratitude are essential to all good relationships. They require *comprensión, entendimiento,* understanding, and the ability to see where the other person is coming from, as exemplified in the story of Minerva and *tia* Mercedes, below.

Tia Mercedes always says no. It is her sacrificial *marianista* way. She never wants anything to eat lest she bother anyone by asking them to prepare it. This is a behavior that is annoying to everyone, but the older relatives put up with it. It is particularly annoying that when the family members invite her to join them for gatherings and holidays, she always says no unless she is asked many times. Thirteen-year-old Minerva gets furious when her mother's aunt behaves that way and tells her mother that she doesn't understand why *tia* Mercedes is so complicated. Out of respect, of course, Minerva never confronts her great aunt. She only tells Martina that she finds it annoying. But Martina feels Minerva should be more empathetic.

Martina sits down with Minerva and tells her what a good *tia* Mercedes has been, and that she loves *tia* Mercedes very much in spite of her flaws. She reminds Minerva that Mercedes lives alone and needs the family's patience and understanding. Minerva's mother reminds her that *tia* Mercedes is always there when she is needed and the beauty of families is that they are there for each other. Minerva learns that her mother at times also feels frustrated with family idiosyncrasies. But she is made to understand that it is important to think of others, especially when they are family.

Because Minerva is young and has little patience for *tia* Mercedes, Martina takes time to teach empathy and gratitude to Minerva by telling her some stories about *tia* Mercedes: how difficult it was for her to be the first member of the family to move to this country; how hard it was for her to accept working as a cleaning woman when back home she had her own maid; how sad it was to lose her husband in an accident; and how brave she was when left alone with big bills to pay. Eventually, *tia* Mercedes brought her entire family to this country and housed them in her own crowded space, caring for them with love and devotion. She helped pay her nephew's college tuition and paid for Martina's wedding. These stories helped Minerva understand how difficult life had been for her ancestors and fostered pride in the family's achievements and in the sacrifices *tia* Mercedes made for the family's success. She was able to feel much more empathic and tolerant of *tia* Mercedes's antics.

Entendimiento *No. 6: Insist on Your Own Well-Being*

The sixth *entendimiento* is essential to both your *familismo* and your parenting skills. This message is simple: Insist on your own well-being. Make being good to yourself a priority. It will help you as well as your loved ones. Make the following affirmations:

- My family is important to me, but so am I. It is not good for my family if I forget about myself.
- I should discard the belief that my family comes before anything else in my life in every situation.
- When I give up buying myself the things I need because constant self-sacrifice defines me as a good mother, I must think of myself as well.
- When I am angry, instead of pushing that feeling aside, I should look into why I am having angry feelings. If they are due to my feeling overwhelmed by doing everything my family is asking me, I need to understand the importance of communicating this to them.
- I must learn the importance of being comfortable with my limitations. I cannot do everything my family asks of me.

- I must remember that it is extremely difficult to have good *entendimiento* when I am feeling angry.
- I must change my belief that if I communicate my feelings in a calm and assertive way, I will hurt others and cause them to not want to have anything to do with me.

The Debilitating Reality of Depression

This advice is particularly relevant to women. As a caretaker of others, you as a mother must recognize the importance of taking care of yourself. You must be very clear that if you do not take care of yourself, you are doing yourself and others a disservice. Mental health professionals know that depression among women, including postpartum depression, is alarmingly high. In fact, depression in women occurs at twice the rate as in men.

Studies such as the Epidemiological Catchment Area (ECA) and the Hispanic Health and Nutrition Examination Survey (HHANES) support this knowledge. Depression before, during, and after pregnancy can have serious consequences in families, most particularly to the children. It is therefore essential to recognize that stress, which can be caused by trying to be everything to everyone (a cultural expectation called *marianismo*) can be exacerbated if you do not take time to rest, regroup, and nurture yourself. This is not selfishness. It is essential for your health and that of your family. You deserve pleasures and joy. If you don't take a break, your immune system can eventually become weakened, making you more vulnerable to illness.

Many Latina mothers and fathers tell me that after having children, they do not have time for themselves. They do not go out, do not buy clothes for themselves, do not pursue their hobbies or pleasures, and do not stay physically fit. They simply become parents. They feel very proud of these sacrifices, but they do not recognize that the end result can be deleterious to themselves and to the family. This is what can bring on the arguments, the lack of time for closeness, the lack of emotional reserves for empathy, and the anger that is then passed to family members and puts severe expectations on them. This is the source of accusations such as: "I have sacrificed so much for you, and look at the way you repay me!" Children do not do what they do to hurt you. If you don't insist on your well-being and do not prioritize your needs, you are actually setting a very bad example for your children. Your son may expect total abnegation from the woman in his life. Your daughter may feel she has to be completely self-sacrificing in order to be worthy of love.

Take a moment to write down your answers to these questions:

- What would you like to do for pleasure alone? With your mate?
- Is it possible to do it? If not, why not? Are you allowing others to help you so that you have fewer burdens to carry?
- When was the last time you had a massage or a manicure?
- When was the last time you took time to have a good, leisurely cup of coffee?
- Do you feel guilty for taking time off to watch your favorite TV program?
- When was the last time you told your mother or relative, "Look, I cannot take you shopping today, I need to take a little time off. I know you understand because you love me and want what is best for me"?
- Would you be able to say to your loved ones, "I am so tired right now, I cannot do that," or, "I cannot go to the party today, but I love you dearly." What would happen? Try it. You'll like it.

Entendimiento *No. 7: Sustain Your Power as a Parent*

The seventh *entendimiento* involves the recognition of your power to balance *familismo* in your life. The most powerful tool you have as a parent is the ability to be consistent in what you teach your children and in what you communicate to your relatives. The same socialization principles that apply to the teaching of *simpatia* apply to teaching *familismo*: it is really you, the parents, who are the most influential teachers, through your role modeling and your specific instructions.

One of the most beautiful and powerful aspects of Latino gatherings is the fun families have sharing food and having a good time. Use this cultural strength to build *familismo* by having celebrations at home and by attending family reunions whenever possible. At the same time, be aware that you may need to use your person/parent power to be there for your child in those moments when the presence, actions, or words of family members stress you or your child.

Keep in mind that what you do sets the tone for what your child will do. There may be times when you must be assertive to stop what could be seen as relatives' abusive verbal behavior, as when thirteen-year-old Blanca is told by her aunt Amelia: "Your face looks horrible with all those pimples, and you need to lose weight, girl, or else you will never find a boyfriend." Derogatory statements require immediate and powerful intervention. Blanca's mother must take her daughter's side and protect her self-esteem. One possible response might be: "Amelia, it is not helpful to Blanca to hear you talk that way." Another possibility would be: "What a pity that you talk to Blanca that way, as she really looks up to you. Why don't you focus on Blanca's worth? She won the science prize at school. She is a lovely, very *simpatica* girl." The point here is that if you allow your family members to make offensive or humiliating comments to you or your child in the name of *familismo,* you will not be viewed by your child as being supportive. Unfortunately, many families have members who are mean or sadistic; it is simply the law of statistics. They should not get away with their meanness toward you or your child just because they are family. Your child will appreciate your power when you assertively confront (notice that being assertive is not the same as being hostile) a family member who has been out of line. Your support will do wonders for your child. You will be teaching the new *familismo,* or the ability to resolve family conflicts, maintain positive family relations, and practice assertiveness.

Entendimiento *No. 8: Mañana Is Another Day*

The eighth *entendimiento* involves remembering that you need to prioritize while your children are young in order to conserve your time and energy. That means putting aside duties that are not crucial. It will require asking yourself, Do I have to do this? Is someone pressuring me? Why do I feel so compelled to do this? Who can help me? Remember, you cannot be everything to everybody. You can always support your family in ways that are realistic and feasible for you. You must forgive your shortcomings. Many Latinas feel they must make the bed every day and wash the dishes every night or they are bad wives and mothers. They'll let sixteen of their children's friends sleep over when it is too taxing for the parents, because that will make their children happy. They'll celebrate their child's first birthday with so much fanfare that they nearly make themselves ill with all the planning and effort.

Remember that *mañana,* tomorrow, is another day. You are the one who will have to be assertive and say no and not feel guilty. Recognize your limitations. You are not Superwoman. A friend of mine told me that since her daughter was born, she feels she must keep a cleaner house for her child and has little time to take her to the park and enjoy leisurely moments together. I laughed and said, "Do you think your baby daughter cares what the house looks like? She just wants you to be with her, relaxed and loving." But I understood her feelings. The important point is that if you exhaust yourself doing too much, you are going to be the one who is left out of the good, fun times. Perhaps having a clean and organized house while the children are young is not realistic. You can do that later, when they are older.

Entendimiento *No. 9: Old Is Important, but . . .*

This last *entendimiento* reminds us that tradition is important, but we must sort out what traditions are truly important and essential to keep. Our children will learn to love their past by our role modeling, not by forcing them to go along with dictates. Expose them to what you value; they will remember it with *orgullo.*

Our past may be deep-rooted and precious, but just like antique furniture or art, some beautiful things from the past need some fixing in order to be enjoyed today and to endure for tomorrow. Fixing what needs fine-tuning does not mean that we are denying who we are. Remember, it is the balance of old and new that matters.

When it comes to the importance of the family, ask yourself what is important to you. Why is it important? How is it affecting you and your children? Then make your decisions.

Showing your children how to exercise freedom within cultural traditions does not spoil them, and it does not mean you are allowing them to do only what they think is correct. It means that you are ensuring that the values that are important to you become your child's values in a genuine way, perhaps for the rest of her life.

You must trust that you can instill important cultural beliefs through modeling and instructions, and you must show your child that you have *confianza* in him. He needs to know that you feel he is capable of making good decisions and following what you have taught him. Your children cannot be carbon copies of you, regardless of how good a role model you are. But by helping them develop who they are and by instilling *orgullo,* you will be putting them on the right track.

~

By now *las reflexiones* should be familiar (and I hope helpful) to you. Remember to write down your responses, and take time to ponder them and compare them to the results of the quiz you took at the beginning of this chapter. Do this as often as needed. Ask yourself: What have I learned? How far have I come on the cultural adjustment continuum?

Las Reflexiones

- Are you struggling with feelings of right versus wrong when it comes to dealing with family obligations based on traditions? What are these feelings? Why do you think you feel this way?
- To what extent do you feel that familial responsibilities, loyalty, and solidarity are the only ties that bind family members?
- How important is it to take your eight-year-old daughter to Uncle Mike's fiftieth birthday party instead of her best friend's birthday celebration on the same evening? Is it possible to stress love for the family while allowing her to go to her friend's celebration?

- Are you capable of not following your sister-in-law's advice about disciplining your daughter? Can you do so without feeling you have disrespected her?
- How important is it for children to always be *simpaticos* with their relatives?
- What memories do you have of those familial duties you feel were imposed on you as a child? How do these memories affect you now?
- Is it very difficult for you to consent to something your child wants when you feel it is okay to do so but fear that other family members will not approve? How would you explain your choice of action to each party involved?

Be Mindful of the Past

In closing our discussion of *familismo,* remember that *entendimiento* begins with knowing ourselves. We must be in touch with how it was for us in the past. Many Latino parents I have worked with tell me, "I don't know why I am doing this to my child. I hated it when I was forced to do what I was told, regardless of my wishes." From that awareness *entendimiento* can grow. I have no doubt in my mind that you will balance *familismo* for you and your children beautifully!

CHAPTER 4

Fostering Friendship:
The New *Simpatia*

5=Always 4=Frequently 3=Sometimes 2=Rarely 1=Never

1. Do you get upset when your seven-year-old's letter to Santa Claus is rude and greedy? _____
2. Are you upset or embarrassed when your four-year-old daughter ignores your friends' greetings? _____
3. Do you blame yourself when your child does not follow the rules of courtesy appropriate for his or her age? _____
4. Do you feel that your six-year-old lacks social skills? _____
5. Do you forbid your child to go to friends' houses for play dates? _____
6. Do you discourage your child from joining groups and sports of her choice? _____
7. Do you consider your child's peers unimportant for his social development? _____
8. Do you feel you are a good role model of *simpatia* for your child? _____

Seven-year-old Juliana comes home from school so upset that she doesn't even say hello to her godmother Martina, who is visiting that day. Her mother, Betty, reminds her of her manners. Juliana complies but is not perceived as *simpatica* and *bien educada,* as she should be, by her mother, Betty, who apologizes profusely to Martina, saying, "I don't know what is wrong with Juliana today!" When Martina leaves, Betty calls Juliana to account and reinforces the importance of always being well mannered and polite. She even asks her, "What is wrong with you?" not in an empathetic manner but with annoyance. It turns out that Juliana had a very difficult day in school because she had a disagreement with her best friend, Cynthia. What she needed was for Betty to have been there with full O.R.G.U.L.L.O. techniques. However, Betty's main concern was her embarrassment in front of Martina and the thought that Juliana was not being *bien educada* or *simpatica.*

Niños Bien Educados—A Very Important Affair

All parents love to see their children develop into generous, friendly, loving, and popular individuals, but for Latino parents there is a special *orgullo* when they are told: "*Tu niño es muy simpatico y bien educado*" (Your child is brought up well; he is nice, friendly, and well mannered). This is why it is so important for Latino parents to teach their children the value of *simpatia.*

Although there is really no completely equivalent translation of *simpatia* in English, it is quite close to good manners and common courtesy. But *simpatia* goes further, because it connotes conformity. That is, you will do things you may not want to do but feel you must for someone else's sake. For example, a traditional Latino will never ask the guests to leave if they are staying too late, even though he has to be at the airport at five o'clock the next morning. Similarly, if a friend shows up on the worst day possible, a well-mannered Latina will not show her frustration or say that today is not a good day to visit. She will smile and be the best hostess she can be. These are behaviors based on what I like to call the Golden Rules of *simpatia,* which are adhered to by traditional Latino parents who want children to be *bien educados:*

The Golden Rules of *Simpatia*

- Importance of the individual being liked
- Importance of the individual being attractive
- Importance of the individual being a fun person
- Importance of the individual being easygoing
- Importance of the individual possessing flexibility and conformity
- Importance of the individual behaving with dignity and respect toward others
- Importance of the individual avoiding negative behaviors

Often, the teachings of these wonderful behaviors by and large do not pose any major conflicts between Latino parents and children in North America—except when it comes to developing friendships in the new culture. It is here that we begin to see cultural clashes.

Although the concept of friendship in North America includes beautiful values also found in Latino culture, such as comradeship, solidarity, support, and goodwill—just like *simpatia*—North American friendship differs from *amistad*. The difference lies in the emphasis in *amistad* on sacrificing to the limit, if needed, for a friend. It is more important to be loyal and a good friend than to be popular. Popularity of the individual does not take precedence over *amistad,* whereas in North America popularity is highly valued and fostered in children, and peer pressure is recognized. This is not to say that Latino children do not experience peer pressure, but many of their parents do not always see it as something that needs to be addressed or understood in their upbringing. One Latina mother told me that having a *simpatico* and *bien educado* child was more important to her than having a popular child.

This chapter will redefine *simpatia* in order to minimize stressful cultural clashes that could wound your children's self-esteem in daily social interactions. If you employ the parenting techniques I recommend, your kids will be able to maintain their good manners Latino style with *orgullo* while attaining a cultural balance that will allow them to make friends and be popular.

Amistad **and Socialization**

It is a given that Latino parents know how to foster the development of *amistad,* or friendship, in their children, but, here again, many choose to follow in their own parents' footsteps, enforcing old rules that may not work so well in the United States.

A child's parents or main caretakers are the most influential teachers of what are considered appropriate behaviors in one's culture. Parents reinforce in their children what are considered appropriate behaviors, which encompass preferred ways of relating to parents, relatives, and other important people in the child's world, including teachers and peers. In the social sciences, this is called *socialization.* For most socialized individuals, not following ingrained cultural mandates can be anxiety producing.

Socialization mandates the instruction by parents of many different skills critical to a child's social well-being. It is here that the blind promotion of old *simpatia,* with an emphasis on politeness, pleasantness, agreeableness, holding one's temper, and *aguante* (enduring stress, passively if necessary), could clash with the social values of your child, as in the case of Alfredo:

Ten-year-old Alfredo is unjustly accused by his neighbor Mrs. Smith of breaking her front gate. Mrs. Smith screamed at him and complained to his mother, Margo, that Alfredo was a problem and a difficult child. After Margo punished Alfredo for breaking the door, his father, Ramon, went to Mrs. Smith to apologize and offer to either fix or pay for the damages. Mrs. Smith told him to forget about it—that it was really her own son who broke the front gate, and that she had gotten very busy with a project and had forgotten to let him know that Alfredo had not broken the front gate.

Mrs. Smith did not apologize to Alfredo, Margo, or to Ramon. However, Alfredo was instructed by Margo to smile and be friendly with Mrs. Smith whenever he saw her. Alfredo refused, saying, "I don't have to be nice to her; she was not nice to me, and I got punished unjustly." Margo was very insistent that Alfredo be friendly and nice as the *niño bien educado* that he was, because Mrs. Smith was an adult and he needed to be respectful and polite to adults at all times.

If Margo would have asked Alfredo not to be nasty with Mrs. Smith, that would have been fine, but she was asking Alfredo to suppress his feelings and have *aguante,* to hold back his feelings and ignore what Mrs. Smith did. Margo certainly missed the point and the opportunity of applying the O.R.G.U.L.L.O. *consejos.* Her main effort in this case was to have Alfredo be a polite and *bien educado* child.

Cultural Scripts / Social Collisions

When I suggest that *simpatia* may not translate directly into North American values, I mean that it falls into what is called a *cultural script*—a specific model of how to relate to others that is tightly adhered to by members of a particular culture. Every group has its own cultural script, which is much prized and required to be passed on to children. In the United States, for example, a higher value is put on practicality, promptness, and individuality than on the formality of *simpatia,* which we Latinos esteem.

The value Latinos assign to the cultural script of *simpatia* is exemplified by how much time and effort a Latino family I met spent in correcting their seven-year-old's letter to Santa Claus, which began "I want a car, a truck . . ." and continued as a no-frills wish list. The parents were displeased by their son's bluntness and attempted to impress on him the importance of saying politely, "Dear Santa, I hope you are doing well. If at all possible, I would very much appreciate your considering bringing me the following . . ." They were trying to instill very early the importance of good manners in their child. This is part of being *un niño bien educado.*

The importance of good manners is definitely a priority to keep, even if it takes a few minutes out of a business call to first say "How are you, how is the family?" and then proceed to the professional matters.

According to the North American cultural script, it would be considered bad manners to show up at a friend's house without calling first, as it would be to arrive at a dinner party two hours after the appointed hour. However, Latinos invented the phrase *mi casa es su casa* for a reason: to us, it's always an open house. Likewise, to be on time for dinner at a friend's home in traditional Latin countries is considered impolite because your hosts might not be ready and are not expecting you on the dot.

Cultural scripts can create clashes between groups and between parents and children if social behaviors are misinterpreted, but social collisions can be prevented. You must begin by revising the traditional Latino cultural script and redefining *simpatia* to include validating your child's feelings, as in Alfredo's case, and learning how to make friends within a bicultural context.

Facilitating the New *Simpatia*

Like *respeto, simpatia* can present conflicts for families when blindly imposed. This blind imposition often leads to children doing things behind the parents' backs, or feeling forced to behave in ways they find embarrassing or, worse, that could undermine their self-esteem. Now we might ask ourselves:

- Does this mean we must do away with *simpatia?*
- Does this mean that *simpatia* is something bad, not to be passed on to Latino children?
- Does this mean that *simpatia* must be taught to our children the way we learned it and trust that they will learn it as we did?

The answer to these questions is an absolute no! What you need to do is adapt some of the components of the *simpatia* cultural script so that they work harmoniously with corresponding aspects of the North American culture. Note that I say *adapt;* adaptation is a healthy behavior and implies control and mastery on the part of the individual. It is a choice, not an imposition, and in this case it is a choice that will be beneficial to your child.

You and Your Child's Everyday Ways of Life

Since child-rearing practices are intimately connected to cultures, Latino parents who are bringing up their children in a culture different from theirs are constantly faced with clashes about nearly every important aspect of the child's life, such as:

- What is the appropriate bedtime?
- How late should children be allowed to stay out?
- What is the acceptable age for having sex?
- Should children be allowed to go and play at a friend's house?
- When is the right time to let them choose the clothes they want to wear?
- Should children be allowed to play on the streets?
- What is the proper way for children to relate to adults?

In summary, what is the right thing for everything the child does? These questions are asked by many parents in many cultures, but different cultures have different answers to these questions. When you join a culture that has very specific guidelines for how a child should be parented that differ from yours, it gets very complicated.

For instance, it can be very disconcerting to hear your daughter say, "You never let me go anywhere. What is wrong with going to Mary's house? You know her mom well, and Mary comes here. Why can't I go there?" You might be tempted to answer, "Because we are different, that is the way it is, period." However, scientists tell us that we seem to be programmed to make sense of our environment by asking questions and wanting answers. This way of communicating leads to an active dialogue.

Understanding Your Own Motives: The First Step

In my work with families, I have seen parents benefit by gaining an understanding of their fears and reactions—especially when they lead to denial of a child's wish that does not pose any danger or sacrifice to anyone.

If you feel anxiety when you need to make a decision about any of your child's requests, it can be useful to consider why. Keep in mind that I am not suggesting that you should let your child do what is not agreeable to you, but you do need to be aware, for example, of why you are encouraging your daughter not to learn things that will place her on par with her peers and lead to good habits later in life, such basic activities as learning to swim, riding a bike, and choosing her clothes—or other issues that are not so simple, such as going away to college or sleepaway camp or going to play at the house of a friend whose parents you know and approve of.

If, for instance, you don't encourage learning sports because that is the way you were brought up and you have managed quite well in this world without these skills, think again:

- Are you really being fair to your daughter?
- Could it be that you are really imposing your own fears on your daughter?
- Are you struggling to keep aspects of your culture that you value but that maybe now need to be adapted?
- Why are you so adamantly against adapting some things?
- Are you afraid of losing control of your child?
- Lastly, do you fear that your child will not want to embrace your own culture? Perhaps, by imposing your rules too rigidly, you may accomplish just that.

Rewriting the Cultural Script: The New *Simpatia*

Although rewriting the cultural script of *simpatia* does not assure instant good results, many Latino parents whom I have helped feel very comfortable with the process. They have been able to maintain important and crucial aspects of *simpatia* that have been welcomed by their children and not rejected as something obsolete. By following the following eight steps of the new S.I.M.P.A.T.I.A., they have managed to maintain its essence. Let's see how this can be done:

1. S   Self-concept—priority within the new *simpatia*
2. I   Interaction redefined—the importance of friends
3. M   Mind-set is essential—state what you value
4. P   Peer influence—a new understanding

5. A Allowing the unfolding—your child's development of the new *simpatia*

6. T Trust but verify—developing *new confianza* through age-appropriate responsibility

7. I Independence and individualism—fostering self-determination and uniqueness in your child

8. A Adaptation—the way to go

~

Step No. 1: Self-Concept—a Priority Within the New Simpatia

Self-concept is the totality of your child's thoughts and feelings about himself. It is developed primarily through all the relationships that the infant experiences. Once a baby is born, she is given a social identity: a gender is assigned, a name is given, and she fits into a birth order—for example, as the firstborn, the middle child, or the youngest child in the family. All of these labels or categories become a defining part of this newborn. She becomes part of that family, and that family is part of a culture.

Many people's competence is affected by having had parents who did not think that they were capable of doing certain things well. This sense of incompetence persists even though they know rationally that they are capable. This is why the first caretakers of the child, especially mothers, must be very aware of the importance of fostering a good self-concept.

The following skills are essential to a good self-concept and are needed to foster friendship:

- A good self-concept cultivates **resiliency,** another key skill for the development of friendship and popularity.
- A good self-concept cultivates **flexibility,** which is fundamental to resilience, very important for a successful life for your child, and a component of good mental health and of being popular and holding on to friends.
- Most important for our purposes, studies conducted by mental

health researchers indicate that Latino children who are **bicultural** are less likely to be delinquent.

Here is an example, closely related to culture, of how to facilitate in the development of a good self-concept.

Seven-year-old Paloma comes home from school looking sad and avoids playing with other children. Her parents, who value their daughter's sociability, notice and become concerned.

The Old Way

PARENTS: Paloma, we were wondering why it is that since we moved to our new home, we don't see any friends coming by. Is there a problem?

PALOMA: I hate the kids in this new school. They are mean. They laugh at my name; they tease me, saying it means pigeon. I hate my name—why did you give me this name? I want to change it. It is silly.

PARENTS: Paloma is a beautiful name and you should not pay attention to those kids. They are really not as sophisticated as you are. They will forget about it; don't pay attention to them. They are silly kids.

The New Way

Paloma's parents take action they know will help her feelings. They do not blame either culture; they do not say "Americans are ignorant"; rather, they give her ammunition to resolve this situation. They acknowledge that this is a case in which culture plays a role, because Paloma is an unusual name in the United States and second-graders are notorious for being merciless teases. But they also recognize that it is up to them to bolster Paloma's self-concept, which includes an appreciation of her culture. This is what they did:

PARENTS: Sweetheart, Paloma is the name of Our Lady of the Paloma and your grandmother's name as well. It is also the name of the daughter of a very famous Spanish painter, who herself makes lovely things that make people happy. Paloma is a beautiful name and that is why we gave it to you. We feel that the children do not want to play with you because you are a new arrival in the school and they have to get to know you. This happens in many cases to children in second and third grades, regardless. The best thing to do is try again to join the group; if they tell you no, then play with other children. Give it a little time.

PALOMA: But I don't like my name!

PARENTS: You never felt this way until you joined this school. This is something that you may have to remember every time you join a new group. When our turn comes on Parent's Presentation Day, we will tell the class the meaning of Our Lady of the Paloma. And listen to how beautiful *paloma* sounds. Oh, this is like music. *Paloma*. Paloma is a beautiful name and that is why we gave it to you. This is how you must think about it and then you will see that others will find it beautiful as we do. *Paaloomaaaaa* (both parents singing).

Paloma laughs and says, "Oh, you guys are funny!"

Paloma is being helped to understand that change must come from within herself. She is going to need time to absorb this concept, but, with her parents' support, it will come, and she will be proud of who she is. Once she functions with *orgullo* of self, the children in school will see she is not bothered by what they say, and their desire to tease her will quickly disappear.

This way of fostering self-concept works very well in my private practice with families, who may come with good reasons to feel bitter and angry about the prejudice and ignorance they have encountered in their new country. Eventually they realize that they have a tremendous inner power to prevent others from defining them.

You must teach children that when they are strong within themselves, they will be *muy simpaticos,* popular among their friends, polite, and definitely their own person. These are beautiful attributes to possess with great *orgullo*.

Step No. 2: Interaction Redefined—the Importance of Friends

The second step of S.I.M.P.A.T.I.A. looks at how to encourage your child to be a popular participant in two worlds.

During an interview with Magdalena, a very intelligent and self-described "modern" professional Latina, raised in this country from the age of two, I heard the following contradictions: "I believe it is important for my eight-year-old daughter to have friends, but they have to come to my house so that I can supervise and monitor them. I do not allow her to go to anybody else's house."

I asked: "Is this also something that you practice with your two sons, as well?"

"No," she replied, "boys are boys."

I then asked: "If we consider drugs and AIDS, don't you think your boys are in as much danger these days?"

Laughing nervously, she admitted, "I never saw it that way."

Getting in Synch with the Times

As an only daughter, Violeta grew up with all the adults in her life hovering over her and granting her everything but not allowing her to have friends. She never learned the importance of taking turns, and now as an adult she gets furious when she doesn't get her way with her husband. She says she does not get along with her daughter, but that is because she screams at her rather than communicates with her. In fact, she says that she finds it very difficult to listen; she often interrupts and does not know how to initiate or end a conversation. She has no friends and is very upset that her eighteen-year-old daughter, Consuelo, is just like her. She forces her to do things and to be with friends, but it does not work. It takes family therapy for Violeta and Consuelo to work things out, but they do!

What is most important to note here is that Violeta has realized that not letting Consuelo have play dates or go over to friends' houses in the past was all based on a fear that something could happen to her. Friends were allowed to play in the house, but after a while they stopped coming because Violeta objected to the noise they made and scolded them for not saying thank you or please all the time. She also did not allow her daughter to ride a bike or go swimming. In fact, Consuelo still does not know how to swim. Violeta has two younger children and fears they may develop problems as Consuelo has.

At first, Violeta could not see herself allowing Consuelo and her two younger children to do things that were normal for her friends, who were good kids but "different." But at the same time, she could not ignore how important it was to the development of lifelong relationship skills to allow her children to make friends. Violeta learned in time that it was through exposure to diversity that her children were able to feel proud of who they were. She dealt with the reality that children today are prey to more dangers than when she was a child— but that the best way to protect them was to help them be aware of these dangers. Although her mother felt she was exposing the children to unpleasant things without cause, Violeta at last chose to trust her own emerging bicultural understanding.

Step No. 3: Mind–Set Is Essential—State What You Value

Scientists who study bicultural competence have found that what they call "the alternative model"—maintaining both culture scripts—is the best method of adaptation for individuals who immigrate or whose descendants are born into another culture.

In order to adapt to a new culture, parents and children need to possess a strong personal identity, be aware of their cultural values and beliefs, have sensitivity to how affection is displayed and by whom, communicate clearly in the language of that culture, be able to perform socially sanctioned behaviors, maintain social relations within the cultural group, and know how to negotiate the institutional associations of that culture.

Here are some effective strategies:

• Share with your children your experiences as an immigrant or person whose background is from another culture.

- Tell them about the heroes of Latin America whom you admire.
- Explain to them why it is so important to be kind to the elderly neighbor.
- Watch that you practice what you preach and do not speak badly of those who are rude or demeaning to you. Simply acknowledge that they are wrong in their assessment of who you are.
- When you have friends over, be aware of how you come across in front of your children; they are always watching.
- Do not enforce your way of making or treating friends on your children, but do tell them why you think it is important to do what you do. And demand good manners always, assertively if necessary, but without being hostile or rude.
- Never promote a sense of humbleness that implies your child is not as good as others. Validate real humiliating actions done to your child, as in the case of Alfredo mentioned earlier in this chapter. You don't have to encourage a hostile response, but you need to validate your child's feelings.
- Encourage survival techniques in your child that will not foster bullying or the teasing of their cultural selves, as in the case of Paloma.
- Do not allow rudeness or meanness toward your child's friends, even if they are mean and nasty themselves; encourage inner-strength techniques such as seeing that the other child is not to be taken seriously, or to be ignored, or encourage walking away from these types of acquaintances.
- Share with your children your feelings of anger or disappointment with your own friends and what you feel are your choices in handling these situations, for example, not paying attention, communicating your feelings, ending the friendship if needed. These are all potentially appropriate behaviors.

Step No. 4: Peer Influence—a New Understanding

Your understanding of the importance of peers in your child's life is crucial. Peer influence helps children to begin the healthy separation from their parents and development of their own identity; it peaks during adolescence when parental influence tends to decline. Children who have been helped to gain a sense of who they are, who have been taught a strong value system from their families, and who have felt loved and supported are much better prepared to be their own person and resist the negative influence of their peers. That is why it is imperative to help your child make informed decisions and to communicate freely with you without feeling you will be critical or judgmental. To best protect your child from negative peer influence:

- Help him to make appropriate decisions.
- Encourage independent thinking while staying aware of what is happening in your child's world. Sometimes the communication you will have with your child will require a great deal of patience and understanding because he will claim everyone else is doing it or that some parent allows his son to do it or that you are being old-fashioned or ruining his fun.

The key component here is to really communicate with your child, not impose your values blindly.

Give Your Child the Gift of Making Mistakes
Studies indicate that children who are taught responsibility and who are presented with reasonable choices by their parents are less vulnerable to the influence of peers. The challenge for Latino parents in North America is to love kids enough to sometimes allow them to make their own mistakes, within reason. Parents have to learn to deal with their own anxiety in ways other than overprotecting their children by controlling their choice of friends or by being conspicuously present in their daughter's room when she brings a friend home from school.

In age-appropriate language and without judgments, parents should communicate to their children their feelings about issues such as sexuality, morality, drugs, and alcohol while making sure they leave communication channels open. Remember that their peers will be influencing them, and you want to know what they are saying, but if you are too rigid and anxious, there is not going to be a dialogue and they won't tell you much.

Parents sometimes shut down communication by not understanding the importance of peer influence on their children. In the example below, parents didn't underestimate the importance of peers and helped their daughter navigate a difficult situation:

Thirteen-year-old Rafaela starts a new school in a new state. She begins to change her dressing habits and hairstyles, and her grades start to slide. Her parents, Manolo and Zoraida, meet with her teacher, but it doesn't help. Manolo and Zoraida decide that the best thing is to ask their daughter what is bothering her.

Rafaela informs her parents that her new friends tell her she comes across like a Latina who looks very *presumida* (self-assured and conceited), and that they say with disdain, "Who does she think she is, a *blanquita?*" Rafaela understands that this pejorative term referring to whites is a rejection. To her, the implication is that to be good, to look good, and to excel is considered wrong.

This is what transpired when the family met:

PARENTS: Rafaela, *cariño,* sweetie, we are very concerned by the way you are dressing these days. Your hair is not as pretty as before, your choice of clothes has changed, you don't wear the beautiful jeans, loafers, and sweaters you got for Three Kings and loved so much.

RAFAELA: I am fine, don't worry, I am fine.

PARENTS: No, you are not fine. Also what is of great concern to us is that your grades are really slipping. This is not like you. We feel something is bothering you. What is it? Please tell us.

RAFAELA: You must promise that you will not stop me from being with my new friends Anita and Yamila.

PARENTS: Why would we do that?

RAFAELA: Because if I try to be *blanquita,* they won't like me and they are my friends.

PARENTS: Well, let's see, what is it that they feel you should be? It sounds like they are saying that by looking nice, getting good grades, and being smart you are trying to be who you are not.

Are they saying that you should be inadequate or bad? Sweetheart, you are our *princesa,* our princess. We are not saying that you should be conceited, but you should not put yourself in a second-class position, either. You must go back to getting your good grades and being who you are.

You are going through an adjustment period and it might take a bit of time until you feel better. Remember what we have told you about the time we moved to this country and what it was like for us?

RAFAELA: Yes, I do remember, and you are right. Maybe I can be myself and still keep my friends.

Here the key to parental success is maintaining a dialogue that emphasizes positive behaviors without adamantly forbidding Rafaela to continue being friends with Yamila and Anita.

Step No. 5: Allowing the Unfolding—Your Child's Development of the New Simpatia

This step stresses the importance of allowing and supporting your child's participation in age-appropriate social activities. We will see in chapter 6 how many parents have not only allowed but actively fostered the development of popularity and social competence in their children within the new *simpatia* format. By following the *consejos* of O.R.G.U.L.L.O., these parents have facilitated a culturally balanced level of *simpatia* and *amistad* in their children.

Latinos value *amistad* and guard it with zealousness: a good friend, like family, will always be there for you. But how are you going to foster social competence and individuality if your daughter is not allowed—with your supervision—to choose who she wants to play with? The friendship-making skills she will develop with practice will help build empathy and resiliency in future relationships.

Most popular children are invited to and participate in birthday parties, sleepovers, team sports, and plays. Children who are not allowed to participate in safe peer activities feel their popularity and self-esteem suffer. This is not to say that children have to do everything their peers do. But North America's cultural script, to which your child is exposed daily, considers going to a friend's house to play, without the parents coming along, as a very normal aspect of a child's development.

Does this mean that we have to conform and allow our children to do everything that is being done out there? Again, the answer is no, but you should consider doing the following:

- Remember that you must start *simpatia* training early. Do not expect that you can let your preschooler do things that are not correct—such as smearing jelly on the sofa—laugh it off, and then expect that he will magically develop responsibility and empathy when he is older.
- Appreciate your child's feelings; hear what she is telling you and then assist her to understand your position. Explain why you feel as you do.
- Reinforce both the information and your rules, and make sure that your child understands what you are asking and why.
- Know what is going on with your child in school and with his peers so that you can talk together. Do not judge, do not criticize. Express your feelings and opinions and listen to your child's.
- Validate and appreciate your child's world. Show empathy and be mindful that lessons in good manners might have to be repeated over and over, so be patient.
- Do not despair if your very young child is not being mindful or showing the social graces you value, just keep teaching them through action, role modeling, and clear communication.

Step No. 6: Trust but Verify—Developing New Confianza through Age-Appropriate Responsibility

This step urges you to help your child learn by negotiating, not forcing your way, as in Osvaldito's story:

Fourteen-year-old Osvaldito is having trouble with his mother, Alba. After school, he wants to hang out with his friends, many of whom are not Latinos, and enjoy a different kind of freedom from what his parents had been permitted when they were growing up.

Alba admonishes Osvaldito by saying: "You are a Latino. You are not an American. I don't care what goes on out there. In this house you do what I tell you to do. This is a Latino house." She goes on to insist that Osvaldito call her from wherever he is every half hour to tell her exactly what he is doing. Despite Osvaldito's perfectly reasonable objections, Alba refuses to discuss the issue further.

Although Osvaldito continues to rebel against his mother's untenable demands, she continues to make them—since, to her, expecting absolute obedience is part and parcel of proper Latino child rearing. All she will say in defense of her position is that her forty-five-year-old brother still feels obliged to blindly obey their father. The sadness about this situation is that Osvaldito continues to act out, his grades are bad, and everyone is unhappy. We will see in chapter 5 how these parents followed the O.R.G.U.L.L.O. *consejos* to resolve this problem.

Parent Power versus Peer Pressure

Ignoring peers or minimizing their importance as Osvaldito's mother did was virtually universal among the Latino parents I interviewed. It is not that they do not value interpersonal relationships; on the contrary, the fostering of *simpatia*—emphasizing good manners, common courtesy, and the development of friendship—is highly valued. But their good intentions are hampered by a lack of understanding of what their child is really facing. It is as if they are putting all their energy into anxiety about what could happen to their child if he or she has bad friends, rather than developing an inner sense of responsibility in their child.

Parent power with proper communication is more influential than peer pressure!

This step suggests that in order to facilitate trust in your child, you must begin by asking yourself the following:

- Do I understand the friendship-making skills required in the world that my child is now facing at school or with his friends?
- Does it make sense to try to maintain the old values that we cherish when they clash with my child's everyday experience?

- Are there new skills that my child might need to be exposed to but that may present problems for me, such as play dates, going away to camp, or sleepovers? Am I opposed to these experiences, even after I get to know the adults my child will be visiting? If so, why?
- What do I do when I feel that I cannot allow what my son is asking? Do I dialogue with him as to why I am saying no?
- When I say no, have I considered O.R.G.U.L.L.O. *consejo* No. 1: Organize your feelings? Then have I thought about the opportunities he is being deprived of—opportunities to develop friendships that offer him an arena to practice other necessary skills?

This self-examination process is the beginning of the development of *confianza* (trust) in your child, which is essential for instilling responsibility.

There is no question that your child will at times break the rules or disappoint you, but, on these occasions, dialogue and mutual understanding are key, even if you subsequently take disciplinary action.

Likewise, it is unrealistic to expect that you can spare your child every possible mishap in the earlier years and that, as if by magic, she will absorb the proper values once a specific birthday milestone is reached. It is the earlier years, in fact, when you can most easily instill your values in your child by fostering trust and communication.

Step No. 7: Independence and Individualism— Fostering Self-determination and Uniqueness in Your Child

You may say, Let me give them my values first, and then when they are old enough they can choose between Latino and North American values for themselves. The problem is that in the meantime, they can go through a great deal of anguish when we say no without age-appropriate consideration and negotiation.

Keep in mind that your children will be exposed to a great deal of cultural stress; they are not only commercial targets and very impressionable but they want to belong. You can communicate through example and by dialogue what moral values you uphold, and know that your children want and need your guidance in striking a balance between the culture of their heritage and the very different circumstances they are confronting.

Here again you must do the following:

- Trust that when your children perceive your sincerity and love as you convey your messages, they will respect your point of view and may be more likely to follow your way of thinking.
- Incorporate their feelings at every opportunity and acknowledge that they are facing a challenging situation. Understand that in order to develop friendships, your children must be helped to learn to negotiate the world they face every day in school.

Talking the Talk

As part of modern life, we acquire new knowledge that can improve the quality and ease of our lives such as the cellular telephones that can keep parents within easy reach of their children and permit better socialization and development of *simpatia*.

Step No. 8: Adaptation—the Way to Go

The last step of S.I.M.P.A.T.I.A. highlights the importance of adaptation. Many Latina mothers I have talked with remember growing up primarily around the adults in their family and going everywhere with their parents, who were utterly devoted to them. They do not dispute that the dedication was felt as love, but they do resent that they were deprived of the opportunities to form friendships at an early age, to share and learn how to relate to peers. They would have loved to have been allowed to go to play dates.

Interestingly, despite their regrets, many of these young Latina mothers also feel that allowing play dates for their daughters is not acceptable, even if they know the other parent well and rationally know there is no danger to their child in going to a house with supervising mature adults.

You've Got to Have Friends

In the Latin culture in the past, there was no need to seek friends outside of the extended family, because a myriad of cousins and siblings provided a stable of playmates. You may often hear parents saying there are too many dangers "out there," and complaining that many non-Latino children are allowed to do whatever they want. There is the belief that many non-Latino children are left alone at home unsupervised. But have you made an honest effort to meet the parents of your children's friends, or are you resisting doing so? If the latter is the case, you might need to explore your feelings to see if you are resisting adapting to that aspect of the *new simpatia* that involves the ability to navigate in the two worlds.

There is no question that there will be times when your child will be exposed to experiences that are definitely not right, and perhaps even risky. Your goal is to build trust, instill a strong self-concept, and teach behaviors that will guarantee that she is not only safe but well equipped to deal with any of these situations later in life. For example:

Old Way: Julie

Julie, a young Latina mother, knew that having open trust and communication with her daughter, Andrea, was the best way to protect her. Julie understood that peeking in on her daughter at every moment when she had friends visiting or not allowing her to go to friends' houses was counterproductive and was symptomatic of her transferring her own anxieties and fears to her daughter.

As a child, Julie was never allowed to go visit friends' houses, and she went through a very unpleasant and abusive experience in her own home with her grandfather, who instead of protecting her was taking sexual advantage of her. Yet Julie could not tell her mother of the abuse because they had never developed a sense of *confianza,* a sense of trust. She was blamed and scolded when she tried to find solace and open communication.

New Way: Andrea

When Andrea was still a toddler, Julie recognized where her own fears of letting Andrea visit friends were coming from, and she acknowledged that her own anxiety was discouraging her daughter from visiting with her friends as she grew older. She did not want Andrea, her only child, to grow up shy and spoiled, not knowing how to share, or to grow up to be mistrustful and *antipatica*. Julie began allowing play dates for Andrea from age one and sent her daughter with a babysitter if she could not take her herself. She was very clear that the sitter needed to be watchful and allowed Andrea to visit only those people she knew well.

When Andrea was seven years old, she went to visit her friend Matilde. Matilde's twenty-three-year-old uncle was visiting, and he paraded in front of the girls in very skimpy underwear. Andrea trusted her mom enough to tell her when she got home. Julie called Matilde's mother and the uncle was told to stop this behavior immediately, which he did.

Julie adapted her own anxieties and experience into knowing exactly what to do to protect her daughter, not allowing her own traumatic experience to be passed on negatively to Andrea.

LAS REFLEXIONES

Look at *las reflexiones* that follow and ask yourself how much you have learned and how far you have come in the cultural adjustment continuum. Write down your responses, review them, and compare them with the results of the quiz you took at the beginning of the chapter. Do this as often as you feel it is necessary. Ask yourself what you have learned.

- In your opinion, what is it that makes play dates such a taboo behavior for children?
- Do you think your fear of not letting your child go with appropriate friends to appropriate houses is a carryover from your past?

(continued)

- Could your past include some bad experiences? What are these? How could you work through them so that you don't pass your fears on to your child?
- Do you think that instilling the new *simpatia* skills in your child is too overwhelming for you?
- How much do you value *simpatia*? Do you believe that *simpatia* is to be achieved at all costs?
- Do you resist *simpatia* because it was forced on you?
- Do you think *simpatia* is old-fashioned?
- How do you feel when your child is not showing *simpatia*? Is it a source of embarrassment? Do you overreact?
- How do you react to people who are *simpaticos* and to those who aren't?
- How do you define yourself in terms of *simpatia*?
- Were you ever called *gorda, antipatica, sangrua, pesada,* all adjectives that imply being unfriendly? How did you feel about this? How did your parents handle it? Does this affect your child-rearing skills?
- How do you feel about holding one's temper through *aguante* (enduring stress passively) if necessary?
- Do you give your child realistic options to practice assertiveness within a *simpatia* framework?

Orgullo **and the New** *Simpatia*

Teaching and maintaining the new *simpatia* in your child is very possible if you remember that you have the power to be the teacher and role model.

I hope you have gained some insights that put you in a better position to balance *simpatia* skills in your child in a way that fits his bicultural situation. Keep practicing with *orgullo* the eight steps of S.I.M.P.A.T.I.A., and:

- Don't be afraid of letting your children have experiences different from yours.
- Do share those personal experiences you value. Do talk to your children and help them develop their own individuality and decision-making abilities within a realistic safety level.

I feel very strongly that your children will blossom!

CHAPTER 5

Setting Appropriate Limits: The New *Obediencia*

Before we begin discussing *obediencia,* please rate yourself by answering the following questions.

5=Always 4=Frequently 3=Sometimes 2=Rarely 1=Never

1. Do you agree that you turned out to be a polite, respectful person because you got spanked whenever you misbehaved? _____

2. Do you believe that children are allowed too much freedom these days? _____

3. Do parents have a responsibility to spank their children when needed? _____

4. Do you agree that the only effective way to get your child to listen to you is with a spanking? _____

5. Do you feel that talking to your child about why a behavior is not allowed is not time well spent? _____

6. Do you feel that explaining to your child why a behavior is not allowed will diminish your authority? _____

7. Do you find yourself disciplining your child in a way that really doesn't sit right with you—simply because your mother, mother-in-law, or others say so? _____

8. Do you find yourself resorting to being too permissive because you don't want to discipline your child in the way you were brought up? _____

Four-year-old Elisa demands to know why her mother, Francisca, won't buy her the toy she promised she would get her at the mall. Francisca explains that there isn't time today because they have to get home before Elisa's six-year-old sister returns from school, but the explanation doesn't make a dent in the little girl's persistence.

When Elisa's *abuelita* sees her granddaughter's behavior, she tells Francisca she is concerned that Elisa is being spoiled and will grow up disrespectful and selfish—particularly because Francisca tells the little girl she understands how frustrated and angry she is feeling and assures her that she will keep her promise the next time they go shopping. Grandmother is firm in her belief that children are to be taught *obediencia* above all and must be told "no" with no explanation offered.

The Rule of Law

Like *orgullo, respeto,* and *familismo, obediencia* is a central cultural concept to us Latinos, particularly when it involves bringing up children.

Obediencia—and its English equivalent, obedience—is intrinsic to all religions and is a prerequisite to civilization: by obeying laws and practicing self-restraint, we impose order on a chaotic world. It is very important, for instance, to know that when the traffic light turns red for cars and green for pedestrians, the pedestrians can proceed to cross the street safely. It is equally reassuring to know that those who break the law will be punished and, one hopes, will not transgress again.

Although *obediencia* and discipline are important concepts to be taught to children, in my work with Latino families I have seen a need for some adjustment in the definition and application of *obediencia*.

Absolute *Obediencia:* **Open Discipline**

When I asked a number of parents how they defined *respeto* in their children, the consensus was absolute *obediencia*—behaving according to what parents think is proper and leaving decisions in the hands of the adults. The setting of limits for children in Latin America traditionally is the right and responsibility of all family members and adults interacting with the child. That includes a teacher, a storekeeper, or any responsible adult who may see that what the child is doing is not appropriate. It is not uncommon to see an elderly person in the park scold a boisterous child without a reaction other than gratitude from the child's parents. This is considered "open discipline."

In contrast, in the United States the setting of limits and discipline is primarily the responsibility of the parents, but with periodic involvement of other professionals, such as teachers, psychologists, pediatricians, judges, and others intimately concerned with the welfare of the child. For example, if a child arrives at school showing some bruises, the teacher may explore the situation with both the child and the parents. If the parents' practice of discipline is deemed too harsh, they not only are called to task but could face serious legal consequences.

Many Latino parents find these regulations ridiculous, largely because they love their children dearly and feel they are only protecting them and teaching them to be *obedientes*—and they don't need any outside agency to tell them how.

These differences can be very challenging for Latino families who have moved from their country of origin to the United States or who grew up in places where traditional Latino child-rearing practices were customary. These parents may feel frightened, confused, and deeply resentful of being told that they cannot spank their own child—which may be the only way they know to discipline an unruly child. Unfortunately, there are disciplinary situations in some families where the need for an outside regulator arises.

The Force of Habit

Often, spanking is something done out of habit. Similarly, many Latino parents and grandparents in North America, simply out of habit, continue to discipline children according to the rules of absolute *obediencia*. If you follow this tradition, however, you might inadvertently be teaching a child conformity, blind compliance, submission, and automatic deference, which may adversely affect his future.

A thirty-two-year-old Latina, Petra came to see me because she wasn't moving up from her present position as an accountant. Petra was unable to say no when she was given assignments that were not in her job description, such as ordering lunch for her boss and other top-tier executives in the company. She also realized that she was seeing similar behaviors in her daughter, Flor, who let herself be pushed around by the other girls in her class. Petra was very clear that she was terrified of authority figures. It was as if they knew more than she did: she always deferred to their opinions.

She was equally incapable of asserting herself with telemarketers. She either listened to the sales pitch while her dinner got cold or told them "I am the maid, I do not leave here" to get them off the phone. At times she simply got so angry that she lost her temper with the salesperson. She could not assert her rights and calmly say, "I do not want this call. Do not call again."

Petra's problems came directly from the harsh punishment disguised as discipline she received as a child. She described being spanked daily and made to kneel on rice if she transgressed. As a result, she either complied or lashed out when she could no longer suppress her rage. It took a great deal of work for her to gain the necessary insight into her habits of submission and deference so as not to pass these behaviors on to her daughter, Flor.

Discipline as Protection, Not Pain

The true purpose of discipline and obedience is to protect and provide safety for our children and to teach them the skills necessary for successful functioning in society, not to make them submissive or hostile. However, there are times when this purpose is not followed, and parents veer from one extreme of the cultural pendulum to the other in setting limits.

Some parents conform to the values they grew up with too rigidly, while others totally disregard what they learned from their parents, claiming they do not want to have anything to do with the old values and becoming much too permissive with their children. I have seen too many of both kinds of parents facing disciplinary difficulties with their sons and daughters.

I find that, in many cases, disciplinary difficulties can be avoided if parents use O.R.G.U.L.L.O. *consejos* to help them evaluate their own motivations, asking themselves:

- How do I feel about explaining my actions to my children? What is my position on this issue?
- Am I afraid to see my daughter's point of view if I disagree with her? If so, why?
- What are my most painful memories of being disobedient?
- How difficult is it for me to contain myself from spanking and not lash out when my son misbehaves in front of his friends? If I spank him, what options do I have?
- Am I overextending myself and constantly feeling tired and angry? Is this taking a toll on how I deal with my children's behavior?
- Is it difficult for me to accept my children's differences? That is, do I push them to see my point of view and feel that the only way of doing things is my way? If so, why is it so difficult for me to view things from their perspective?
- Why do I insist on absolute *obediencia*? Where did I learn to think and feel that way? What would happen if I discussed my feelings with my children?
- Am I modeling absolute obedience for my daughter when I interact with others? Who are these others? Am I satisfied with the way I am treated and how I react in stores, school, institutions, clinics, hospitals, at work, with my in-laws?
- What do I do when I am not satisfied with the way someone treats me or when it feels I am being oppressed? Why do I do what I do? Do I like it? Am I compliant or assertive?

Armed with heightened self-awareness, you are now in a position to confront a troublesome subject for many Latinos: enforcing discipline through what may today be considered abusive behavior.

I Spank You Because I Love You

If you believe that you must spank or verbally abuse your children because these are the only methods that keep them in line, think again!
As you will see, there are other, much more efficient and less damag-
ing ways to teach children to obey.

In my work with Latino families, I help them see that when they
expect too much compliance from their children, they are in a losing
battle. I assist parents in adhering to two major guidelines in the setting of reasonable limits: (1) being clear about the purpose of their
disciplining, and (2) being consistent. The purpose of discipline, as I
have said, is to keep children safe, to teach them how to function in
society, and to develop healthy behavioral patterns that will assure
success in the future. Discipline does not have to be harsh and abusive
in order to work. I appreciate that this is not an easy issue to address,
since most Latino parents believe that a little spanking and name-
calling are both appropriate and harmless; after all, many of us were
spanked and harshly scolded as children, and we turned out pretty
well. But at what price?

So many Latino parents grew up with the motto "I spank you because I love you" or "It is better that I hit you now than that the police
do it later on." It is as if the only way to discipline is by spanking and
causing pain. But doesn't it seem contradictory that parents who only
want the best for their children so frequently resort to corporal punishment or insults? We do it, Latino parents tell me, because we believe in our traditions of *respeto* and *obediencia;* we do not believe in
North American permissiveness.

Ironically, North Americans also use spanking and abusive methods to discipline their children. So when Latino parents criticize
North American permissiveness, what they really might be criticizing
is the idea of doing things differently. However, in my direct work or
in my supervision of others working with Latino families, I have seen
that spanking and unrealistic expectations of absolute *obediencia* are
quite prevalent problems for Latinos. And what might be more salient

for us is that this way of disciplining children comes from deeply rooted cultural expectations of absolute *obediencia*.

While spanking, hitting, or harsh punishment were acceptable in the past, there is now a consensus among child-rearing professionals that better and more efficient disciplinary techniques exist. I am in no way endorsing complete permissiveness, but, rather, disciplining in a way that will promote good results in your child, such as a high self-concept, self-discipline, moral behavior, and an ability to make decisions based on these attributes. These characteristics will foster development of a successful, resilient child who stands a good chance of becoming a resilient, successful adult.

Setting New Limits:
Why *Obediencia* Must Be Redefined

Many well-meaning Latino parents who are bringing up their children with Old World techniques have indicated to me that they really do not believe that any other methods work. They say, "You do not know my child." That is true, but I have encountered many situations through my professional work with Latino families, and I have children of my own. I know that you can discipline effectively without spanking or using harsh language. I also know that spanking and using abusive language can actually harm children, making them angry, disrespectful, and "down" on themselves. That's why it is critical for Latino parents to redefine *obediencia*.

I often tell the families I work with, "There was a time when a diagnosis of juvenile diabetes was close to a death sentence. Nowadays, the illness can be monitored with insulin and the child has a much better chance of having a good quality of life." The point is obvious: mental health professionals and social scientists know that there are better ways of setting limits and applying the proper discipline. Discipline, after all, comes from the Latin word *disciplina,* which means to teach. This is a marvelous way to regard discipline—we are teaching our children to be productive and respectful members of the society in which they live, not training them to develop a high tolerance for physical pain and verbal insult. Let's see how this redefinition of *obedi-encia* works in the old and new ways:

Old Way

Despite a hectic home and career schedule, Esperanza is planning a weeknight dinner party featuring her specialty, *sancocho*—a complex stew that requires a host of Caribbean vegetables and meats, and that tastes extra good if prepared the day before it is served. The night before the party, Esperanza stays up cooking till the wee hours, since she will be at work all the next day and will not have much time to prepare things when she gets home.

The following afternoon her eight-year-old daughter, Alma, invites some friends over after school. Everybody's hungry, so Alma rummages around in the fridge and discovers a big pot of something delicious. You can imagine what happens next, as well as Esperanza's horror when she comes home to find that most of the *sancocho* has vanished.

Esperanza loses her temper and proceeds to tell Alma everything she is feeling—most of which cannot be printed here. She also grounds her for a month. When Alma protests, "But you didn't tell me! I wasn't even here when you were making it—I spent the night at Grandma's house. I didn't know it was special. I thought it was for us, like always!!" she resorts to hitting her without listening to her valid explanations.

It is difficult for a parent not to get upset in a situation like this, but Esperanza could have avoided imposing absolute *obediencia* on Alma if the mother-daughter communication about boundaries were better. In this household, before she goes to work Mom always prepares food for the kids to eat after school. When they take advantage—by leaving empty juice bottles in the fridge instead of throwing them away and alerting their mother that more juice is needed, for instance—she simply gets furious and feels victimized. She never sits down with her children to establish clear house rules. As a result, when a big infraction occurs, such as eating the *sancocho,* she explodes. As we are learning, it is far better to be proactive and head off problems by communicating clearly so that children know what is expected of them. This is the new way:

New Way

Following the O.R.G.U.L.L.O. *consejos,* Esperanza can resolve the situation in a different, nonaggressive manner.

Esperanza acknowledges to her daughter that she did not explain that some foods were indeed going to be off-limits to the family. She also confesses to Alma that she forgot Alma had slept over at Grandma's and wasn't even aware there was going to be a dinner party. To teach Alma and her siblings about boundaries, Esperanza tells them that she will make it a habit to tell them when a particular food is off-limits to them or tape a note on the pot so that they will have no excuse for poaching.

Most important, Esperanza is now teaching Alma that name-calling and grounding do not constitute effective lessons in respecting others' property. Esperanza then solves the immediate crisis by calling the local rotisserie that specializes in *pernil.* Luckily, they still have some left, and she asks her husband to pick it up on his way home.

Essentials of the New *Obediencia*

As I've said, the purpose of disciplining children is to teach them to protect themselves and to function effectively within society. It is not to hurt them or make them suffer. On the contrary, most of us excel when someone we deem important tells us how proud they feel about us. We then try as hard as possible to deserve and preserve their positive view of us. The reverse can occur when we are humiliated or abused or feel unworthy: we just don't try as hard, and we may grow anxious and depressed—two behavioral components that lower performance and reduce our sense of competence.

You might find it very difficult to apply new discipline techniques when you are in a rush, feeling stressed, or your child is not cooperating—particularly if you have told him many times, for example, that candy is not to be eaten before dinner, or to clean his room, or to not yell indoors. We are creatures of habit, and we tend to resort to behaviors that are familiar, even though we might know there are better ones. Becoming more flexible as a parent requires vigilance and a great deal of practice.

The Ten Reference Points of the New *Obediencia*

I would like to share with you ten points of reference defining the new *obediencia* within *El Nuevo Tradicionalismo* that have helped many Latino parents who consult me about disciplinary problems with their children, and who want to learn new ways of setting limits while maintaining the traditional cultural values they honor:

1. O   Open a dialogue with yourself
2. B   Beware of behaviors that keep you stuck in the past
3. E   Encouragement can work miracles
4. D   Democracy has its merits
5. I   Independence must be promoted
6. E   Emotions are valid
7. N   Negotiating is not surrendering
8. C   Channel the child's natural energy
9. I   Inconsistency encourages disobedience
10. A   Aggression is contagious

Point of Reference No. 1: Open a Dialogue with Yourself

You know by now that understanding your own feelings is the cornerstone of *El Nuevo Tradicionalismo*. When it comes to *obediencia*, you are almost certain to assume a position based on your own experiences.

You were once a child and were subject to *obediencia* and discipline. The lessons you learned have affected you for better or worse. As you reflect on your past as a child and your present situation as a parent, try to maintain a very open mind and be as impartial as you can. Begin by assuming that the absolute *obediencia* with which you may have been raised was not the result of intentional cruelty. But also do not assume that your childhood experience reflects the only effective manner of setting limits.

You might open your inner dialogue by asking yourself if there are aspects of the way you are disciplining your children now that you feel you want to change. If you are screaming at your children a lot or find setting limits a chronic struggle, perhaps the techniques you are using are not working so well. Naturally, you recognize that teaching *obediencia* and self-discipline to your child is an ongoing process that lasts many years. But there are child-rearing methods that will encourage your child to be obedient and self-disciplined *without coercion*.

Go to page 115 at the beginning of this chapter where you were asked to evaluate your own motivations and again reflect on the exercise that was presented. The best way to make lasting changes is through inner exploration.

Point of Reference No. 2:
Beware of Behaviors That Keep You Stuck in the Past

My work as a therapist has made me certain that accessing and understanding dormant and sometimes unconscious hurtful or angry feelings can enhance overall functioning and diminish hostility and aggression within us. The painful behaviors of the past must never be allowed to be repeated.

If You Don't Understand the Past, You're Doomed to Repeat It

Many Latino parents practice the type of discipline that they grew up with. That is fine if that discipline nurtured a flexible and well-adjusted outlook in life. On the other hand, if adherence to *obediencia* did not promote self-discipline without significant anger or pain, then replicating the rules you grew up with is an invitation to disciplinary disaster. For example:

Mario and his brothers and sisters were raised in a household where absolute discipline was practiced to the letter. Rather than guiding them when they did something wrong, the parents scolded the children and often spanked them. Now a parent himself, Mario told me that although he has sworn to himself he will never spank his kids, sometimes when they really get out of hand, he finds himself doing precisely that. It is as if he feels at that moment that the only technique that works is spanking. Mario was trapped between the manner in which he was brought up and the style in which he would like to bring up his children.

When he brought his ten-year-old son, Hernan, to see me out of sheer desperation, Mario was not aware of how powerfully the past was affecting him. It was as if his anger blinded him so that the only disciplinary option he could see was spanking or what his father referred to as "*puño* therapy," therapy of the fist. Mario knew that Hernan had to be taught how to behave in school and at home. He could not be allowed to scream at or hit his younger sister, Ana, but spanking was not working. When I asked Mario what childhood memories he had about spanking or disciplining, Mario related several stories where he was disciplined by the belt and the fist. The day he learned to ride a bike, he received the beating of his life: he was sent to the supermarket to get groceries for dinner, but when he got an opportunity to ride bikes with his friends, he simply forgot about the groceries. He repeated several times that he did not mean to spank Hernan, but that sometimes the only method that worked was what he received as a child himself. Result: Hernan is disciplined in a way that Mario thinks is best for him, not based on Hernan's needs. Let's see how this happens:

Old Way

Mario gets a note from school that Hernan is not doing well in his classes. Hernan's favorite school activity is soccer. Mario tells the boy to shape up or he is going to have him taken off the soccer team. When Hernan brings home a failing grade in math, Mario follows through on his threat. Needless to say, there is pandemonium in the house. Hernan screams that his father is a bad parent, Mario ends up hitting Hernan, and, worst of all, nothing is really resolved. It never occurs to Mario to have a serious talk with Hernan and establish rules based on both their understandings of the situation. His actions are guided solely by old habits.

New Way

Mario applies the O.R.G.U.L.L.O. *consejos* he learned in therapy. He is getting in touch with old feelings that are serving as barriers in the present and makes the connection between his behavior with Hernan and his own father's behavior with him: while Mario was consciously saying he would not spank his children, he was doing just the opposite. Mario realizes that he has been reverting to habits learned in the past, the only model he knew to follow during a crisis. Mario learns to calmly explore all the issues that Hernan is facing, which include his being an excellent athlete but not the math whiz Mario would like him to be. However, focusing on Hernan's strengths brought much better results in all domains. It turned out that Hernan had great difficulties in math due to a learning problem, not because of laziness. We will see in chapter 9 how to identify undiagnosed learning problems and what to do about them. For the time being, the point is this: Mario could have avoided a great deal of conflict from the get-go by understanding and changing his ingrained habits of disciplining, reducing the pressures and punishment, and providing his son with the kind of help students with learning disabilities need.

Point of Reference No. 3: Encouragement Can Work Miracles

Many parents do not realize that constant harshness, be it physical or verbal, is without exception detrimental to their children. You must always take your child's self-esteem into account. Even though the word may be overused, self-esteem remains a critically important component of your child's future.

You are your child's most influential teacher, with the power to boost his self-esteem virtually single-handedly. As such, constructive discipline and encouragement can work miracles.

Ask yourself how many times you have been able to get through something very difficult because there was someone involved telling you they believed in you.

Old Way

Like little Mary in the nursery rhyme, nine-year-old Susana was quite contrary: if she was praised for an achievement, she insisted, "You don't mean that, you are just feeling sorry for me." If her parents commented on her grades, telling her not to worry that she got a B, she would say, "You say that because you care more for Mariela," her sister, who consistently got A's. Her parents would lose their temper and tell her how frustrated they were. There was simply no winning with her, they said; it was very difficult to be supportive with Susana.

When Susana's parents came to me for counseling, it quickly became clear that they were constantly reinforcing or encouraging her to be oppositional by telling her, "Nothing pleases you. You are the only person in this house who does not appreciate our compliments; your sister is so appreciative, so different from you." But they never suggested how she might express herself differently. What she needed was a different understanding of her feelings.

New Way

Through our work, Susana's parents learned to help her to accept compliments by expressing their feelings, rather than comparing her with her sister or calling her difficult, even though she was. They began saying things such as: "Let's hear why it is that you don't feel we are truthful when we tell you it is okay to have a B?" It turned out that Susana was a perfectionist and quite jealous of her sister. By allowing Susana to express her feelings, her parents helped Susana to feel more competent. Susana's feelings were viewed as valid, not as disobedience and defiance.

Point of Reference No. 4: Democracy Has Its Merits

Many Latino parents I have talked with feel that democracy doesn't work well in child rearing. They are aware that dictatorship is not effective, but feel there are times when *obediencia* requires a forceful application; after all, parents cannot expect a child to angelically comply with requests to behave. I know what they are talking about, since I brought up two children of my own, but democratic parenting is never to be confused with allowing a child a place of equality with the parent, in which the child is allowed to call the shots. It means affording kids an opportunity to be heard and to participate in constructing effective solutions to discipline problems. It encourages children's participation in establishing "house rules." This will not only increase the chances that they will obey those rules independently of you, but also that they will learn the essential components of the democratic process, including self-discipline, freedom of thought, and morality. In chapter 6 we will discuss in more detail how to apply and teach democratic ideals beginning as early as the child is able to understand words. For now, let's observe how the process can work:

New Way

Remember Osvaldito from chapter 4? He was the young boy whose overprotective Latina mother wouldn't allow him to interact with his peers by, for instance, forbidding him go out for pizza with them after school. These are the specific techniques they applied to settle the parent-child dispute using the O.R.G.U.L.L.O. *consejo* of dialogue:

PARENTS: Osvaldito, we know that you want to be like the other kids, but we really worry about you. Do you understand why?

OSVALDITO: Because you think I am a baby, and because you worry about everything.

PARENTS: That is not it at all. Remember what we said to you about your homework and grades? We are concerned that you will not have enough time to do your homework if you go for pizza every afternoon and watch TV every night.

OSVALDITO: But all the other kids are allowed to go for pizza. Besides, I'm doing great in school.

PARENTS: That is true, but it's just as true that hanging out with your friends and watching TV for hours could really cut into your study time. Where do you think we can find the extra time you'll need to study?

Osvaldito: I know! I'll tape my TV programs and watch them over the weekend!

It turned out that this is exactly what Osvaldito did, and it worked because he was allowed to participate in devising the rules. The earlier rules were clear, but they did not take into consideration important aspects of his social development and did not allow him to feel understood by his parents. The new solution helped Osvaldito to practice responsibility and self-discipline skills that will stay with him forever, because he knows that in order to go out for pizza after school he must fulfill his part of the bargain by getting his homework done and keeping his grades up. If he doesn't, he will not be able to have the privilege of doing those things that he values. His parents also assured themselves that the activities are really harmless, by checking into the pizza place and the kids whom Osvaldito hangs out with. They realize that this actually is a good opportunity to develop Osvaldito's social skills with North American kids and practice *simpatia*, as well.

Point of Reference No. 5: Independence Must Be Promoted

Independence is a trait that needs to be promoted from day one. We will see in Part Two of this book how to encourage independence in children of all ages. For now, consider that the best protection against drugs, alcohol, and other forms of self-destruction is to foster the uniqueness of your child by instilling self-discipline and leadership qualities.

The best way to do this is by helping her to feel competent, able to graciously acknowledge her qualities, draw on her strengths, and be proud of who she is. Here is a good example of how healthy independence can be fostered:

Anita's sixteen-year-old daughter, Eva, and fourteen-year-old son, Pedro, want to cook a Mother's Day feast from scratch. They decide on a menu they've seen Anita prepare many, many times for special occasions—*pernil,* a roast, and *moro,* rice and beans cooked together. Anita's feelings about the project are mixed: she's touched but she's also worried that the teenagers are going to make a mess and perhaps burn themselves; it might turn out not to be worth the effort. She is on the verge of telling them not to bother when she decides to apply the O.R.G.U.L.L.O. *consejos.*

After a frank dialogue with herself (O.R.G.U.L.L.O. *consejo* No. 1), Anita faces the fact that although it seems her concerns are about order and safety, they are really about herself: about the trouble she has accepting affection and her need to retain control. Cooking a *pernil,* after all, requires only seasoning it and baking it in the oven at the proper temperature. The rice and beans will be cooked in her special pot, which practically does the job by itself. So Anita puts her feelings aside, tells her children how much she appreciates their marvelous gesture, and cheerfully answers any questions they have about preparing the meal.

At last she understands that Eva and Pedro are proud of being self-sufficient and realizes that she has taught them enough self-discipline to be able to handle the task at hand. The result is the best Mother's Day celebration the family has ever had!

Point of Reference No. 6: Emotions Are Valid

We are only human, and sometimes we lose patience with our children. But nothing weakens parental authority as much as parents' losing their tempers in front of kids. What can you do to get it back as fast as possible? Apply the O.R.G.U.L.L.O. *consejos.*

The most important *consejo* in moments like this is no. 1, which deals with self-examination: Organize your feelings. Ask yourself if your lack of patience and frustration are related to your child—or whether they are actually related to your boss, your mate, your parents, in-laws, or a friend. If your issues really are with your child, you must be very careful not to allow your emotions to bring you down to your child's level—leading you to either beg her to be nice to you or to accuse her of behaving in a certain way specifically to annoy you.

Next, use open communication to determine why she is being so difficult. It might be helpful to ask your child if she is having problems at school, or perhaps she has overheard a difficult conversation you had with your mate that was not intended for her ears. Could this information be making your daughter upset but baffled as to how to deal with her feelings?

In that case, you will want to straighten things out before her anger escalates:

Old Way

Mercedes sometimes can't help screaming at her twelve-year-old daughter, Marisa, calling her insensitive, scatterbrained, irresponsible, and selfish and accusing her of doing things purposely to annoy her. She has even been known to yell, "I can't stand the sight of you! Get away from me!"

Recently, for instance, Mercedes lost her temper when she realized she missed a very important business call because Marisa left the phone disconnected after a friend called—even though Mercedes had told Marisa she was expecting the call and stressed its importance.

New Way

Mercedes realizes that name-calling and screaming are not in Marisa's best developmental interests. It is true that Marisa was wrong in not being more careful about the phone and that there will be occasions when Marisa's mother will feel very angry and frustrated with Marisa. But when Marisa bursts out crying and says, "Why do you talk to me like that? You don't love me!" Mercedes realizes that she has gone too far and acknowledges it to Marisa.

She begins a dialogue with her daughter by accepting responsibility for losing her temper and acknowledging she was wrong to call Marisa names. She tells Marisa that she lost her temper and that this is not the example she wants to set for her. Marisa then tells her *mami* that she forgot to reconnect the phone because she was very upset by the call from her friend. Mom offers help in sorting out Marisa's hurt feelings. After a productive conversation between mother and daughter, Marisa tells Mercedes, "I am sorry, Mami, I let you down; I forgot and this is not right."

Mercedes reports that Marisa has begun to change as she understands that emotions need to be checked and talked about, and that while Mami loses her temper at times, that does not mean she doesn't love and value her daughter. Both mother and daughter are learning the importance of keeping emotions in check.

Point of Reference No. 7: Negotiating Is Not Surrendering

Negotiating with your child does not imply you are giving in. In fact, it can instill in kids a strong sense of self-discipline, responsibility, and the ability to be assertive.

First, reflect on what the concept of negotiating means to you. If you see it as the opposite of confrontation, as a process of give and take, and as a way of cooperation, then it is clear that such teamwork and negotiation are extremely beneficial.

Just as important, though, sometimes the negotiation has to be with yourself. You will not be helping your daughter, for example, by resolving every little problem she may face. You need to strike a balance between offering your help and allowing necessary failures. It might be very difficult to resist the urge to step in. You have to tell yourself that you are not failing or abandoning your daughter but, rather, instilling a sense of perseverance and competence. These might just be the best gifts you can give her.

Old Way

Ten-year-old Otile is basically good-natured and responsible, but she is forgetful. Only when her mom, Betty, is ready to go to bed does Otile tell her about a big science project due the next day on which the entire grade for the course will be based. There is clearly no way that Otile can handle this project alone at this late date because it requires a great deal of research, typing, cutting, and pasting. Otile needs her assistance. Betty spends the whole night helping her.

This is what many devoted Latina mothers would do: bail out the child by being there and offering the necessary help. But Otile's problem goes deeper than the deadline: Otile does not like to ask for help, and she also has a time management problem. She will never learn otherwise if her mother continues to rescue her. Their pattern has been that Betty often makes suggestions, but Otile always says: "I need to do this by myself; it is my project." Yet Betty always ends up helping her when the deadline looms. Here the mother needed to help Otile by first making changes within herself, understanding her own feelings as suggested by O.R.G.U.L.L.O. *consejo* no. 1: Organize your feelings.

New Way

Betty decides not to help Otile with the assignment; consequently, it is not as good as it could have been. This upsets Otile, since she is a good student, but she begins to realize that she needs to structure her time better. In this situation negotiation begins only after Betty has allowed Otile to fail. Betty negotiated with herself first, then with Otile.

She tells Otile that Otile needs help in structuring her time and makes it clear to her she is never again going to help her at the last minute. The two of them devise a calendar on which all Otile's assignments are entered. The moment an assignment is given to Otile, she sets a reasonable completion date and lists the assignment on the calendar—which she and Betty check once a week.

This is a good mother who wants to help her daughter remain a good student, and she found a more constructive way to do so. She realized that Otile needed to feel she was in charge in order to develop better time management skills. The discipline strategy they negotiated enabled Otile to practice those skills. The strategy also consisted of exploring with Otile the reasons for her resistance to ask for help. It had to do with Otile's perception that if you ask for help, you are not as good as if you do everything yourself. Betty explained to Otile that asking for help, when needed and working in a team, is a sign of maturity and can yield better results. But Betty also realizes that Otile was reacting to her constant hovering over her, making suggestions. This was a behavior that required a great deal of inner work and reflection for Betty to change. But Betty was motivated: she did not want to be a negative role model for Otile.

Point of Reference No. 8: Channel the Child's Natural Energy

I do not need to tell you about the unlimited energy that a healthy child possesses. If parents do not recognize this reality and help the child to minimize the possibility of destructiveness, then the child is going to be seen as a nuisance.

A child who runs into the corner of the coffee table because he has not been outside all day cannot be blamed for his excess energy. If the weather is bad, there are countless activities that are great fun for the family to do together, including reading stories, working puzzles, or playing educational games or videos. Many Latino parents shy away from the Internet, but remember O.R.G.U.L.L.O. *consejo* no. 4: Update your media awareness often. There are many educational Web sites (see Recommended Resources).

For now, simply be aware that a child cannot be expected to behave the same as an adult. Many Latino parents take the children to church, to the movies, or visiting and expect the child to be perfectly behaved, which to her is a form of punishment for a "crime" she cannot help committing. It is often the case that when a child has the space to play, be it in a park or in any open area, her behavior is much more appropriate.

The five-year-old twins Margarita Elena and Juana Elena were very difficult to control at home, where space was limited. However, when they visited their aunt in New Jersey and had space to run in her backyard, they were two happy little angels who could sit and behave through dinner. This was not the case when they visited their grandparents' tiny apartment in the city or when they went to church on Sundays.

Desperate, the twins' parents asked for help to learn new ways to be less demanding both in their own small home and when visiting relatives or friends with limited space. They learned to bring puzzles when they went visiting or took the children to restaurants or doctors' offices. The parents happily reported in our sessions that on rainy days at home they helped the children to assemble puzzles, and they had great fun. The mother also prioritized taking the girls to the park, instead of constantly admonishing them to be good while she did endless household chores. Once she began to see the importance of keeping young children busy rather than demanding good behavior from them, she was able to see that this was in everyone's best interest. She also did not insist on having the children sit at the table like two little *señoritas*. The girls did have to ask permission to leave the table, but their parents were more aware and tolerant of the level of energy natural to five-year-olds.

Point of Reference No. 9: Inconsistency Encourages Disobedience

There is nothing more confusing to a child than to be faced with disciplinary rules that contradict each other. For example, when parents are having a party or are busy and the child insists on being allowed to watch a TV program later than he is allowed to, many parents break their own rule simply because at that moment they are very busy. If they do so without any explanation, however, and then later deny their child the same behavior that they had once agreed to, the child becomes confused about the rules. What is he going to do? He is going to keep trying until he gets what he wants. After all, it worked before. Sometimes the inconsistency arises from the parents' not agreeing on how to set the limits, perhaps because they have different ways of seeing the world or because they are separated or divorced and are allowing the children to pit them against each other in order to get what they want. Thus, inconsistent discipline only leads children to further test the limits to see how far they can go. Often this is not done out of mischievousness but out of genuine confusion: children feel lost and do not know which way they are expected to behave.

Developing Rage Control

The most challenging situations that lead to inconsistent discipline have to do with punishing out of desperation or under tremendous rage. It is in these instances that you can lose your composure and apply punishment that could have repercussions later on.

For example, if your six-year-old is scheduled to be the ring bearer in a weekend wedding and you punish him for a transgression by saying "You are grounded and not permitted to leave this house for the entire weekend," are you going to refuse to let the child attend the wedding? Are you not going to let him enjoy the festivities? If you say "I will punish you tomorrow," you are still breaking your word. Losing your temper has created a very complicated discipline situation. That's why it is crucial to keep a cool head when you are setting limits and not act on an impulse or out of anger. These are not good ingredients for establishing good discipline in your children.

By being constantly in touch with your feelings, you can take steps to avoid becoming overextended and stressed. I encourage you to ask for support if you need it. In chapter 9, we'll explore in detail when it is important to ask for professional help and how to know when you need that help.

It is better to give yourself some time to cool down than to respond in a rage at the moment of your child's transgression. When I was a child, one of the things that my mother consistently did if I transgressed when we were out or had guests was to say to me: "We will talk later." She'd never forget to have those talks, and I knew she wouldn't. Since she was consistent, I understood what to expect. The disciplinary effect was the same or better than if she had acted angrily in the moment. She had some time to sort out her feelings and thoughts, and I had time to mend my behavior.

Point of Reference No. 10: Aggression Is Contagious

Spanking, hitting, punching, and using harsh, humiliating, and belittling language with your child is never to be done, because it is undisguised aggression. Causing pain may result in temporary compliances, but it does not instill lasting self-discipline, only unnecessary feelings of anger and hostility. I have talked with innumerable parents who tell me that when they were being spanked or hit with the belt as children, they simply took the punishment in a stoic way and told themselves, "It will be over soon: big deal." Their thoughts were not "I should not lie because it is not right," but, rather, "Next time I do this I had better make sure I am not caught." What parents are really teaching their children when they spank them is to conceal their bad behaviors, not abandon them.

Many of my adult patients have told me that when they were children and were spanked, once the spanking was over they put the transgression out of their mind and did not think about it again. So we can see that when you use verbal and physical humiliation as punishment, the learning accomplished is not what you had in mind. What is learned is to be hostile and angry—and to more than likely use this behavior on others. I cannot emphasize enough how much imitation of aggression I have seen in both adults and children in my many years working as a therapist with families. The case of Ramiro and Francisca's family is only one of many:

Ramiro and Francisca, their six-year-old daughter, Maria, five-year-old son, Manuel, and three-year-old son, Agustin, came to see me because Maria and Manuel were very difficult to control and hit Agustin as a matter of habit. This is what transpired upon exploration:

RAMIRO AND FRANCISCA: The situation at home is difficult, but we also have seen that Agustin is being affected by Maria and Manuel because he is now hitting everyone in the park and the mothers are complaining.

MARIA: We hit the baby because he breaks our toys and is always whining, and you blame us. You let him get away with everything. Besides, you tell us not to hit the baby, but you hit us.

I find out that Ramiro loses his temper and screams at everyone, calls them names, and spanks the children when they misbehave.

This family needed to implement a great deal of behavioral changes for different children of different ages. We will look at these specific changes and their application in chapter 6. The point here is twofold: (1) physical punishment and harsh language are not only unproductive and harmful to the child, but the child will imitate these behaviors, and (2) it is ironic to see a parent hit a child because that child is hitting a sibling. The excessive guilt you may cause in the child by harshly chastising him can be a form of harassment, too.

LAS REFLEXIONES

As you write your responses to the questions below, compare your answers to the results of the quiz you took at the beginning of this chapter. Ask yourself: How has my outlook changed? How far have I come on the cultural adjustment continuum?

- What was your experience with discipline when you were a child? How does this affect your disciplining your own child now?
- Do you fear that unless your child is spanked and scolded harshly when she disobeys, she will quickly become spoiled and undisciplined?
- How do you set limits? According to the infraction? According to your instincts? According to what your parents or in-laws determine is appropriate—so that they will not label you a bad parent?
- What is your opinion of those stories you hear about spanking, in which parents relate that as children they almost welcomed the spanking just to get it over with? Have you ever been in that situation?
- Would you consider yourself a disciplined person? How do you feel about your answer?
- Do you consider first what your child's violation of the rules is before you discipline, excluding, of course, emergency situations?

Orgullo **and the New** *Obediencia*

I think that the old way of thinking about discipline adheres to the myth that disciplining or teaching a child to be obedient is an easy task: the parents say "You do as I say, period," and the child obeys. If he doesn't, he earns a beating. It has been my goal in this chapter to convince you that hitting not only is unhelpful but causes more harm than good.

Keep in mind that physical punishment is not the only harmful way of disciplining a child; many children are humiliated or belittled with words. For example, to be told "You have failed me, you are a total disaster" or to go over and over an issue that a parent disagrees with can be as much torture as the hitting or spanking. Words can be very powerful, so please watch what and how you discipline your child.

Remember, discipline is teaching, and it takes a long time to accomplish the task. Many children will require a great deal of patience in the process of their instruction. You can always label the wrongful act as what it is, not as a label for the child. Here is where you must remember the *consejos* of O.R.G.U.L.L.O. Think how you feel when you know you have made a mistake and someone tells you: "It is your fault, you asked for it." Understand that children do not have the level of maturity of adults and need to be taught discipline that will be internalized. This teaching can be achieved by applying components of the new *obediencia* within O.R.G.U.L.L.O.

Think how wonderful it will feel to bring up your children with O.R.G.U.L.L.O. and feel *orgullo,* the pride of passing on our wonderful Latino values—but only the wonderful ones!

Common Child-Rearing Issues

Part Two takes a developmental approach, dealing with specific problems that may be expected to appear as the child progresses from infancy through adolescence, including the child's world at home, at school, and in the community—with friends, relatives, neighbors, teammates, and others in the child's life. Issues range from bilingualism to dating, from corporal punishment to peer pressure.

Part Two ends with a look at those problems your child and your family may be experiencing that are intertwined with adjustment to a new culture. You will see the relationship between culture and some of these problems, and I will provide some guidelines for knowing when you may need to seek professional help. These safeguards will inform you by developmental stages so that you will know what to look for in your child's behavior that may be cause for concern—as well as when a family crisis mandates professional guidance. I'll also describe exactly how to choose the most effective counseling to resolve your dilemma.

CHAPTER 6

The World of the Preschooler: Instilling O.R.G.U.L.L.O. from Day One

Please rate yourself on how often the following questions apply to you.

5=ALWAYS 4=FREQUENTLY 3=SOMETIMES 2=RARELY 1=NEVER

1. Are you unclear about the proper time to take the bottle away and to begin toilet training your child? _____
2. Do you worry about what language to teach your child first? _____
3. Do you feel you cannot deal with telling your four-year-old that his pet died? _____
4. Do you allow your two-year-old child to sleep with you rather than let her cry? _____
5. Do you feel that it is better to wait until the baby is born to tell your three-year-old he has a new sibling? _____
6. Do you feel that you must take your child with you everywhere in order to feel you are a good parent? _____
7. Do you feel it is not vital for your preschooler to have friends? _____
8. Do you feel guilty when you are tired and do not wish to get up in the middle of the night to feed the baby? _____

Ana Maria, who was born in this country, describes herself as a Latina who wants her only daughter, Eliza, to maintain some of the values that Ana Maria grew up with. She finds herself in a sea of confusion:

Her oldest sister tells her to speak to Eliza only in Spanish. Her best friend, who is a non-Latina, tells her: "You don't want your child to go to school not able to speak fluent English! She will suffer socially and academically. Besides, we are in the United States; English is the language she should speak."

Her mother lectures her, "You are being too accommodating to Eliza. Let her cry. It will only make her strong."

When Eliza is eighteen months old and Ana Maria wants to switch her from the bottle to a sip cup, the *abuelita* urges her, "Let her keep the bottle. Pamper her! It is better that way."

When Ana Maria considers toilet training Eliza, her mother-in-law tells her, "Don't worry about toilet training. We don't even have a word in Spanish for that kind of thing. Nature will take its course. This is the way we Latinos do things. That is how I did it with your husband, and look at him—he turned out fine."

Ana Maria's husband does not want the baby to sleep with them; he is not only afraid he might crush the baby but he strongly believes that children should sleep alone. But Ana Maria feels that since she used to sleep with her parents, it has to be all right.

～

I have heard many stories similar to Ana Maria's over the years, because many Latino parents tend to revert to tradition when they have children. This means that too often they opt for the values with which they grew up without considering whether they apply in today's world. Like Ana Maria, they find themselves so overwhelmed by the contradictions between cultural traditions and modern times that they simply don't know where to turn or what to do.

In the first part of *Parenting with Pride,* you learned how to balance traditional Latino cultural principles with the demands of modern times by applying the principles of *El Nuevo Tradicionalismo*—or O.R.G.U.L.L.O. in action, redefining *orgullo, respeto, familismo, simpa-*

tia, and *obediencia.* You were also provided with the basic guidelines of *El Nuevo Tradicionalismo* through the seven *consejos* of O.R.G.U.L.L.O.:

1. O Organize your feelings
2. R Respect your child's feelings
3. G Guide and teach your child; do not dictate
4. U Update your media awareness often
5. L Love your child for who she or he is
6. L Listen to your child
7. O Open the communication channels—and keep them open

In the second part of *Parenting with Pride,* you will be guided in applying these tools to specific parenting problems that many Latino parents have found difficult to resolve successfully.

To commence our discussion, I want to list the four most important ways in which *El Nuevo Tradicionalismo* departs from traditional Latino child-rearing practices:

- *One rule does not fit all: every child is an individual.* Every person grows up to have a unique history, and even children who grow up in the same household have very different interpretations of their experiences. Children are born with their own temperament and each one is unique in terms of their behavior, capacity to learn, and how their parents relate to them.
- *One age does not fit all: what you can expect from a child is determined by developmental stage.* This is very important for knowing when to let go, and in fostering independence and responsibility in your child.
- *One parenting method does not fit all: circumstances alter cases and times change.* Parents may follow the values they grew up with, or they may reject these values. Circumstances also may play a role in determining what method to follow in bringing up children. For example, when it comes to deciding what first language to teach the child, most North Americans will say it should be English, but not

many traditional Latinos feel that way. They feel children should be taught Spanish first or both Spanish and English.

- *One value system does not fit all: you grew up then; your kids are growing up now.* There is no question that different times bring different trends that can be confusing for all parents, such as whether it is considered acceptable today to sleep with the baby, when to introduce solid foods, how to relate to relatives, and much more.

These directives will help you in raising your child Latino style in modern times; we will return to them frequently in subsequent chapters, as they apply to the point we are trying to illustrate. Let's proceed now to the template issues that we will explore in this chapter:

- Babies have a great capacity to learn, but they need a great deal of teaching
- The teaching of the Latino values
- Should we let our baby sleep with us?
- The dos and don'ts of toilet training
- How to survive the terrible twos (and threes and fours)
- New traditional child care
- Selecting a nursery school: a practical plan for letting go with O.R.G.U.L.L.O.
- Protecting your child with O.R.G.U.L.L.O.

Babies Have a Great Capacity to Learn, But They Need a Great Deal of Teaching

One of the most beautiful things about teaching children is their huge capacity to learn, but each child learns differently. The present scientific view is that the data-processing power of a child's brain is equal to a computer's *before* age three—and better thereafter. What is also known is that infants are born with a biological readiness to learn.

Through a series of experiments using specialized computers that measure brain waves and reactions, it is now known that newborns recognize what their tongues look like and as early as six months of age can tell the difference between languages, as well as identify changes in facial expression, such as a parent's smiling or frowning. This is important evidence that at a very young age children have the capacity to perceive a significant amount of information. This was not understood in the past. In fact, it was believed that babies were completely "blank slates" and did not possess a biologically programmed capacity to learn. Naturally, application of this capacity to learn requires instruction and modeling. In other words, the more you teach, the more your child will learn. Getting to know and work with your child early in life will establish a solid foundation for acquiring the bicultural balance you want your baby to possess and developing good parent-child relations.

Keep Your Expectations Realistic

When my son Jaime was about two years old, he hit me in my right eye with a key. I got both frightened and teary-eyed and he began to soothe me, saying, "Don't cry, Mommy," and he kissed me. Jaime was aware that I was suffering and wanted to make me feel better, the way I had done with him on other occasions. We now know through scientific experiments that babies "come equipped with" such seemingly adult capacities as empathy, which further develops over time. Here is where you must be quite clear on what to expect according to age. Your expectations must be realistic. The teaching of values, even to the youngest children, must take into account the importance of age appropriateness in the development of self-discipline and self-reliance.

If you are dealing with a five-year-old who is suffering from night fears and asking to sleep with you, the solution will be totally different than for a three-year-old who is traveling with you to another country and is not comfortable with the new surroundings—and different from your child's crying because he is sick and needs you to be with him in the middle of the night. However, it is also unrealistic to expect that *you* will be able to anticipate your child's every possible need at every age. I hope that this section of the book will better prepare you for myriad eventualities, but, as they say in the world of baseball, "Nobody bats a thousand." No parent perceives correctly a child's needs and desires 100 percent of the time.

When You Set Limits, You Encourage Self-Discipline and Self-Respect

From the day a child is born, believe it or not, parents consciously or unconsciously teach that child by setting limits.

Every limit imposed on your child by you or by the people who love him basically has to do with the deprivation of a desire: something he wants that we are not giving to him. Imposing limits becomes even more difficult when we are talking about an infant, whose cry commands us to go and see what his distress is all about. We automatically want to soothe him and stop his discomfort. The basic task of parenting is to find a balance between responding to the child's needs and wisely setting age-appropriate limits around those needs.

Keeping a rigid schedule or adhering to a very rigid way of relating to the baby is no better than constantly giving in. You will need to use your judgment. Children cannot be dealt with as if they were a dish we want to make for tonight's dinner: there is no foolproof recipe. Each child is unique. This awareness of children's uniqueness and the need to use your judgment while bringing up children apply to *all aspects* of their development, including passing on your linguistic and cultural values, toilet training, and helping them with shyness. Putting these teachings into practice often requires a balancing act, not devoid of sacrifices for you and for your child. Quite often, it might be easier to give in, but we both know that this is not the best option for all involved. The point is that when you teach a child the appropriate behavior, you are giving your child a beautiful gift, not taking something away. Although the process can at times be difficult and require a great deal of work, the end result is the development of a person who will be more successful with others and in all aspects of their society including the ability to adhere to valuable democratic ideals of self-respect and self-discipline.

Now let's continue with the template issues of the preschool years where most of you have experienced problems:

The Teaching of the Latino Values

Teaching Language—the Beginnings of O.R.G.U.L.L.O. in Action

Here in the United States it is a given that once he starts school, a child will be conversing in English with his peers. For the Latino child and his parents, the language issue is considerably more complicated. Over and over, traditional Latino parents ask: Should I teach English first, then Spanish, the other way around, or both at the same time? And to whom do I turn for advice on this?

This Is Difficult and Confusing

Julia, a young Latina mother, desperately wanted to make the best language decisions for her first child, Martita, but she didn't know where to start. Her sister Amelia, who was studying to become a bilingual teacher, lectured her with great authority: "You should not teach Martita English and Spanish simultaneously; it is going to confuse her and she will not learn either language properly because learning one language will interfere with learning the other." Amelia then compounded the problem by passing on, as a fact, a theory she had actually misinterpreted: that some children who learn English and Spanish simultaneously became learning disabled.

Julia consulted me about this dilemma and I helped her to see her sister's concern as misinformed. Learning two languages simultaneously does not have to be harmful. In fact, it may well encourage educational achievement across the board. Scientific studies have found that the learning of a second language improves mastery of the first, and is positively related to learning and intelligence.

Even so, Julia was not sure where to begin, since her husband was not Spanish speaking. I helped her to see that by assigning one person to teach the baby Spanish (the one-person, one-language method), someone else could take on the teaching of English. She hired a Spanish-speaking nanny and she herself talked to Amelia only in Spanish in the baby's early years, while her husband spoke to the child in English. I'm happy to report that the baby is doing wonderfully in her bilingualism.

Here I want to stress several points:

- There is no scientific evidence that teaching two languages at the same time is harmful to a child; in fact, the ability to speak several languages is without question a major source of *orgullo*—an enrichment and expansion of one's mind and ability to communicate, which boosts *respeto* for the self and the capacity for *simpatia*.
- Latinos who want to take the bilingual path in teaching their children simply don't always know how to do it.
- The prospect of teaching both Spanish and English simultaneously to a small child is seen by Latino parents as a demanding time commitment, but it does not have to be that difficult.
- Consistency is the way to go! Language requires practice. In the early years, it would be best if your child hears only English from one person and only Spanish from another (the one-person, one-language method). Often in families following *El Nuevo Tradicionalismo,* the responsibility for teaching Spanish is taken by the grandparents. This was what I did with my son Jaime. It is a great example of the new *familismo,* giving the grandparents a new way to continue to hold a very important place in the Latino family in the United States.

You Have No Idea How Busy I Am

Many Latino parents say that they simply do not have time to teach Spanish to their kids. Since these days many mothers and fathers work outside the home, they are exhausted by evening. The weekend is full of chores that must be done for the house, the children, and their own parents. Many Latino parents feel that they have to move faster than Speedy Gonzalez.

However, we have a saying in Spanish: *La escasez es la madre de la invencion.* (Scarcity is the mother of invention.) In that spirit, many Latino parents have found solutions that work quite well:

- Send the child regularly to visit relatives in their country of origin, if possible, providing the child with what is called a language immersion experience. (If you do this, always make sure during the early years that the child travels and stays with a relative he knows, if he is going alone; otherwise, the separation from you can adversely affect the child.)
- Maintain a consistent but separate focus of teaching each language. This refers to having one person talk to the child in one language. This could be arranged between the two parents themselves, or between parents and the babysitter, the mother or mother-in-law, or any relative who interacts with the child regularly.
- Make an effort to meet other Latino parents and invite them to your house to have the children play together and speak in Spanish with each other.
- Gather regularly with Spanish-speaking friends and/or relatives. The best way to learn a language is through communication and exposure. Regular gatherings could be quite enjoyable to the children and provide a socialization experience promoting *simpatia* for all. If the different households rotate the burden, all the work need not fall on one family alone.
- Update your media awareness often (O.R.G.U.L.L.O. *consejo* no. 4) Educational programs in Spanish and/or English are available to children from infancy through adolescence, encompassing videos, books, music, and toys. For instance, on the Web site SpanishToys.com, you can purchase age-appropriate software, such as *El Conejo Lector* (or Peter Rabbit in English), and other programs from the Spanish Software Educativo. This is a site where you have to purchase the products, but refer to the Recommended Resources section for other possibilities that are free of charge.

This educative software in Spanish comes in the form of games, enabling children to have fun while learning such skills in Spanish as vocabulary, reading, pronunciation, and math in an incremental manner according to age.

Implementing Bilingualism

Ask yourself: If we have scientific evidence that bilingualism is not harmful, that in fact it helps to improve language acquisition and higher intelligence, isn't it worth trying? Of course this is your decision, but I can tell you that it can be done.

It is important to keep in mind that the degree of bilingualism attained by a child is not related to whether the languages are acquired simultaneously; however, if it is possible and you wish to teach two languages to your child from birth, the process will feel more natural to both you and your child.

Whatever your decision, it should be based on the available facts about bilingual child rearing. Both my children are bilingual, but let me cite as an example how my husband and I dealt with my elder son, Jaime, regarding language issues:

Jaime's first language was Spanish. We all made an effort to talk to him exclusively in Spanish, and he was cared for by a Spanish-speaking nanny. Jaime also visited his grandparents in our country of origin and his Spanish was constantly reinforced through these visits. Later on, he had formal schooling in Spanish for the entire summer while visiting my parents. But we also had English-speaking friends, and when they came to visit us Jaime was exposed to English, as well as to English-language children's television programs, such as *Sesame Street*. When Jaime began nursery school, he did not speak English, but he caught on to the language quite quickly. He is now a bilingual/bicultural adult.

We allowed Jaime to "do what came naturally" to a great extent, learning Spanish first, and then English.

Remember that one of the most wonderful things about children is their fantastic ability to learn, but in their own unique way. If you adhere to teaching consistently, simply by making an effort to talk to your child using the one-person, one-language method, in Spanish first, it is quite possible to teach her Spanish and English simultaneously.

Simpatia *Begins with "Thank You"*

To instill the new *simpatia,* parents would be wise to pay particular attention to the second and fifth O.R.G.U.L.L.O. *consejos:* Respect your child's feelings and Love your child for who she or he is. Good manners—what falls under what we psychologists call "socialization"—are taught to children by parental modeling. Expectations must always be age appropriate.

If you say thank you when your child gives you a toy or does something that is pleasant, she will learn to say thank you when appropriate and will probably make this phrase a part of her vocabulary for life. Teaching good manners includes appreciating the good things a child does, even at the toddler stage. In fact, aspects of *simpatia* can be taught from the moment you start talking to your child. When your baby gives you a smile, you can say thank you. Many parents do these things automatically, but sometimes this habit must be learned, particularly when there are expectations of absolute *obediencia* and a belief that children are best taught by giving orders, rather than by *respeto.*

For example, a traditional Latina who came to see me for help tells me that she grew up being given orders, "Give me that" or "Do that," and never being thanked for anything she did well as a child. She now finds it very difficult to say thank you to her husband and even more difficult to teach these niceties to her children. By no means am I suggesting that you must plead with your children to behave. I am simply suggesting human respect: "Marquito, could you please hand me that book?" and then saying, "Thank you, sweetheart."

Being **Simpatico:** *The Beginning of Self-Reliance*

It is very important for your child to learn to be with others as a stepping-stone to developing self-reliance. He will learn to use language to ask for things he wants, for example, instead of gesturing or grunting in ways that only parents understand. As language develops and the child gets older, expectations for socialization can be more consistent, but they must always be age appropriate.

Your toddler's emerging sense of independence can be respected and reinforced if you allow your child to do certain things that he might not be able to do too well at the moment, but that he will master with your teaching, time, and patience. If you feel reluctant to let your child try his skills, consider the first O.R.G.U.L.L.O. *consejo*, Organize your feelings, and ascertain whether you are dealing with your need to be in control or to keep your baby dependent on you. Then respect your child's feelings and individuality. When he says, "Let me do it," listen to him and permit him to dress himself, if that is the issue, even if he is not doing it too well.

For tasks like brushing teeth, you can always say, "Let me show you; watch how Mommy does it." Then give her the opportunity to try. If she wants to dial the telephone, show her how to do it. I realize that parents are very busy and may find it a bit difficult to be patient, but many times a child is not allowed to try things on her own simply because parents do not realize how important these things are to learning independence.

Nip Shyness and Aggression in the Bud

Rosa and Jose, like many traditional Latino parents, believe that their children must be *bien educados* and *simpaticos*. They feel great *orgullo* about how loving, outgoing, and friendly six-year-old Magda and four-year-old Mickey have always been at family gatherings. The same cannot be said of two-year-old Enrique. In social situations Rosa and Jose feel that Enrique always comes across as *mal educado:* he cries and screams, and refuses to smile at or kiss his aunts and uncles, and he is very shy.

Rosa and Jose are uncomfortable with and resent Enrique's behavior, even at this tender age, because they see it as a poor reflection on their parenting skills. They believe that if he isn't taught proper behavior right from the beginning, he will be shy and unsociable all his life. They persist in dragging him along to gatherings on the assumption that enough exposure to groups will sooner or later make him less shy and more *simpatico*—like his brother and sister—but Enrique's behavior does not improve. The only corrective approaches that occur to them are scolding the little boy or simply ignoring him—both equally ineffective. Here are the mistakes Rosa and Jose are making:

- The techniques they are using to alter Enrique's behavior are based on unrealistic expectations; they are not, for example, taking into account factors such as age appropriateness and situational specificity.
- They are not applying the O.R.G.U.L.L.O. *consejos*. In this case, *consejo* no. 2: Respect your child's feelings.
- They are judging him by his siblings without appreciating that he is an individual, which violates O.R.G.U.L.L.O. *consejo* no. 5: Love your child for who she or he is.

Coping with the Shy Toddler

Although it is true that *simpatia* or socialization skills are inculcated very early, Rosa and Jose are not justified in worrying about Enrique's shyness. He is still too young to be very social, and he is still not comfortable in family gatherings because they are not his everyday world.

Children at this age are prone to reacting to strangers as they do to loud, unfamiliar noises—with signs of distress such as crying and throwing tantrums. It is unrealistic to expect a two-year-old *not* to become upset when overstimulated and overwhelmed. A child's level of shyness varies according to the inborn temperament of the child. Attempting to force a child to stop being shy almost always fails. Practicing the new *familismo* involves considering Enrique's needs and being less concerned with having him, at this tender age, be present at all family gatherings in order to follow the traditional *familismo*. Togetherness is a beautiful part of *familismo,* but there are situations where the new *familismo* necessitates explaining to Grandma or to other family members that it is better for Enrique to stay home with a babysitter until he feels more comfortable at family gatherings. More than likely this is a stage that will pass, but what Enrique needs at the moment is for his parents to focus on *his* needs, not their own.

Coping with the Aggressive Toddler

Although the toddler is learning to become independent and au-
tonomous, parents need to guide the child and not allow certain behaviors, such as hitting or biting others. Even at this age, children
need to know that what they are doing is not allowed. This is an important part of beginning to instill *simpatia*. But always keep in mind
that the process of instilling socialization skills takes time and is very
dependent on maturation.

Also, do not expect your preschooler to say thank you all the time.
There will be days when he is sick or bored or tired and might not be
capable of being *simpatico*. Don't worry. Using the O.R.G.U.L.L.O.
consejos will help you understand these ordinary vacillations in your
child's behavior and will help you know when to insist on his compliance because the behavior is becoming a bad habit—which may eventually become a real problem in school, at a birthday party, or on the
playground.

Physical aggression demands immediate parental attention before
it becomes a habit, in which case a child will have very few friends. If
he keeps hitting other children, bear in mind his age. He is going to
need your help. Take him out of the room to help him cope with whatever he may be feeling. Maybe he needs a break; or he might be tired
or overwhelmed easily in crowds, as Enrique was. He will have plenty
of time to acquire his *simpatia* skills. Don't yell at or hit him, because
your aggression will only reinforce his aggression.

Situational Discipline Could Boomerang

Situational discipline refers to parents allowing certain behaviors at
home that later could become problematic when the child is adjusting
to other settings, such as school. For example:

Marcelo went to bed at eleven or later because Clara and her husband felt that nighttime was the only chance they had to be with him.
This seems to me a serious misinterpretation of the new *familismo*. If
this behavior continues and Marcelo is not taught a sleeping schedule,
in the future, on nights when they decide he must go to sleep earlier,
he will be just as resistant as he is about using the potty, as we will see

later. In this particular case, parents were advised to begin with a modified schedule that gradually moves Marcelo toward an earlier bedtime.

Below is a list of steps to take in implementing what I call enlightened discipline. They will help you develop an overall structure within which you situate specific discipline strategies. They have proved helpful to many Latino parents whom I have counseled and I found them very helpful while I was raising my sons:

- Provide your young child with an organized routine. Do not put him to bed at 11:00 p.m. regularly in order to spend more time with him, as Marcelo's parents did. This is to your benefit; it may be fun for you or ease your guilt at being away from your child all day, but it is not to his benefit.

- Maintain consistency in your discipline, and include your child's babysitter in this process. For example, if you do not approve of your child's eating in bed, do not allow it according to your mood—that is, sometimes you let him eat if you are in a good mood, but you forbid it when you are feeling angry or guilty for being too permissive. Make sure your babysitter follows your guidelines as well.

- As your child gets older, begin showing him how to put his toys in a handy basket or trunk. He might not obey you immediately, but keep at it. It might be easier for you to pick up the toys yourself, but you are teaching good habits. In the earlier years you can play Simon Says: "Simon says put the toy away." The important thing is to establish routines.

- If during mealtimes your child is allowed to leave the table while you follow him around with food in order to coax him to eat, you are setting a bad precedent. Eating must be done at the table and at a prescribed time.

- This is the age to begin helping your child to handle her aggression. If you allow her to break her brother's toys and find it cute because she is very young, you could be teaching her that it is acceptable to do this in school and with other children. The thing to do is to say, "No, you cannot do this." Stay with that position. Do not spank; take her away from the situation after explaining to her that toys are not to be broken.

Picking Your Battles

If you are not sure how to begin the daunting job of enlightened discipline, follow the first O.R.G.U.L.L.O. *consejo:* Organize your feelings. It may very well be that you were raised in a climate of absolute obedience and find it difficult to imagine an alternative—especially when you will probably be urged by well-meaning family members to stick with the old, tried-and-true ways of raising your children. The first step to mastering enlightened discipline is to move away from the "one rule fits all" approach and to start picking your battles. Let me give you an example of how this works:

Your *niña* is one and a half years old and is getting into everything, with a special fascination for pots and pans and kitchen utensils. You have already childproofed your home by installing special locks on cabinets that contain potentially toxic substances, and you are mindful of making sure that handles of hot pots and pans are safely out of her reach. But you also need to teach your toddler that the hot stove is dangerous if touched. To do this, most parents use their common sense and teach their toddler through role playing—they point to the stove or oven and tell the toddler in simple words, something along the lines of "Ouch, no touch." This needs to be done while always taking precautions to keep the toddler safe.

One night, as you are in the middle of preparing dinner, your little girl wants to play with every utensil in sight. You can take action the traditional way and shout, "Juanita, don't touch that!" but it won't work, because at this age toddlers are driven to explore their world and that of their parents; their curiosity is at a high peak.

Or you can begin implementing *El Nuevo Tradicionalismo:* although the interruption is annoying, you appreciate that it's to be expected in a child your daughter's age. You also realize she's too young to be reasoned with. So you pick your battles: you let her play safely with these objects that fascinate her. No parent wins them all, and this battle definitely is not worth fighting. You give Juanita several pots and pans to play with in a safe area of the kitchen. She will soon find other, more interesting things to do and will outgrow this interest.

Should We Let Our Baby Sleep with Us?

This is another issue that many traditional Latino parents find confusing. Many North American psychologists and pediatricians caution that sleeping with the baby is not a good idea, but in many Latin countries it is seen as a natural occurrence. The truth is that there are different theories in this regard, and different cultures have different ways of raising children, which can create tension in the household.

Before deciding whether or not you want to sleep with the baby on a regular basis, make use of the first O.R.G.U.L.L.O. *consejo:* Organize your feelings. Ask yourself, "Why do I want to do this?" If this is something you are struggling with, be aware that many parents allow their newborn to sleep with them because it is easier, particularly if the mother is nursing the baby. But this is for their benefit, not the child's. The issue becomes more complicated when the child is older than a newborn. Ultimately, it is a personal decision; many professionals do not feel that it is necessarily bad for the baby to sleep with the parents, when practiced within reason, but it's not a good idea when the child is three or four years old to be sleeping with the parents in a regular basis. It is always problematic when it creates friction between the couple.

Some parents find that allowing their child to sleep with them is a bonding experience, even an aspect of the new *familismo,* helping to offset their busy schedule by meeting their need for rest as well as quality time with their baby. In fact, for those reasons, there seems to be a trend now for many parents, not necessarily Latinos, to sleep with the baby. But consistency within limits is important here.

When You Make a Rule, You Must Follow It

If you plan to have your baby sleep with you regularly, you need to have a clear rationale for why you are taking this step, and this is your decision, which is fine as long as it works out for the family. You cannot bring your baby into your bed often and then expect that he will peacefully sleep by himself when you want him to. Many children either fall asleep in the parents' bed or come in crying with a wet diaper. Sometimes they are frightened by a dream or they are cranky from not feeling well. These situations are different from allowing your child to sleep with you on a regular basis, which is a conscious parenting decision that both parents need to agree on.

I was consulted by Minerva and Francisco because their three-year-old son, Andres, refused to go to sleep in his crib and insisted on joining them every night. Since Francisco was very unhappy with this situation, the couple was arguing and very unhappy with each other. I asked why Andres had been permitted to do this. They explained that when Andres was put to bed in his room, he would scream so loudly that the neighbors could hear him. The real reason, however, was that Minerva had slept with her parents for most of her early childhood. She felt that this was a part of loving a child, when in fact it had been more as the result of the very cramped quarters the family lived in when they moved to this country. Of the two, Francisco was the more opposed to Andres's constant presence at bedtime, and his feelings were putting a strain on the marriage. These parents needed to implement a program to change Andres's habits before the problem mushroomed into a bad domestic situation.

What the Parents Did

When Minerva followed the first O.R.G.U.L.L.O. *consejo,* Organize your feelings, she discovered that she was feeling very guilty about having to go to work and leave Andres with a babysitter. She saw this as not being a good Latina mother and depriving Andres of family togetherness. Minerva also came to see that she was angry with Francisco because she had to work to support the family while he finished medical school, and she had been unconsciously punishing him by bringing Andres to bed with them, thereby depriving their relationship of both comfort and intimacy. Minerva realized that the combined demands of her job and motherhood left her exhausted. It was less taxing for her to bring Andres to their bed than to help him outgrow a habit that was growing increasingly burdensome for both parents—but they both needed their sleep and couldn't get comfortable with a three-year-old between them. When they tried at times to stop this habit, Andres expressed his dissatisfaction loud and clear.

I advised the couple to prepare themselves for the fact that Andres was going to cry for a few nights when he was put down in his crib. Once they understood that they were not depriving him of love, they saw this not only as the beginning of discipline but as the necessary ending of a parenting behavior that had made sense when the boy was an infant but was no longer appropriate. It had helped Minerva not to have to get out of bed to breast-feed Andres when he was an infant; now that he was no longer an infant, the parents were not resting properly while Andres was with them in bed.

Strengthened by the knowledge that they were following the dictates of *El Nuevo Tradicionalismo,* Minerva and Francisco were able to alter Andres's sleeping arrangements without feeling that they were depriving him of love. They took turns sitting by his crib, singing to him and soothing him. After crying for a while, Andres would get tired and fall asleep.

Remember that one parenting rule does not fit all: you should use your common sense about this issue as you would about any other. If, for example, you have just brought home a new baby or have moved, it is quite possible that your preschooler will react to these stressful changes by wanting to come to bed with you. In these cases, a preferred toy in the crib and special attention when it is time to go to sleep, such as singing, reading, or playing soft music, can be very helpful. A child this age may verbalize that he does not like his baby sister. By letting him know that the new baby sister is here to stay, but that you understand his feelings, you are applying helpful O.R.G.U.L.L.O. *consejos.* Even at this tender age you are respecting and listening to his feelings and opening the communication channels (*consejo* nos. 2, 6, and 7). There is no need to tell him "You must not feel that way" or "Do not talk like that about your sister." In most situations, these feelings, if handled properly, resolve themselves.

The Dos and Don'ts of Toilet Training

Toilet training can be seen as one of the earliest opportunities parents are given to teach children self-discipline and autonomy; as such, it must be regarded as a bestowal of love on your son or daughter. How and when to toilet train—even in traditional Latino culture—varies from family to family and can be either rigid or flexible. Still, the fact remains that you cannot delay the process until your child is over four and expect her to cooperate with you. It is not that your child will not eventually be toilet trained—since any normal child sooner or later becomes toilet trained—but it's important that she be on par with peers when she starts attending kindergarten. She will be at a disadvantage if other children laugh at her, pointing at her on those occasions when it is obvious what has happened. On the other hand, if you begin toilet training at twelve months, your expectations of success in most cases will be unrealistic, because most children need to mature more in order to be ready for toilet training. Although experts never take a "one age fits all" stance, they do indicate that the appropriate age range for starting to toilet train is between twenty and thirty-six months.

Toilet training also follows cultural beliefs and varies according to the times. Every ten years or so, opinions change on the proper form of toilet training. It is always very important to do the teaching in a pleasant manner: full of love, kissing, hugging, praising, and patience.

Your chosen method of toilet training will reflect your parenting style. As a Latino living in North America, you have three options: absolute *obediencia;* its opposite, absolute permissiveness (what I call the pendulum swing); or *El Nuevo Tradicionalismo.* I am going to give you examples of the first two styles, which have been known to cause a lot of problems for many parents, and then describe how, through the child-rearing practices I advocate, those problems can be resolved or avoided altogether.

Toilet Training and Absolute Obediencia

Toilet training leads to greater autonomy and independence, but it is also connected with self-discipline or *obediencia*. As such, it can lead to power struggles between parent and child.

Yamila is quite proud to say that she was toilet trained at nine months of age and connects this with the beginning of her good self-discipline habits. She wanted her daughter Nelly to follow in her footsteps, and she puts Nelly in training pants by eight months. The results were not good: Nelly was having temper tantrums whenever Yamila tried to show her the potty or put her on it. In fact, Nelly began having difficulties going to the bathroom and had to be taken to the pediatrician. Yamila could not understand why this was the case, since all of her siblings had been toilet trained back home much earlier than children in this country. Of course, they had been carefully supervised by numerous caretakers in Yamila's house who basically had anticipated whenever the children wanted to go to the potty. Yamila did not have time to do this, but she was expecting similar results. Yamila got angry whenever Nelly went to the bathroom behind the curtains or in other places, and she would severely scold her.

Yamila came to see me because she was having a great deal of problems with Nelly, such as difficulty with sleeping, eating, and temper tantrums. By now Nelly was three years old and Yamila was very upset and depressed. Yamila felt that there had to be something wrong with Nelly and tried harder to force Nelly to obey her. But the more she tried to stop Nelly's tantrums and make her comply with what Yamila wanted, the more Nelly refused to do what Yamila wanted.

Yamila and I worked on helping her apply a more relaxed attitude toward Nelly's toilet training. She began to use a lot of hugs, praise, and kisses, allowed Nelly to take a doll to the potty, and said to Nelly whenever she had an "accident," "Don't worry, baby, it is okay." Yamila applied the first O.R.G.U.L.L.O. *consejo*, Organize your feelings, and realized that she felt she had to bring up Nelly exactly the way she was brought up in order to be a good mother and a good Latina. She also learned to follow the second and third

O.R.G.U.L.L.O. *consejos,* Respect your child's feelings and Guide and teach your child; do not dictate, by not getting angry, respecting Nelly's feelings, and guiding without dictating, in a fun manner. These tactics helped Nelly to be toilet trained with less controversy and to be more compliant in general.

Toilet Training and the Pendulum Swing

Clara, the daughter of a second-generation Latina-American, grew up in a household where absolute *obediencia* was avoided at all costs. Clara's mother was insistent that the Latino values she had been forced to follow not be passed on to Clara; in fact, her parenting style was extremely permissive. Now a mother herself, Clara imposes no discipline whatsoever on her four-and-a-half-year-old son, Marcelo, including not guiding him toward using the potty and letting him go to bed whenever he wants, which is very late at night. The little boy's nanny, obeying Clara's orders, also permits him to more or less run wild. Now, with kindergarten only months away, Clara is frantic. It is imperative that Marcelo learn to use the toilet, because most school programs will not accept a child who is not toilet trained (although "accidents" are usually understood), but he steadfastly refuses. The issue has escalated into a battle between parent and child.

Adding to Marcelo's problems with toilet training and *obediencia* is his isolation from other children. Because of the busy schedule that both Clara and her husband maintain, they do not have time and do not consider it important to socialize and expose Marcelo to other children.

"It's already July," Clara told me, obviously upset, "and he's got to be toilet trained by September, when he starts school! But he's so defiant, he starts screaming when he even *sees* the potty!" She went on to explain that their pediatrician wasn't alarmed but did suggest that Clara start Marcelo on a schedule to begin toilet training him. "I don't know anything about schedules," she said. "I wasn't raised with one. My mother didn't believe in them."

In our work together, Clara learned how to apply the first

O.R.G.U.L.L.O. *consejo:* Organize your feelings. Clara came to see her own free-form parenting style as a continuation of her mother Francisca's rebellion against her own rigid upbringing. Clara applied the fifth O.R.G.U.L.L.O. *consejo,* Love your child for who she or he is, distinct from his or her siblings and from yourself as a child. "I was always a very well-behaved little girl," she admitted one afternoon. "I guess I needed a lot of approval, and for whatever reason, I didn't require much structure. I sort of went along with what I sensed my mother wanted from me. Marcelo definitely *isn't* like me in that respect! He seems to need guidance, but I do not know how to give it to him without feeling guilty, as if I am punishing him." Clara felt that being a good mother meant allowing her child free rein. She also recognized that her mother's permissiveness had been good for her in some respects, but it had harmed her by being too extreme in its permissiveness and not teaching her to function within boundaries or to set limits.

Clara came to see that in failing to discipline her appropriately, her mother was in fact misinterpreting many of the *consejos,* including the third O.R.G.U.L.L.O. *consejo:* Guide and teach your child; do not dictate. Consequently, Clara found it very difficult to guide Marcelo on much-needed aspects of his development.

Here are two tips on toilet training that Clara learned. They will prove useful no matter what your parenting style:

- Either too much or too little intensity when toilet training a child will usually produce unsuccessful results. As in all other aspects of parenting, balance is key. As Yamila learned, pressuring a child to use the potty is almost a guarantee that she won't—either because she's not developmentally ready or because she's at that stage where any request, much less a demand, is rebelled against. In Clara's case, absolute permissiveness proved equally ineffective. Although she initially thought she was respecting and loving Marcelo by giving him carte blanche, she had to face the fact that she was too busy with her own life to really concentrate on the little boy's needs. She was also so isolated from other parents that she could not benefit from sharing experiences and learning how other parents might have resolved similar problems.

- Make sure your child interacts with other kids in her age range, who will serve as role models, and encourage her to want to acquire behaviors that involve autonomy. Since Clara did not understand the importance of Marcelo's being with other children, she did not make it a priority that he go to the park or visit other children with the babysitter. She said that it was easier for her to have Marcelo cared for at home by the sitter, since that way she did not have to worry that he was being exposed to any outside dangers. Since he didn't have exposure to other children his age, he insisted on running around the house all day in diapers.

How to Survive the Terrible Twos (and Threes and Fours)

The year from age two to age three is often called "terrible" because it marks the inception of children's ability to say no. And once they know they can, they seem to say nothing but! This is the very beginning of independence. Children this age say no to everything—even to things that they like, such as eating or taking a walk. It is as if children suddenly understand themselves as being separate from the adults in their life, and they are putting their independence into practice. This is not to be seen as *desobediencia*. It is a normal, transitory stage; it will pass.

If you have the time, be patient and wait when, for example, two-year-old Martin sits down on the sidewalk and refuses to walk. Allowing him to sit will not make him disobedient for life. If, on the other hand, you are in a rush and must get to school to pick up your five-year-old, then gently pick him up and keep walking without explaining; simply keep walking. This is what *El Nuevo Tradicionalismo* recommends: you send a calm message that we have to move on, without screaming or accusations.

As your child reaches three or four years of age, he is able to speak in full sentences and has enhanced motor (physical) ability. He may use these skills to test your patience, and obeying the rules of the new *obediencia* and the new *respeto* becomes a challenge. You can meet the challenge if you bear in mind that you have two essential tasks to perform: teaching him that certain objects must not be touched because they either can break or can be dangerous to him; and remembering that if you want to be listened to, you must practice consistency in the way you relate to him.

For example, when Pedrito throws a glass, you must tell him in no uncertain terms that breaking things is not allowed. You must make sure you relay this "house rule" to him clearly and repeatedly until he gets the message.

What you should not do—although your parents may have done it with you when you were young—is attempt to get him to behave by screaming at him or spanking him; this will only make him more defiant. You must also not laugh in amusement at his antics. This can be difficult because toddlers can be very cute. If you do laugh, however, you're courting disaster because he will assume that what he did was a *good* thing and will keep on doing it.

New Traditional Child Care

As you probably know from firsthand experience, Latino cultural tradition holds that children be cared for primarily by family—because throughout the centuries we have received from our family members the love and dedication so necessary for teaching kids the Latino values we treasure. According to the traditional way, employing nannies and babysitters is frowned on: if Mami must work outside the home (which also is not seen as the ideal), then *abuelita* Leonora or *tia* Luisa must supervise the raising of little Angela. We know that the economic demands of life today are far more rigorous from what they were even a decade ago, no matter where we reside. We also know that the society of which we are now a part is vastly different from that of our country of origin. As parents, we must deal with a whole new set of realities and expectations, including the area of child care. But that doesn't mean we won't feel guilty about hiring a nanny or babysitter—even though we know that the guilt is unwarranted and puts more pressure on us.

Although I am not necessarily advocating child care outside of the family as the best choice for everyone, I am asking you to consider that having your child cared for by someone other than a family member may be a reality of modern life. Do I think that doing it will be a guilt-free and problem-free situation? Of course not. However, you can minimize a host of potential difficulties by thoroughly interviewing candidates before you even think of hiring them, using your powers of observation, and following the suggestions below:

- What is her philosophy of bringing up children? Does she practice the second and third O.R.G.U.L.L.O. *consejos:* Respect your child's feelings and Guide and teach your child; do not dictate?
- Ask if she has children of her own. This discussion will give you an opportunity to assess if she has had firsthand experience in child care and whether or not she finds it rewarding.
- How does she feel about *obediencia*? Her answer will give you an idea of how she will deal with your child. If she believes in absolute *obediencia,* she might not follow your guidelines and will probably use hers—in which case you might not want this person to care for your child.
- If this applies, ask how she feels about working for someone younger than she. If she is older than you, is she likely to consider herself more experienced than you at child rearing and feel that gives her license to do things her way?
- Determine whether she is a *savelodotodo*—someone who thinks she knows it all. If that is how she strikes you, she might not be the right person for you. After all, she will be exerting an influence on your child. If she herself has an unpleasant personality, how is she going to teach your child *simpatia*?
- Visit her at her own house and examine her housekeeping habits. Is the house too fastidiously clean or too messy?
- Ask her if she is a person who feels frightened by certain things.

What are these things? You do not want her passing her fears to your child.

- Talk to her about her own childhood. Does she characterize her childhood as good or bad? Listen closely to how she handles the answer.

- Use the O.R.G.U.L.L.O. *consejos* as a basis for your interview questions, to get a sense of how she feels about these points and how receptive she is to following them.

- Invite her over for a day and observe her playing with and handling your child. Children's responses are quite telling. If your child is comfortable with her and she has qualifications that are suitable to your needs, then you may decide to hire her. By so doing, you will be following the second, O.R.G.U.L.L.O. *consejos:* Respect your child's feelings.

Hassle-Free Child Care? Only in Our Dreams!

Even if we hire the nanny from heaven, problems will inevitably arise. Be prepared for "trouble spots" that frequently occur when your child care provider is not a trusted family member:

- Ideal bonding, where the nanny or babysitter becomes a surrogate family member, was more possible back home. To expect such bonding to take place today may lead you to experience the babysitter as cold and detached when she is just being professional. On the other hand, if she is not being loving toward your child, you might need to look for another caregiver.

- Many Latino parents tell me that they cannot let go of worries when the caregiver travels outside the home with the child, because in many Latin countries children have been kidnapped. News accounts of abductions in the United States add to their fears. When you have a competent babysitter, yet you continue to worry, what you may be grappling with is your guilt, perhaps over not following the traditional parenting guidelines or over not being with your child all the time.

- Sometimes a mother's resentment of the babysitter is really resentment at having to work instead of being with her baby. If you have no choice but to work, you can still be a great mom when you come home and during the weekend and other free time. You can make being with your baby a priority during your free time. The truth is that if you are with your child all the time and end up feeling overwhelmed, you might not be as good a mom as when you come home eager to spend quality time with your child. Many Latina mothers tell me that in order to minimize their worries, they give their babysitter a cell phone. That way they can be in contact with each other if needed, and they can check in with the babysitter periodically to be sure that everything is fine.

Having found the right babysitter, you may find yourself jealous of her, afraid that your baby loves her "too much" or that she loves your baby "too much." These feelings are normal and quite common. I have found that the first step toward resolving them is through practicing the first O.R.G.U.L.L.O. *consejo:* Organize your feelings. You may find that you are dealing with old unconscious feelings of competition, perhaps with a sibling who you felt was loved more than you were. I can tell you that although this feeling is very real, it is more your own fear of not being loved as you need; it is not necessarily the case that your baby loves her babysitter more than she loves you.

If you find quality time to be with your child, she is going to love you always and you do not need to fear she will love the babysitter more than she loves you. Your child is used to your smell from birth; your child can love more than one person simultaneously and you will not be less loved than the babysitter. Most important, you will be there with your child for the major milestones, such as the first haircut, the first day of school, birthdays, graduations, and other occasions. Your child will always know that you are Mommy.

Selecting a Nursery School: A Practical Plan for Letting Go with O.R.G.U.L.L.O.

Although nursery school—or prekindergarten—can be seen as an important component of a child's beginning to develop interpersonal skills, parents of all ethnic backgrounds tend to feel anxious about their son or daughter moving outside the safety of the home for the first time. Traditional Latino parents say they feel that the experience at first is fraught with anxiety for them because they see their babies' place as being with the parents or extended family in the safety of the home. I have heard so many Latino parents say, "Why can't I wait to start him at school until he is older and better equipped to take care of himself?" Other two-career families prefer to employ a full-time babysitter who can closely monitor children in the safety of their home.

There are of course perfectly rational reasons for feeling that your child will not receive anywhere else the same level of love and care that he will receive in the safety of home. Media accounts of abuse of children and other dangerous situations may make you feel compelled to exert absolute caution. But once you make the right choice of both babysitter and school, focus on how your child is going to be enriched by the experience, not on dangers and harm.

Protecting Your Child with O.R.G.U.L.L.O.

Yes, there are all sorts of dangers out there. And there is no question that your role as a parent is to be as protective as is reasonably possible. Yet you must also make sure that your child gets the best upbringing possible, and that includes the opportunity to mix with other kids. There is a second catch to absolute caution: if you adhere to this way of thinking, you will feel more and more overwhelmed by trying to protect your child, since each age range brings new risks. Realize that no parent can anticipate every potential danger that their child may encounter.

Many traditional Latino parents feel that by sending their child so early to a non-Latino school, the opportunities for solidifying Latino cultural teachings at an early age are weakened; therefore, it is better to keep the child at home for as long as possible. I definitely understand that it is much easier to instill cultural values at an early age without any other interferences. However, the exposure to other children in nursery school can be very helpful to the socialization of a child. Although exposure to a diversified environment is not essential at such an early age, it can be a very good learning experience in every aspect.

Remember that in the past children had the opportunity to play with their siblings, cousins, or with friends of the extended family. Nowadays, most children must be taken outside the home, such as to a preschool or day care, in order to begin many aspects of their social learning.

Rosa and Jose, the parents of four-year-old Mickey, whom we read about earlier, wrestled with the preschool issue from all angles, Old World and New, before coming up with a process by which they selected a preschool for him:

1. By using the first O.R.G.U.L.L.O. *consejo,* Organize your feelings, Rosa and Jose discovered that they were finding it difficult not to use the same method of training they grew up with. They had both been raised in a dangerous neighborhood and had not been allowed to go downstairs to play. They realized that this was not the case now: they lived in a beautiful neighborhood where children could be quite safe during supervised play outside the home. So they put aside their own old fears and saw Mickey as a separate individual in a world very different from the one they grew up in. Only when they were clear on their own inner conflicts did they proceed to the next step in making decisions about Mickey's future, including the issue of sending him to a bilingual nursery.

2. Rosa and Jose decided to enroll Mickey in a school close to their home and asked the other parents in the neighborhood for suggestions. They had sent their daughter, Magda, to a bilingual nursery, but since they had moved in the interim, they decided that it was too far from their house and that they could easily help Mickey acquire Spanish at home.

3. Rosa and Jose visited prospective non-bilingual schools, attended classes, and spoke with staff, always making sure to be clear about the fact that, by their own choice, Mickey was more proficient right now in Spanish than in English—something that the staff needed to be sensitive to. Since Rosa and Jose timed their visits to the end of the school day, they were also able to talk to parents when they came to pick up their children. It was clear to Rosa and Jose that although the staff at the school they chose was not bilingual, they were attentive to Mickey's needs, such as needing to go to the bathroom or needing a drink. This also helped Mickey's English skills to develop faster.

4. Once they had chosen the preschool, Rosa and Jose immediately became actively involved: they got to know other students' parents, many of whom were Latino. In time, this parents' group teamed up to help organize fun events such as cultural fairs.

Rosa and Jose also followed the fourth O.R.G.U.L.L.O. *consejo,* Update your media awareness often, to find the best TV programs for Mickey in both English and Spanish.

The Many Ways of Raising a Child Latino Style

As Rosa and Jose's example shows, there are many ways to raise a child Latino style. By becoming involved at Mickey's school, they not only were satisfied that they had as great a say as possible in their child's first educational experience, but they also were able to share their cultural pride, bringing the riches of Latino culture to other parents and children.

An Integration of Cultures: The World from Kindergarten Through Junior High School

Before we begin discussing the early through middle school years, please rate yourself on how often the following questions apply to you.

5=ALWAYS 4=FREQUENTLY 3=SOMETIMES 2=RARELY 1=NEVER

1. Do you feel that you must stay with your daughter during the first day of school after you can tell your child is doing fine and the teacher tells you that it is perfectly okay for you to leave her? _____

2. Do you feel that you and your child's teacher do not agree on how your child should be allowed to behave?

    _____

3. Do you feel you are unprepared to separate from your child and let him visit friends even when you know the parents? _____

4. Do you hang up your child's school clothes when you ask her to do so and she doesn't listen to you? _____

5. Do you find yourself always doing your child's home-work rather than guiding him in completing it himself?

    _____

6. Have you learned about the Internet and computers in general so that you can help your children and protect them from inappropriate information? _____

(continued)

7. Do you avoid asking your husband or partner to help you with your child, even though he might not do things the way you do? _____
8. Do you compare your children's school progress with others and share your feelings with them? _____

Five-year-old Angelita is taken to school by her mother, Claudia, for the first time. As the teacher invites Angelita to join the other children, Claudia looks visibly sad. Angelita clings to her mother's skirt and refuses to join the other children. After this happened for two consecutive weeks, the teacher suggested that Claudia quietly leave and see how Angelita handles herself. Claudia leaves the room, but not the school. It turns out that Angelita gets happily involved in a drawing project. The following week, Claudia, who is now the only parent staying in the room, wants to stay, but the teacher motions for her to leave. Claudia finds it difficult. She has cared for Angelita from day one at home and has never left her with anyone other than her family. She feels guilty for leaving her at preschool and feels she is not a good mother. She fears that her daughter will not be able to handle herself if there is a problem, and that her daughter might not eat appropriately at school.

~

I have talked to many Latino parents who closely identify with the anecdote above. Many of these parents also have indicated that the eight questions asked at the beginning of the chapter are issues that they face in navigating the transition from home to school.

Before we continue our discussion, let's review the most important areas in which *El Nuevo Tradicionalismo* departs from traditional child-rearing practices; a review of these differences will guide you toward raising your child Latino style—with *orgullo*—in modern times.

- One rule does not fit all: every child is an individual.
- One age does not fit all: what you can expect from a child is determined by developmental stage.
- One parenting method does not fit all: circumstances alter cases and times change.
- One value system does not fit all: you grew up then; your kids are growing up now.

Having revisited the basic guidelines that pertain to all age groups, let's proceed to the template issues that will define our exploration of the early and middle school years:

- Facilitating the transition from home to school.
- Continuing to teach Latino values.
- Teaching age-appropriate independence and autonomy with love—Latino style.
- Loving your child's individuality.
- Talking about sexuality with your child.
- Getting a head start on the fight against the lurking demons of alcohol, drugs, and cigarettes.
- Maintaining the comforts of home in the school years.

Facilitating the Transition from Home to School

The Years of Smooth Sailing, but . . .

Conflicting cultural expectations and interpretations between the world of the Latino child at home and the outside world start to become apparent during the early and middle school years. It is still the case that this stage—what some professionals call the latency years—is generally regarded as the calm before the storm of adolescence for the child. Still, you as a Latino parent may find dark clouds brewing around the cultural conflicts manifested by the following issues:

- Accepting your child's budding independence/autonomy.
- Disagreement with the school and the teacher's philosophy, particularly over how to foster age-appropriate independence/autonomy.
- Allowing the child to visit nonrelatives and non-Hispanic friends.
- Knowing when to be less solicitous or accommodating: for example, not picking up clothes or toys for your child.
- Concern about how the child's character or progress compares with siblings or peers.
- Treating children differently based on gender.
- Confusion about how to continue teaching Latino cultural practices and language.

The beginning of school for most children marks the beginning of a long transition from home to school, and eventually to the larger world. However, for many Latino children this transition not only requires adjusting to different rules and regulations, but also a major adjustment in ways of viewing the outside world.

As mentioned in chapter 6, many Latino parents feel strongly that it is best to keep their young children at home or with relatives, rather than send them to preschool or day care before beginning kindergarten. They do this sometimes to protect their children from outside dangers, and often to build a strong basis of Latino traditions, or *costumbres*. But this early isolation can make the beginning of the school experience more difficult for the child, as well as for the parents. When a child starts school older than his peers, he is bound to find the adjustment to kindergarten more difficult than if he had started in nursery school or prekindergarten. In part, this is due to having had less opportunity to adjust to being with other children. Granted, many Latino children at home play with their siblings or relatives, but many do not, and siblings may be more similar and tolerant of one another than are peers.

The point is that there are better alternatives than isolation for establishing a solid basis of the Latino cultural values. These values can be attained while the child goes to school if you continue what you have already started teaching at home. While you are teaching and re-inforcing these values, you can and should simultaneously prepare your child for the first day of school.

Let's see what preparation for your child's school should include:

- Begin playing a pretend game of being at school as early as possible.
- Talk about how much fun it will be to be in school.
- Tell your child how happy you are that he is going to be with other children who will become his friends.
- Make a point of being as relaxed as you can when you reach school on the first day.
- Do not show your apprehension or fear to your child.
- Meet the other Latino and non-Latino parents and see if you can get together at a later point—find out if they have an interest in teaching Spanish to their child and form a parents' group.
- Find out how you can participate in school activities.
- Once school starts, ask your child to tell you about the day's activities.
- Have your child tell Grandma and other relatives how grown-up he is now that he is going to school.

The early and middle school years, or latency stage, also mark the beginning of the different expectations parents and other adults have of girls and boys. It is during the middle school years, around the sixth, seventh, and eighth grades in particular, that these expectations increase and conflicts can arise between children and parents if not handled appropriately. This is the stage when your child's hormones begin to kick in, causing the development of pubic hair, bodily odors, onset of menstruation and breast development in girls, and changes in voice in boys, among other things. And it is around this stage that the cultural expectations of *marianismo* and *machismo* begin to take hold. Girls are protected and boys are given the message that they must be tough, can't cry, and mustn't act like a baby.

Let's see what continuation of the teaching of the Latino cultural values entails:

Continuing to Teach Latino Values

The teaching of Latino values that began in the preschool years takes on a different dimension in the middle school years, because at this point your child is spending more time in school and probably in an environment different from what she experiences at home. But many Latino families have succeeded in teaching their values to their older children.

A Latino family said to me: "We brought our cultural *orgullo* out into the outside world of our children." They said that they felt it was not enough to teach a child about his Latino culture and keep it in the domain of the home; it must be brought into the open and into the school. They became involved in celebrations. They organized the parents from their child's class to have a multicultural fair in school. Parents from all cultures brought special food dishes and objects of art, and each child related stories describing their countries' heroes and heroines. This is something that they have repeated yearly throughout middle school. This family sees their involvement as a way of empowering the child to communicate his cultural uniqueness and also to celebrate being part of this culture. The children were taught *cuentos* (stories) in Spanish, and then they read the translation of these stories to the class.

Another family's ten-year-old daughter, Felicia, has been taught from the very beginning to have pride in her language and culture. She has put together a girls' club composed of seven girls who meet once a week to do art projects, bake cookies, listen to Spanish music, dance, watch movies picked with the permission of the parents, and read books that relate to Spanish culture, such as *When the Garcia Girls Lost Their Accent*. Felicia is very comfortable speaking Spanish or English.

The Language Situation—Issues

Most Latino parents are very busy and may find teaching Spanish to their school-age child a bit difficult, particularly now that the child spends more time away from home. You do have choices at the school.

Children can take Spanish beginning in fourth grade in many schools. You can also visit many Web sites and either retrieve or buy software that will make learning Spanish fun. You can go to the public library and borrow educational materials. You can also have your child attend Spanish-language school programs over the weekend. My younger son, Miguel, attended a weekend school in Spanish called the Escuela Argentina, in Queens, New York. See what institutions in your area can provide a formal teaching of the Spanish language for your child. Ask around, check the Internet and the phone book to find ways to teach Spanish to your child. You can also use the one-person, one-language method that I discussed in chapter 6.

Parenting children at this age is not as physically draining as during the preschool years, when your child needed your full and nearly constant attention. At school, your child will be expanding her learning of the values taught at home, including self-discipline, socialization, and of course academics. But the Latino child might not necessarily be in a situation where the Latino values taught at home are reinforced at school. I have seen that many parents have mastered the teaching of these values by being inventive. As I have said, *La escasez es la madre de la invencion* (Scarcity is the mother of invention). As always, you must consider your child's age and have realistic expectations. Each age is going to bring a different challenge. Sometimes your child might refuse to speak Spanish, which may alarm you. Your child might be facing and reacting to differences between him and his peers, wanting to be like them, only speaking English. What to do in a situation like this?

- Apply O.R.G.U.L.L.O. *consejos* no. 2, Respect your child's feelings; no. 3, Guide and teach your child; do not dictate; no. 6, Listen to your child, and no. 7, Open the communication channels—and keep them open. By respecting her feelings and not getting upset about your child saying "I do not want to speak Spanish," you set the stage for communication. Ask her why she feels this way. Help her see how she can speak both languages and fit in well in both worlds she inhabits.

- Suggest a peer group party where both Latin and North American music can be played.
- Propose to her that together you will suggest a cultural fair at the school where students will make presentations on their culture of origin. She will see how much fun this can be and that many of her peers are unique, as she is.

If none of this works, do not worry. Continue practicing those aspects of your culture that you value with *orgullo*. See this as a phase that will eventually pass. She will more than likely learn to feel proud of her language and culture. Just keep at it gently and persistently.

The New Respeto *in the School Years*

As we saw in the opening anecdote of this chapter describing Angelita and her mother, Claudia, most Latino parents find themselves caught between different interpretations and applications of child-rearing issues, those in the home compared with those in their child's school. These differing interpretations can cause cultural clashes unless there is adaptation to what I call the new *respeto*.

The new *respeto* primarily requires an understanding of the child's needs. He should be allowed to ask for an explanation of your actions when appropriate. The new *respeto* also incorporates issues of age-appropriate independence, privacy, and sexuality. Perhaps the most difficult aspect of the new *respeto* in the early, middle, and high school years is determining how much freedom to give your child. It is a fact of life that your child is going to be increasingly exposed to others and needs sufficient freedom to feel a sense of independence from you.

The new *respeto* also requires an understanding of your child's feelings. You may need to explain why his North American friends are allowed to do certain things that he is not allowed to do. You may do this in terms of what you value and what the rules of your household are, but not in terms of your ethnicity. Remember that cultural pride is not going to be passed on by saying "This is a Latino home and we do things Latino style." Doing so will only create animosity, not *orgullo*.

- The new *respeto* Latino style emphasizes the need never to talk back to mother, father, grandparents, or any adult, for that matter. This is not to be changed.
- The new *respeto* Latino style might include your rule that there is to be no cursing.
- The new *respeto* Latino style might include your rules for how your child or his friends should conduct themselves in your house. If your child feels that you are being too strict, at least hear him out and consider whether he might have a point. Consult with well-informed friends and people you trust to guide you.
- The new *respeto* Latino style should include having *confianza* in your child. A sense of trust quite often leads to good behavior. When this trust is broken, then a productive dialogue is in order and, if needed, application of discipline that includes removal of privileges.

Remember that the new *respeto* Latino style requires that you not compare your child with siblings or peers. This is definitely not respectful of your child's character.

Averting Clashes between Familismo *and School*

Angelita's transition from home to school is more difficult for her mother, Claudia, than it is for Angelita. Claudia's behavior is not making it easy for Angelita, who perceives her mother's apprehension and becomes anxious. Claudia is letting her own needs rule, not Angelita's. Claudia grew up with ten siblings and found the support of her family wonderful. She wants her girl to have the same experience as she did, and she decided to keep Angelita out of preschool and at home with her and her family. Claudia told me with great pride that she purposely kept Angelita isolated in order to preserve the unity of the family, or *familismo*. From our discussion it became clear to me that she was equating maintenance of *familismo* with isolation from others who were not family. But Claudia was also concerned that harm might befall Angelita in school. She feared that Angelita might leave the classroom and cross the street or go with strangers. If you have similar fears, it might be helpful to consider these ideas:

- *Juntos pero no revueltos* (Together, but not entangled). *Familismo* can be maintained by the support that each member of the family gives each other. Your child will see it and follow your lead.
- The safety of your child is a priority, but there are different ways of assuring safety other than constantly watching your child. One way, for example, is to encourage your child to tell you about her day at school. Also, teach issues of safety from the very beginning: never to go with strangers, never to cross the street alone, and other safety rules. Explain how to tell if someone is a stranger, what to do if a stranger approaches your child, and that your child should tell you immediately what happened. By teaching your child how to be cautious and well aware of safety issues, you are giving him the help he needs to stay safe when he is not with you.
- Ask yourself if your policy of not allowing your child go on play dates to "permissive North American houses" is always warranted. Is your young Latino child only safe in your presence? I have seen that many of these messages passed on to a child can negatively affect his smooth sailing through school.

There is no question that when a child enters school, his tolerance for frustration and structure is limited. He is going to need you to help him make the transition by establishing age-appropriate communication about his fears, if any, and about how he can navigate his new environment.

This also means helping your child do things he is mature enough to do, such as picking up his clothes, choosing what clothes to wear to school, fastening his buttons by himself, fastening his seat belt, and staying with the teachers and other children when it is time to do so.

What about the New Simpatia?

Simpatia is a concept that is very relevant to the world of school at this stage. It is also one that needs to be adapted but that is definitely worth keeping. The most salient cultural differences you will notice as your child begins attending school will be in how to socialize with other children. Here is where the by-now famous play dates become more problematic. Here is where the importance of your child's peers, who become progressively more important with age, must be recognized. The primary challenge is to reconcile the differences in a way that helps your child navigate both of his worlds: Latino and North American. Here are some strategies:

- Value and actively foster your child's development and maintenance of friendships.
- Listen to your child. Is he saying things like, "But the other kids are allowed to do that"? I know this is not a good reason to allow your child do whatever he asks of you, but if you listen, and if you view popularity and socialization as important, you will find ways to hear your child's concerns and not simply respond with an absolute no.
- Encourage your child to be a popular participant in her two worlds.
- Allow your child to visit her friends' homes once you get to know the friends and their families. If you insist that "children must always visit us, so I can see what they are up to," you are applying a traditional way of thinking that is not helpful to your child. You are not teaching her a sense of mutuality. In fact, you are saying "Everything has to be my way." This is not conducive to cooperation, sharing, and friendship. One of the requirements of being a good friend is to know how to cooperate.
- Invite your child's non-Latino friends and their parents to your cultural celebrations.
- Invite open communication regarding your child's friends—ask what your child's friends like to do. This way, if you feel that the

friends' behaviors are not to your liking, you can be very honest about your views without implying any ethnic superiority or inferiority.

- Promote cooperation and healthy competition by facilitating your child's participation in clubs and team sports.
- Reinforce the beauty of being part of two cultures—explain the differences that may surface with your expectations of *simpatia*.
- Observe how your child deals with his peers: is he too bossy, always wanting his own way? Reflect on how or where he might be learning these behaviors.
- If in spite of modeling socialization behaviors that are important to you, they are still lacking in your child, explain to your child the importance of being *bien educado*. He should know how to maintain an age-appropriate conversation, to say please, excuse me, and I'm sorry.
- Become involved in school activities. You will be providing a good role model to your child by participating in his world and socializing with others, including non-Latinos. You will also have an opportunity to observe your child in the world of school to see if there are skills that he needs helps with. Is he too shy? Is he too bossy? Is he quitting games when he does not get his way? Is he getting angry or frustrated too quickly? Does he know how to initiate and end a conversation appropriately? Is he playing too aggressively? Is he being too competitive or too submissive? I think you get the idea of how important it is to observe your child in his school world.

Dos and Don'ts of Obediencia and Discipline in the School Years

As your child grows older and progresses in school, several things could happen.

- Your child may see differences between himself and other children that might prompt him to begin to ask you for explanations of your disciplinary actions.
- Your child may want to do things that the other children do.

- Your parenting and discipline methods may be noticed by others outside of the family. Any bruises or indications of physical abuse of a child may be questioned.
- Demanding absolute *obediencia* could make your child overly compliant or submissive with others, and she may experience difficulties defending herself.

The first thing to do is to be in touch with those feelings you learned when reading about *obediencia* in chapter 5. When your child demands explanations of your parenting decisions, focus on keeping an open dialogue, allowing your child to express herself. Explain your thinking and be very sensitive to what she is feeling, but also guide her to do what you believe is right, because your child needs a parent's guidance and periodic discipline.

A Latina mother told me how her twelve-year-old son, Steven, came home from school with a note from the teacher that indicated he was punished that day because he disrupted the class and disobeyed the teacher. She said, "When I read the note I felt quite angry and frustrated, disappointed in him. My first inclination was to spank him and punish him myself, as well, but then I remembered the new *obediencia* and decided to instead have an honest discussion with him to hear his version.

"After he explained to me that his friend Tom had tickled him and he could not help but laugh and struggle to get away, I was able to help him see that it was he who had gotten into trouble, not his friend. I asked how he was going to resolve this. I stressed to him that if it happened again, I was going to punish him and talk to Tom's mother, because I could not allow his school progress and behavior to be affected in any way. In the meantime, I said, I was going to leave it to him to look for a solution. Steven replied that Tom was his friend and that this friendship was very important to him. Through our discussion we were able to come up with a solution: Steven would talk to Tom and tell him not to do that in the classroom anymore because he did not want to get into trouble."

Through careful dialogue, this mother and her son found a positive way to solve a school problem that guided him in *obediencia* without shouting, spanking, or name-calling.

Dialogue and exploration of feelings are powerful tools in parenting older children. A two-year-old child must be shown and helped to put his toys away, but at school age or beyond, he should know how to do this. The problem is that sometimes, children know what they are supposed to do but still break the rules. This is where patient discussion might work best, and, when necessary, withholding of privileges. Do not forget to praise when appropriate. You do not give the child a reward for having done what he is supposed to do, such as brushing his teeth or taking a bath, but you can certainly show appreciation.

Teaching Age-Appropriate Independence and Autonomy with Love—Latino Style

Parents and schools may differ as to what is considered appropriate for a child in terms of fostering his independence and autonomy. This issue presents itself with varying intensity according to the child's age, particularly during the earlier years in school and throughout adolescence, as we will see in the next chapter.

Is there such a thing as independence and autonomy Latino style? I have seen many different practices by many Latino parents. Certainly, Latino parents in no way purposely raise children to be dependent, but their views often differ from those of their child's school. A parent told me that she is very concerned because the school administrators feel that her daughter, now in fifth grade, is ready to go home alone, but this parent feels her daughter is not ready. The school officials feel that this parent is making her daughter's transition difficult, because she is the only child who cannot go home alone and must wait at school for her mom or someone to pick her up.

Some disagreements will require your having a serious discussion with the school executives, and you should be as assertive as needed. However, if disagreements may include your child's choices of extracurricular activities, or participating in sports such as swimming, be careful not to be too controlling and not to apply your own fears to your child. You might want to discuss with her the pros and cons of her choices, but if she wants to play the violin instead of the guitar, let her have her choice.

Parents often ask, "How can I determine whether I am on the right track in fostering my child's level of independence?" In traditional Latino culture children are protected, perhaps because parents in earlier times had more time to spend with children or had a more extensive support system of family and community. That is less often the case for today's families.

Independence also depends on the level of maturity of the child. Sending a child to school should be seen as the beginning of the establishment of age-appropriate independence and autonomy. Every child is different, and knowing your child's temperament and abilities is a very important part of the *consejos* of O.R.G.U.L.L.O.

Loving Your Child's Individuality

By about age five your child probably has developed enough to be able to manage herself for several hours at a time without you and under the supervision of a responsible adult. You are entitled to feel that your child is not better off with anyone but you, but that is not always a fact. Keeping a child isolated from other children and limiting contact to primarily you, the parent, might not be best for the smooth development of the child's character.

The degree of independence and autonomy allowed a child is of course very much dependent on the child's age and level of maturity. For example, a six-year-old should not go to school alone, but a sixteen-year-old can easily do so. Another important aspect of autonomy is to allow your child to solve certain problems on his own. Doing so helps him achieve a sense of competence in life. Here the O.R.G.U.L.L.O. *consejos* need to be applied in full, because they will help you differentiate between your needs and your child's needs while also helping you adhere to your core values:

- Organize your feelings
- Respect your child's feelings
- Guide and teach your child; do not dictate

- Update your media awareness often
- Love your child for who she or he is
- Listen to your child
- Open the communication channels—and keep them open

Remember that school offers your child a different experience from the home environment, not just in terms of academic learning but in terms of getting along with others, respecting boundaries, making independent, age-appropriate decisions, and following rules.

As your child progresses through the middle school years, you will need to revisit and revise your reasons for allowing or forbidding certain harmless behaviors that differ from yours. It is during the school years that children become increasingly aware of the ways other people behave and live. You will need your listening skills in order to guide your child without creating unnecessary battles.

Becoming aware of others' differences and similarities could cause conflicts of identity in your child. Here is where your calming presence and dialogue with your child will offer much-needed emotional support in terms of her language and ethnicity.

Encouraging the following behaviors will help your child in making sound decisions. Some of these strategies refer to specific school activities and others to more general principles, but all will help your child in learning to make decisions, which is a main component of autonomy:

- Ask your daughter what she thinks she should wear today to school based on her listening to the weather forecast. If she is incorrect, gently tell her what would be a better choice.
- Have your son or daughter select thank-you cards to send to family members for gifts given on Three Kings Day, birthdays, or other celebrations.
- Take your child to the library to select games, books, or music. Do not try to invalidate her choices, unless they are harmful.
- Allow your son to help with food preparation, for example, washing and peeling vegetables. Thank him for his help.

- Encourage using a dictionary to look up unfamiliar words in English or Spanish, rather than give the answers.
- Have your son help you address envelopes for his birthday party, your thank-you notes, or the family's Christmas cards.
- Ask your son to help you set the table. This could become a fun project during the earlier years, and then a big help to you later on.
- Ask your daughter what musical instrument she would like to learn to play in school and then guide, do not dictate, her choice.
- When your child arrives home from school or sometime during the evening, take time to hear about her school activities, friends, and teachers. Make a point of asking questions that open the way to dialogues, such as, "How do you feel about what your friend said to you?" Try not to judge her reactions as nonsense or babyish; just listen and ask about feelings. Ask your child what she thinks should be done to solve a problem. Offer support for her feelings, for example, "I hear you are sad" or "I hear you are angry." Rather than decide what she should do, ask how you can help.
- Go thoroughly into her homework assignments, but in a way that involves both of you. Have her show you what she has done in class during the day and ask how she is finding the nature of the work. Find out if she needs help. This is different from doing things for her.

You may want to spare your child from every unpleasant experience. But overprotection is not helping your child. If Morayma's five-year-old son, Peter, wants to fasten his jacket by himself, but his mother feels he is not doing it well or fast enough and says, "Let me do it for you," she does not teach him by taking over the task.

It might be helpful to get your child accustomed from an early age to show you his homework assignment, rather than open his bag and look for it yourself. You can say: "Marcos, let's open your bag and show me your homework." If he has received a note from school, it's a good opportunity to establish much-needed dialogue and say:

"Marcos, let's talk about this." Marcos might say it is not his fault or he does not know anything about what happened. You must be patient and remember that you are teaching him how to communicate. Respect his feelings by saying: "Marcos, I know this is difficult for you, but I am not angry, I am concerned. This is important and I want to hear what happened."

Teaching independence requires allowing the child sometimes to make mistakes so that he can learn the consequences of his behaviors. There are some issues, though, that might not allow the freedom of making mistakes—which brings me to the subject of sexuality.

Talking About Sexuality with Your Child

It is not my intention to provide an exhaustive discussion of sexuality. But I do want to explore how difficult it is for many Latino parents to talk naturally to their children about sexuality. It is often presented as a shameful, sinful, awful thing. This way of viewing sex tends to misinform children, send them to the wrong sources to get information (which is often erroneous), and shuts down the communication with the parents. I will show alternative methods that have helped many Latino parents whom I have worked with.

During the middle school years children begin to develop into sexual beings. While there is no question that children should be protected from inappropriate sexual exploration, they need factual information that will not frighten them and affect their future sexuality. It is essential that children learn to make responsible decisions without being easily swayed by others.

It is your responsibility as a parent to teach your child about sexuality. This way, you are in control of the facts and information your child receives and you can guide your child in a manner appropriate to your values. Sexuality is a topic that makes many parents anxious, and your preference might be to ignore it. I suggest that you do not. Consider it a fact of life that must be dealt with.

If you think about it, many parents do include sexuality in their child's everyday life, but in a negative and frightening way. Fear of allowing a daughter to visit a neighbor or have a play date is one example. Many Latino parents have told me of not allowing their pre-teen daughter visit a friend due to fears that she will be molested. Unfortunately, many Latino adults reveal to me in therapy that they have been sexually molested at home, either by a relative or a trusted friend, and not necessarily while on a play date. Preventing sexual abuse is in fact a key reason for having an honest and open dialogue about sexuality with your child. Awareness and safety measures must be inculcated in your child by dialogue, not by withholding information. Let's see how this can be done:

First, keep in mind O.R.G.U.L.L.O *consejo* no. 1. You need to organize your feelings about this subject and be comfortable with your experiences in order to talk to your child in a calm and relaxed way that will be helpful to him.

Your attitude about sexuality will be absorbed by your child. Keep in mind that your child is probably going to be receiving sexual education in school at about eleven or twelve years of age or by the time he reaches junior high or high school. You will want to know what he has learned and help him to understand it more fully, in concert with your values.

Although sexuality issues peak around adolescence, you cannot wait until then to start talking about sexuality to your child. One way to begin talking about sexuality with your child between the ages of six to eight is to talk about the human body. There are wonderful books that can help you get started (see the Recommended Resources section for some suggestions).

- In the early years, talk with your child in a relaxed way about the body parts that you feel he should know. In fact, it is generally expected that a child will know the location of basic body parts such as eyes, nose, chin, and so on by approximately age four.
- You should view talking about the private body parts as a natural next step. Again, the amount of information will vary according to your child's age, but you would want your six-year-old girl to know the importance of washing her genitals when she bathes, or your twelve-year-old child to know about health risks, preg-

nancy, and AIDS. This teaching can be matter-of-fact and be given the same importance as drinking enough milk or eating the right food.

- Do not talk to your children about sexuality as if it is a shameful or bad thing. Tell them that sex is a natural act that adults do with each other but not with children, and that sometimes some disturbed adults might want to use sex to hurt children, and that no adult should ever touch your child's private parts.

Sexuality has many dimensions and you will need to begin talking with your child in an age-appropriate manner. A young child will probably ask: "Where do children come from?" Do not say "from heaven." This is the time to get a book from the library and let it guide you; there are many responsible and wonderful books on these issues.

Sexuality is essential to the development of an individual. I see it as part of the new *respeto* in the sense that the teaching of sexuality is a way of teaching self-respect, and parents have the responsibility to decide when and how sexuality will be incorporated in their child's life.

Getting a Head Start on the Fight Against the Lurking Demons of Alcohol, Drugs, and Cigarettes

As with the teaching of sexuality, which is an important issue in the development of self-respect and autonomy in your child, you need to consider to start talking at the middle school age about the lurking demons of drugs, alcohol, smoking, and other forms of self-destruction that we referred to in chapter 5. The most important preventive step you can take is not to say things like, "Don't let me catch you using any of that stuff," but rather to establish a dialogue. Explain how much you are against using drugs and give factual reasons for your opinion, such as that these substances can become habit-forming, interfere with school progress, are illegal, and are inadequate ways of coping with life. You may have to amend your urge to say: "I forbid you to go out with Regina; her parents are too permissive." This will only shut down the communication between you and your child. Explain your reasons. This strategy works best in the middle school years. Your approach in the high school years might need to be different, as we will explore in chapter 8.

Your consistent and clear expression of your feelings on these issues should begin as early as the situations may occur. You must also maintain a very clear position on these matters with relatives. A Latina mother told me that when her daughters were six and seven, she was quite upset to have to tell her only brother, who had a drug and alcohol problem, that he could not come and live with them as he had requested. She did not approve of his excesses and did not want her daughters exposed to his example. Which brings us to the necessity of being very mindful of the example you set on these issues. Your child is watching, and the discipline you teach must be the discipline you yourself model.

If you smoke cigarettes and cannot stop the habit, your child may question your sincerity. Through open dialogue you can share with her that the fact that you do it does not mean that it is okay; that you do it because nobody really made you understand how difficult it was to stop smoking and now you are so used to it that you cannot stop. Now you know better than you did when you were younger, and by not allowing her to smoke you are not taking something away from her, but you are protecting her as you wish someone had protected you. We will discuss your approach to the lurking demons in the high school years in chapter 8, but for the middle school years:

- Start educating your children about the dangers of drugs and alcohol as early as they start school.
- Share your views and values as clearly as possible, particularly in the early years, when children will be more prone to listen to you.
- Be as informed as you can so that you have the facts and can share them with your children.
- Open the communication channels so that your children can ask you questions. Do not overreact by getting too anxious about these issues; otherwise, your child will sense your anxiety and protect himself and you by not telling you anything.

- Set the example and be the role model; do not expect that you can do it and your child will not.
- Here is where your media awareness (TV, Internet, print) can be of help. Find out how to block certain unsavory programs from being watched at home.
- Frame your explanations in terms of what you value and what the rules of your household are, not in terms of your ethnicity.
- Know that it is better to establish trust than to demand compliance. If you have followed the guidelines of the new *obediencia,* you will have a child who is on his way toward following your values.
- Restrain yourself from looking in your child's drawers. If you followed the guidelines for developing your child's healthy autonomy, you should be able to talk to your child very openly about anything. Most important, she will be able to talk to you in the same way. You do not need to be sneaky. This is not a way of protecting her, because if she feels that you are going into her drawers, she will find different ways to hide things from you if she has things to hide. It is better to establish trust.
- Make a point of having these discussions alone with your child or only in the presence of your partner and no one else. Privacy respects his feelings, while still making him accountable for his actions.
- Strategic planning might be required when applying the new *respeto.* By now your child and you should have established certain rules about behavior and your reprimands. You can tell him that you will not scold him in front of friends, but that if he has violated a rule, you are going to remind him that he now needs to be alone. It should be his responsibility to tell his friend that he must leave.
- It is very important to maintain boundaries. Your room is to be respected. Your child must knock on the door before entering your room. You will also knock on her door if it is closed or locked. This is not asking permission to enter but an act of respect for her space: a gentle knock and then you enter.

Maintaining the Comforts of Home
in the School Years

A supportive home atmosphere for the school years means providing your child with a safe and age-appropriate environment for
learning—including the completion of homework—providing intel-
lectual stimulation, and being aware of your child's media exposure.
We already discussed the need to talk to your child about the facts and
myths of sexuality.

This is an ideal time to watch movies with your children and use
them as a source of discussion. Once your child turns six, you can use
movies to share examples of behavior that is irresponsible or immature, or that causes harm to others. Look also for examples of behavior that is empathetic and worth imitating. Some other guidelines:

- Remember that whatever happens at home is bound to be used by
  your child as a model. I remember, when my children were in middle school, we had a party at our home and one of the guests asked
  permission to light a joint. We said, "No, we are sorry but we have
  our children here."

- Remember that part of the new *respeto* is to tell your child as often
  as you can that you appreciate his good behavior. The home is a
  good place to put these guidelines into practice. Thank him for listening to your request to turn down the music. Thank him for remembering to turn off the TV when he leaves the room. Express
  your pleasure at the neatness of his room.

- When your children violate the household rules, indicate without
  any hesitancy that this is not acceptable. Be clear and precise that
  what has been done is not correct.

- At home you have the opportunity to establish intimacy with your
  child by expressing your love, your expectations of the new *obediencia,* and your empathy.

- At home your child is entitled to an orderly and peaceful environment where there will be no shouting, no humiliations, no disrespect, no abuses.

Home is the place where you can establish a balance between providing your child with your support and guidance and letting him make some decisions on his own. Maintaining a flexible view will help you avoid what Bartolo's parents did.

Eight-year-old Bartolo starts fights with other students in his school on a daily basis, and his clowning around in class is extremely disruptive. At her wits' end, Bartolo's teacher meets with his parents to discuss the problem. When they ask Bartolo why he is behaving so badly, the parents understand that it is because they do not allow him to bring friends home or to play outside the house. But the real bone of contention is the draconian schedule they force the boy to follow—no TV, no play, only schoolwork.

Through opening this dialogue with their son, Bartolo's parents realized the importance of work and play, which required a great deal of readjustment, since both of them had grown up not being permitted to read *novelas* or play with friends. They realized that they had to step past their fear that allowing Bartolo to have some fun would spoil him and cause him to fall behind in his studies. That was Old World thinking. Bartolo's parents were ignoring the importance of peers and friendship, which are essential to developing a good self-concept.

A Win-Win Proposition

The closing statement in this chapter will be very brief, but I think very powerful. It is something that two Latino parents who came to see me said at the end of a successful family treatment: "If we can keep the good about our culture, although we might have to modify it, and by modifying the good, we spare our children's self-esteem, why not do so?"

CHAPTER 8

The Culturally Diverse Adolescent:
Turn the Stormy Years
into Smooth Sailing

Before we begin discussing the teenage years, please answer the following questions, rating yourself on how often they apply to you.

5=ALWAYS 4=FREQUENTLY 3=SOMETIMES 2=RARELY 1=NEVER

1. Do you feel that your adolescent child is becoming a stranger in ways that you never imagined? _____

2. Do you lecture rather than communicate with your adolescent about sexuality, drug usage, and alcohol? _____

3. Do you avoid socializing with the parents of your adolescent's friends? _____

4. Do you look into your adolescent's drawers and eavesdrop on her telephone conversations, but deny complaints that you are interfering with her privacy? _____

5. Do you impose your cultural values on your adolescent and disregard what he has to say about these issues?

   _____

6. Do you forbid, without explanation and dialogue, your son or daughter to bring home friends you disapprove of? _____

7. Do you disregard the importance of peers in your adolescent's life? _____

8. Do you forbid your adolescent to disagree with you, firmly keeping your initial position without a dialogue?

   _____

Fourteen-year-old Virginia angrily puts her foot down this time: she is going to the school dance without her mother, Graciela, who up until now has insisted on chaperoning her to all school functions, even when other parents had been scheduled to act as chaperones. Graciela claims not to trust anyone other than herself to oversee Virginia at dances because "there are too many dangers out there." Virginia is also furious that her mother has begun searching through her dresser drawers and will not permit her to close her bedroom door when her friend Jennifer comes to visit.

～

We have already established that each developmental stage brings its own specific set of joys and difficulties for parents. Early to middle adolescence is no exception. Although this stage need not necessarily be tumultuous, it is notoriously more difficult than any other, regardless of the child's ethnicity, because it is the psychological bridge between childhood and adult life, rife with both biological and cognitive changes. Adolescence is also the period when children are making major decisions regarding peers, drug usage, dating, sexuality, gender and identity, as well as autonomy and privacy issues.

Latino adolescents may face an additional hurdle: the awareness that their cultural identity is different from North American teens' and that it is often difficult to balance the customs of the world outside the home with their parents' traditional values. As the anecdote about Virginia demonstrates, many Latino teens feel that their North American peers have much more freedom than they do.

This chapter guides Latino parents in helping their adolescent children negotiate the worlds of home, school, and community successfully. You will discover that learning to function in a bicultural climate will actually broaden your child's horizons and make him an emotionally healthy, self-reliant citizen of two cultures. You will also see that you can give your child the space to develop as an individual without falling victim to overpermissiveness.

First, let's review the four major areas in which *El Nuevo Tradicionalismo* departs from traditional child-rearing practices; a review of these differences will guide you toward raising your child Latino style—with *orgullo*—in modern times.

- One rule does not fit all: every child is an individual
- One age does not fit all: what you can expect from a child is determined by developmental stage
- One parenting method does not fit all: circumstances alter cases and times change
- One value system does not fit all: you grew up then; your kids are growing up now

Now, let's proceed to the template issues that will define our exploration of adolescence:

- Independence and autonomy: how much is too much?
- *Confianza:* the gateway to open communication
- Protecting your child is a good thing—within reason
- Template issues and peace terms
- Embedding O.R.G.U.L.L.O.
- Continuing to teach Latino values
- Furthering independence and autonomy with love—Latino style
- When your style and your children's collide
- Redefining gender expectations

Independence and Autonomy: How Much Is Too Much?

Many Latino parents who want to pass the traditional Latino values of *respeto, familismo, simpatia,* and *obediencia,* on to their adolescent sons and daughters face conflicts around the question: How much freedom is too much? My aim in this chapter is to provide you with an understanding of what constitutes an appropriate level of independence and autonomy for your bicultural teenager. To begin with, it is crucial for you to be able to judge when your child is ready to be given a certain level of *confianza,* or trust.

Confianza: *The Gateway to Open Communication*

You might in many instances know better than your adolescent, but perhaps not in all situations. You may also have had a totally different experience when you were her age and were probably not exposed to what she is exposed to today. You therefore need to hear from her how she sees certain things and you must allow her to have opinions different from yours. Do this through dialogue and sharing your opinions, especially on issues that are less threatening or dangerous, such as fashion, friends, and music preference. It is with issues such as drug abuse and other self-destructive behaviors that you need to be very firm, but always still allow for open communication, where you trust but verify. The trick is maintaining that balance, because the adolescent needs your supervision and support but also needs to know that you have *confianza* in her. You must be very careful not to overreact when she confides in you about a sensitive subject. Let's return to Virginia's story to see how open communication will benefit you and your child:

After much hesitation, Virginia confesses to her mother, Graciela, that her friend Pamela has asked her to say that Pamela slept over at their house when she is really planning to spend the night with her boyfriend. It is critical that Graciela listen, not judge, because if she rushes to judgment, she severs communication:

GRACIELA: Virginia, what do you think Pamela is asking us to do?

VIRGINIA: I know she wants us to cover up for her. But she's my best friend and I really love her.

GRACIELA: I want you to think about this and tell me if it is something you feel I would agree with.

VIRGINIA: No, I don't think so, and that's why I am telling you. But Mom, *please* don't tell on Pamela. If you do, she won't be my friend anymore. I put my trust in you. Don't betray me.

GRACIELA: I don't want you to see this as betrayal, but lying is not accepted under any circumstances. I will leave it to you to tell Pamela that I will never agree to lying to her mother. Think about it. This is a big request that Pamela is making of us, and it is absolutely not right. We cannot always do everything that friends ask us to do if we are not in agreement with it. Besides, good friends will understand if we say no when they ask us to do things that will harm us. I would suggest that you call her now and ask her to think this over. I really appreciate that you trust and confide in me and I hope you always will.

VIRGINIA: You don't know what her mother is like with her! She screams. She never listens to her. She accuses her of doing terrible things. She's a nightmare!

GRACIELA: Virginia, there have been times when you thought I was every bit as much of a nightmare as Pamela's mother. Remember when you wanted to get your nose pierced? We talked it over and agreed you could get a clip-on hoop that wouldn't require a piercing. I know Pamela's mother. I admit she is very old-fashioned. She treats Pamela as if she weren't an independent person, and I bet her own mother treated her the same way. I hold no grudge toward Pamela; in fact, if she wants to talk to me about these issues that is quite all right.

VIRGINIA: Thanks, Mom, I think she will appreciate your help. I will talk to her about it.

Do Not Label, Do Not Judge

Many parents of adolescents complain that their adolescents do not talk with them. I never had that problem with my kids. I listened and when I did not like what I heard, I voiced my feelings, but I did not label or judge my children. Listening is the key to communication: do not label, do not judge.

For better or for worse, things are not the same as they were when you were growing up. Times have changed. There are different cultural forces in action. If you want your child to keep Latino values, then there are going to have to be changes in how you interact with your adolescent.

Do not see this as a loss of your authority. As a parent, you still have the power. Do not see this as having to do what your child says. That will hurt you and your child, and it is not what I am advocating. What I am saying is that there is a need to reflect and decide if there is room for making some adjustments.

Protecting Your Child Is a Good Thing —Within Reason

Talking about sensitive topics with your adolescent does not mean that you are exposing them to these issues or advocating them. It is painful to say this, but it would be very difficult for your child to have escaped being exposed to drugs, sex, and alcohol through media and other means, regardless of how protective you have been. And if you have overprotected your child with the best intention of sparing her from outside dangers, you need to have a frank conversation with yourself: by overprotecting her, you are not supplying her with the ammunition she will need to resist peer pressure.

Template Issues and Peace Terms

Good communication can be better achieved when you see the other person's side. I have seen many instances of miscommunication between Latino parents and adolescents as a result of the cultural contradictions expressed in the following trigger issues.

The Latino adolescent living in the United States now wants:

- not to have to inform his parents where he is every minute
- not to have so many rules and regulations to follow
- not to be treated as if she is a baby
- not to have the parents see danger in every action
- not to be lectured
- not to be loved conditionally—that is, loved only if she does what her parents wish
- not to have to do things such as dating, going out with friends, and so on exactly as his parents did when growing up
- to be trusted that he can be responsible

The Latino parent of an adolescent living in the United States now wants:

- to be informed about everything the adolescent does that parents deem important, which is pretty much everything; in fact, many Latino parents expect to be their children's confidant and best friend
- to have their rules and regulations respected and obeyed; in fact, they feel that even though their teenager is more capable of understanding the facts of life, he still needs much guidance
- to feel that their teen does not believe he is invulnerable and to see their teen exercise more common sense and be thoughtful
- to continue their bond with their child and help the child see the world as they do
- to ensure that their child values family, respects adults, and is obedient—all signs that she is becoming a responsible adult

As I was reading this list to a colleague of mine who is also the parent of an adolescent, she exclaimed: "My God, what a tall order to ask of them." Yes, it is probably not realistic to expect total adherence to all of these desires. However, with the proper dialogue you can attain very good results. I have done it with my own children and I have helped many parents do it with theirs.

Battle Zones of the Latino Parent-Child Conflict

Many traditional Latino parents experience struggle and resistance from their adolescent children primarily in the following domains specific to adolescence:

- Cognitive changes: he is now opinionated, demands explanations, and has a mind of his own
- The biological and behavioral process of becoming a sexual being
- Socialization and its discontents
- Having a different philosophy and opinion of the world from her parents'

- Differences of opinion about the degree to which Latino culture and language should be furthered
- Different views of what constitutes an appropriate degree of freedom

You can smooth these differences by taking the following steps:

- Recognize the difference between your needs and desires and your children's needs and desires.
- Learn to discern when you are following a cultural script simply because this is what is familiar to you, as opposed to trying to understand and communicate with your adolescent children.

I have helped many Latino parents of adolescents follow these two principles with very good results. They have been able to continue the process of passing on Latino values and guiding their child through the adolescent years Latino style. But the passing of these values must incorporate your child's need for a certain degree of independence or autonomy, which if not recognized can lead your child to turn away from continuing to embrace Latino values.

Classic Adolescent Protestations

The most salient protests that parents will hear on a regular basis from their adolescent are:

- Do not tell me I don't know what I want
- Let me make my own mistakes
- You smoke; why shouldn't I?
- You drink; why shouldn't I?
- I can take care of myself
- My friend is allowed to do that; why can't I?
- I can drive myself; lend me the car
- You don't trust me
- You don't really know me

- I hate that Latino stuff; I am an American
- I am old enough and I know what I am doing

Latino adolescents may also look physically different from their peers: they may have defining ethnic features such as skin color, hair color, weight, as well as other determinants. These are not always accepted by some individuals in North American society, prompting the Latino adolescent to want to shed his ethnicity or to feel confused and angry about who he is. Latino teens often require support and understanding in coming to terms with these differences. Guidance can be given through the O.R.G.U.L.L.O. *consejos.*

Embedding O.R.G.U.L.L.O.

I hope that by now you have had an opportunity to apply O.R.G.U.L.L.O. techniques not only for the resolution of problems between you and your child, but for their prevention as well. It is very likely that if parents have brought up their children to see themselves as bicultural or bilingual/bicultural individuals who are respected and loved, and if they have recognized the importance of age-appropriate independence and autonomy as suggested in O.R.G.U.L.L.O., the so-called crises of adolescence may be prevented or might not be as intense.

However, if you have not had an opportunity to apply these techniques earlier and now are faced with an adolescent who needs these *consejos,* do not despair. You can still apply them with very good results. For instance, let's take:

O.R.G.U.L.L.O. *consejo* no. 1: Organize your feelings. When you understand where you stand emotionally, this is bound to give you a very assured emotional position that will help you to be clear in making and stating your decisions.

O.R.G.U.L.L.O. *consejo* no. 2: Respect your child's feelings. If you respect your child's feelings by distinguishing them from your own, he is going to notice. He might still feel frustrated because you may not have permitted what he wants, if it is not the best thing for him in your estimation, but everyone likes to feel that their feelings are respected.

O.R.G.U.L.L.O. *consejo* no. 3: Guide and teach your child; do not dictate. If you guide and teach, rather than lecture and dictate, not only will you have better results but you will have a more cooperative child.

O.R.G.U.L.L.O. *consejo* no. 4: Update your media awareness often. By updating your media and technological information you are staying ahead of the game. You need to be informed on what drugs are lurking out there, whether the "in" drug is Ecstasy, marijuana, glue vapors, uppers, downers, herbs, or weight-loss drugs. You must also be informed about the frightening reality of situations in which girls are taken advantage of by having drugs put in their drinks. These issues need to be openly discussed with your child, not by forbidding her to go out or insisting on chaperoning her everywhere, but by making sure that she develops the best common sense possible. Trust but verify: you must be flexible enough to trust your child, but also be a verifier of what is really happening in your child's world.

O.R.G.U.L.L.O. *consejos* nos. 5, 6, and 7: Love your child for who she or he is, Listen to your child, and Open the communication channels—and keep them open. I have seen very good results when Latino parents and their adolescents work as a team. Consider the powerful message you are sending to your child when your words and actions show that your love is unconditional—that is, you love her for who she is, not withdrawing your love when she does not listen to you or does not follow your advice—and when you clearly tell her so. This affirming message is the best preventive measure in protecting her from doing self-destructive things. Once you establish the routine of listening to your child, she will know she can tell you the things that you need to know in order to guide and protect her, and that you will find time to talk. By listening carefully, you are encouraging your child to come to you with her dilemmas rather than trying to protect her by never giving her the opportunity to take risks by herself. To try to be physically present at all of your adolescent's activities can be suffocating to her and can lead to rebellion. You need to trust that you have taught your child enough to know how to survive the risks she will be facing, and let her know that she can come to you for help whenever she needs it. This is the essence of parenting with O.R.G.U.L.L.O., and it will help you and your child come out of the adolescent years with fewer emotional bumps and bruises, and with more cultural *orgullo* and success in life.

Continuing to Teach Latino Values

Adolescence—Prime Time for Teaching Cultural Orgullo

Research studies indicate that individuals do not attain an ethnic identity until adolescence or late adulthood. Given that language is central to one's identity, it can be extrapolated that for the Latino adolescent, speaking Spanish, English, or both can be a crucial issue.

While speaking the language is not a Latino cultural value per se, it is highly cherished and is pivotal to the Latino ethnic identity.

It will probably be of great comfort to know that research on the development of ethnic identity in the adolescent indicates that young adults expressed a stronger desire to embrace their parents' ethnic beliefs if they perceived ethnicity to be important to their parents and when their relationship with their parents was a good one.

Having said that, bear in mind that language takes on a different dimension in adolescence because teenagers do not want to be different from their peers. Not only will your child talk mostly in English with his peers, but he may even state that he does not want to speak Spanish. Rather than panic, argue, or give up with your teen, keep in mind that this problem is common among Latino adolescents. Here is what you can do:

- Understand, understand, understand—that adolescence is going to bring changes and that this is a time when ethnic identity is solidifying.
- Ask yourself if perhaps your adolescent is using language as a way of feeling in control. This will require that you take a careful look at what you are allowing and what you are not and see if you need

to give your teen some latitude in some appropriate areas, such as keeping up with fashion.

- Communicate, communicate, communicate. Open the communication channels and see if your adolescent feels embarrassed about your accent, for instance. Here an acknowledgment of her feelings by indicating that you understand might help, but then you can proceed to speak about your background and language with *orgullo,* with great pride. Try not to feel offended if your adolescent shuns your ethnicity. Nearly all teens say they are embarrassed by some aspects of their parents. This is only a stage and it will pass.
- Ask yourself whether you or other members of your family might be putting too much pressure on your child to speak Spanish with her siblings or friends. It is natural that at this age, children will want to speak English with their peers. Persevere in helping your adolescent to see the importance of mastering another language.
- Provide interesting, age-appropriate books in Spanish.
- Propose to your adolescent that you watch Spanish movies together.
- Observe whether anybody is making fun of how your child speaks Spanish during visits to relatives. Adolescents can be very sensitive and get embarrassed easily.

Here is what you can do if your adolescent is bilingual/bicultural but needs more reinforcement of his Spanish:

- Continue expressing your feelings about the importance of maintaining and continuing to improve his mastery of the Spanish language.
- Continue the reinforcement of the language by speaking Spanish when possible or by seeing movies and programs in Spanish, listening to music in Spanish, and so on. Reinforcing your beliefs through your own behavior is one of the best predictors that your children will follow them.
- Communicate, communicate, communicate. Open the communication channels by first respecting his choice of language study in

school if it is other than Spanish. If the choice is not Spanish, give him advice on the importance of continuing to improve his Spanish. He will hopefully see how relevant it is to do so.

Respeto: *Issuing Your Child a Passport to Adulthood*

When you are dealing with an adolescent, you must view *respeto* differently and incorporate an added dimension—respecting your child's individuality. The new *respeto* must include the changes that are part of the adolescent, including forming her own opinions, asking for explanations from you, having a mind of her own, expecting privacy, becoming a sexual being, and wanting to have friends and participate in her own world.

Your role is to issue your teen a passport to take him from childhood to adult life. You can demand all you want from him, but remember: giving him orders does not guarantee that he will comply with them. If you have already instilled in him *respeto* for himself and for others, your chances for open communication are vastly improved.

Let's look at independence via hot-button issues that perplex all parents of adolescents, but that for many Latino parents are uniquely difficult to deal with.

Familismo: *House Rules and How to Enforce Them with Love*

While your adolescent needs your appreciation of his opinions, you can accept that he sees things his way without permitting certain behaviors that you deem unacceptable as they pertain to the new *familismo.* Your youngster is now old enough to understand that his elders, including grandparents and you, the parent, have rules that must be followed. For example, by now your adolescent may have different musical tastes from yours and might want to impose them on you and the rest of the family at high decibel levels. You may angrily command, "Turn that down right now! I can't stand it!" or you can calmly state the house rules and give the reasons for them:

You: Mark, you cannot play your music so loudly in the house.

MARK: But Mom, this is my house.

You: Yes, it is your house, but you are only one of the people who live here. Your father and I and your grandparents also live here. Your grandparents are no longer young, and the noise really bothers them. Someday when you have your own house and I visit you, I will listen to the music you like. Now I must insist you be respectful of your elders.

You can be firm while also giving Mark some space, by suggesting, for instance, that he may play music when he is in his room with the door closed or if he wears headphones. However you choose to deal with the problem, do not lose your cool, do not scream, stick with your position, and give your teen some reasonable options.

Thus, through dialogue, you have put these principles into practice:

- You have furthered the cultural value of *familismo* by explaining to your son that it is very important to consider other family members' needs as well as his own.
- You have sent the message that you are considering his individuality, since you acknowledge he is free to choose the music he wants to listen to.
- You are respecting his feelings and giving him reasonable options for making his own choices. You are not demanding that he think of the family at all costs; his feelings are included and considered, as well.

Many adolescents are very loving and considerate of their grandparents and other adults; others are not. Understanding that the latter case is a phase will help you to be more patient and to continue teaching. I often hear my grown children say things that I taught them in childhood, but at the time I felt that they were not listening. I love when they say to me: "Mom, I am just like you," or "I am just like Dad," or "Dad taught me well." What this means is that children really do hear what you value. Above all, remember that they will use you as a role model. Be persistent in explaining what you value and in showing it, as well.

Family Matters from Your Child's Point of View

Your child should not be allowed to be disrespectful to his grandparents or to any adult, for that matter, but it is just as detrimental to allow grandparents or other adults to be disrespectful to your adolescent. Your protection, if needed, of your adolescent's feelings might be a new challenge for you, but see it as a necessary one. You may need to step in and take your child's side if any of the following happens:

- Scolding or rejection from Grandma when Julito does not call her to say hello
- Family members showing preference for one child over another
- Family members expecting your child to be their translator and shopping companion when your child may have other plans
- Family members expecting your child to view the world through their values
- Family members criticizing your methods of bringing up your child
- Family members drinking to excess
- Family members making fun of your child in a humiliating manner in front of friends

We have seen what a fantastic value *familismo* is, but when applied blindly in the traditional style it might create problems. The new *familismo* takes on particular importance during adolescence because the adolescent's natural drive at this age is to separate from his parents, to be less dependent, and to make his own decisions. However, he still very much needs the family's approval and support. The following are important points to keep in mind about the new *familismo*:

- Children will go where they are loved. While they need to be with their peers and want to belong, if they know the family is there for them, they will not stray away.
- Do not induce guilt by saying, "Is this the way you repay me after I

have sacrificed so much for you?" You are not developing your child's character by doing this, you are just manipulating.

- Do not expect that your adolescent will see things the way you do: he is not going to want to sacrifice in the same way as you do in many family matters.
- Do express your ideas on the importance of the family to you.
- Do remind your teen that it is important to be there for one's siblings.
- Do encourage communication between siblings. If they have disagreements, try to help by being fair; try not to take sides, but do voice how important it is to you that siblings have a good relationship, and that they share their feelings rather than act on them by fighting or not talking to each other.
- Do encourage respect toward the family elders, but let your children express their frustrations about relatives and hear their arguments.
- Understand that an adolescent might want to go to their friends' gathering rather than to their uncle's eightieth birthday party. If possible, ask him to come to a family gathering for a while and then go to be with his friends.
- Remember that it has been demonstrated in research studies that a supportive family is the best assurance of a child wanting to continue upholding Latino values.
- Be aware that studies have also indicated that when the family has problems, Latino adolescents are much more affected than if something happens to their peers or even or to themselves.

Simpatia: *Peer Pressure Doesn't Have to Be a Crisis Issue*

We established in chapter 4 that the new *simpatia* includes Latino values that we hold dear but that are adapted to the child's exposure to North American culture. *Simpatia* asks that the adolescent be mindful of others, Latino style, but it also includes being liked, being attractive, being fun, being easygoing, being flexible, having dignity, and avoiding negative behaviors.

There are times, however, when some of these attributes clash with what the adolescent is experiencing in his world. He wants to belong and will want to do what his peers are doing. Your adolescent will be dealing with peer pressures. Remember that it is during adolescence that friends become especially important to your child.

All of the O.R.G.U.L.L.O. *consejos* will be very helpful in fostering the new *simpatia,* including *consejo* no. 2, Respect your child's feelings, especially about his friends. *Consejo* no. 3, Guide and teach your child; do not dictate, will be very much needed when you do not see things as your child does. *Consejo* no. 4, Update your media awareness often, is also essential because you need to communicate with facts, not fears; otherwise your child might be respectful and hear you, but she will not listen in the sense of trusting that you are guiding her correctly. *Consejo* no. 5, Love your child for who she or he is; *consejo* no. 6, Listen to your child; and *consejo* no. 7, Open the communication channels—and keep them open, must also be very present in the new *simpatia* so that you are not critical of your child's friends.

Recognizing the importance of friends to your teen, including his wanting to be liked, to have fun, to belong, and to follow their lead at times is fundamental. You need to get to know your son or daughter's friends, become their friends, and include them in your life. If you show interest and follow O.R.G.U.L.L.O. *consejos,* you will be imparting the new *simpatia* to your child in a biculturally balanced manner.

Introducing Quality Time into the Balanced Equation

Family conversations at the dinner table need not stop, even if your teenagers are busy with sports, homework, and friends. Whenever I hear that an adolescent has stopped talking to her parents, I always explore whether the seven *consejos* of O.R.G.U.L.L.O. are being followed, and in most cases they are not.

In my household when my children were adolescents, we tried to spend as much quality time as possible with one another, so we ate together as often as we could. During dinner, we talked about one another's day. Even now, when we get together, I tell them, "Let me tell you what I did today." They tease me by saying, "What did you do,

Mom?" but when they were young, my words modeled how to open up and talk, and we always talked. My boys always told me about their friends, because I was interested in knowing. I knew about Jaime's best friends, Jeffrey, Mike, and Richard. Later on we talked about Miguel's friends, Nick, Sunil, and Katina, who along with Miguel were called the Four Musketeers. I was truly interested in my sons' friends and we all had a pleasant relationship. I knew many of their parents, too. I used to invite my sons' friends to go out with us to eat hamburgers, to plays, and to movies, and these occasions were truly enjoyed by all. They never refused an invitation, which makes me think that they felt comfortable with us as a family and enjoyed the time as much as I did.

Obediencia: *Quelling Teen Rebellion Before It Erupts*

The application of the new *obediencia* during adolescence naturally requires a utilization of the O.R.G.U.L.L.O. *consejos,* in particular *consejo* no. 1, Organize your feelings, because during this stage you may get a great deal of back talk from your child. During these challenges, it is helpful to speak with your adolescent in a firm but calm manner. When she asks, "But Mom, why can't I do that?" you might be tempted to say: "Because I say so." But getting testy is not conducive to teaching; remember that discipline and *obediencia* necessitate teaching.

You want to instill permanent values of empathy, responsibility, morality, and independence in your child. Rather than using fear and manipulation—which can lead to your child finding a way to break the rules at the first opportunity—you want your child to develop an inner voice that coaches him on what is right and what is wrong. If you are not aware of your own inner feelings, you may easily follow what you grew up with as a kid, which may take one of two extremes:

- Do as I was told and forced to do
- Do as you wish because I am not going to make you do as I was told to do

Neither extreme works well. What you want to instill in your child is *balance*.

Pick Your Battles and Lead the Way

Fifteen-year-old Caridad is walking barefoot on what her father, Manuel, considers a very cold floor, which he feels is not healthy. When Manuel orders Caridad to put on shoes, she claims she is old enough not to be told what to wear, especially at home, then adds, "But Pop, you know I never like to wear shoes in the house."

Manuel counters by insisting: "I do not want to hear any back talk from you. You have gotten too many colds this year and I'm the one who has to take you to the doctor and pay the bills. Do as I say, and don't argue. You are always arguing with me!"

It seems clear that Manuel grew up in a "Do as I say; do not question me" household. He needs to ask himself if he is following old habits and expecting Caridad to obey just as he was. In addition, it happens that Manuel is having a hard time with his boss at work and has been very unhappy. *Consejo* no. 2, Respect your child's feelings, needs to be applied here because Manuel is not thinking of Caridad's feelings. She feels that she wants to be without shoes, and this is not such a big deal. *Consejo* no. 3, Guide and teach your child; do not dictate, must be applied here fast, especially with something as innocuous as wearing shoes in the house. Manuel is concerned for Caridad and is acting out of love, but he is not showing his love in a way that Caridad can accept. He is also risking that Caridad disregard him on other discipline issues of more importance. If Manuel follows *consejo* no. 4, Update your media awareness, he will become aware that colds are not caused by walking barefoot on a wooden floor in a heated apartment.

Consejo no. 6, Listen to your child, would have helped him to ask Caridad why she likes to walk barefooted and accept it as something that she likes; she might feel freer this way. This is a choice that Caridad is old enough to make. If Manuel sees it that way, he will avoid getting into needless arguments just for the sake of control. Caridad should be seen as a unique individual with unique needs and preferences. Battling over these unimportant issues can only create animosity and power struggles between father and daughter. Pick your battles and lead the way.

When Your Angry Teen Talks Back to You

When their child talks back to them, many Latino parents often do not know what to do other than punish and scold. I am not suggesting that talking back is always acceptable, but I have seen that if you apply O.R.G.U.L.L.O. *consejo* no. 7, Open the communication channels— and keep them open, you can tell your child that this manner of talking is not acceptable and acknowledge that you want very much to talk with her when she is feeling calm.

Overly frequent punishment or the constant demand of absolute obedience are often indicative that the parent does not have any other means of reaching the child. Do not confuse teaching your adolescent to do what is appropriate in terms of being a moral, responsible, and self-disciplined person with simple submission to your wishes. Bear in mind also that you might be asking your child to do things nobody else is doing or that may be capricious or based on misinformation, as in the case of Caridad and her father, Manuel.

At the other extreme of the cultural pendulum are Latino parents who are afraid to set limits for their children. These parents fear that their children will get angry with them or will not love them. Being a good parent requires teaching a balance between extremes of behavior by maintaining a balance yourself. That balance at times will require that you risk making your child angry at you. Once you are clear that the reason why you have established the limit is a fair and reasonable one,

- Remember that in order to teach self-discipline and self-control, you must dialogue with your child, following all of the *consejos* of O.R.G.U.L.L.O.
- Involve your adolescent in problem solving and decision making.

Do not tell her how she should do everything. Ask her what her views are and listen to her views; do not interrupt and state yours.

- When a rule has been broken, remember that the idea is to teach, not just get your teen to submit to your will. Sit down with your adolescent to recap the situation and find ways of preventing it from happening again. Do not fall in the old trap of giving commands and rules with sternness and anger. Often the end result of that is irresponsibility and confrontation, rather than cooperation.

- Throughout this book I have indicated that hitting, shouting, and verbal abuse are not effective or efficient in general. I cannot stress enough not to use any of these methods during adolescence. They only lead to anger and more rebelliousness.

- Use democracy as learned in chapters 5 and 6: for example, if your daughter tells you, "Mom, you are always screaming at me," listen and consider, and then talk to her to discover what is causing your mutual frustrations.

- Discuss the consequences of an action with your adolescent so that she understands the potential outcome of what she wants to do.

- If you must punish your teen, be consistent and make the punishment appropriate to the violation. Removal of rewards is often a good deterrent, but make sure that your teen understands the wrongfulness of her transgression. State very clearly that the trust between you has been broken and discuss how to establish that trust again.

No Scolding, No Screaming

Be very attentive when your adolescent wants to talk to you about something painful to her. She may preface it by saying something like, "Don't scold me, because I've already learned my lesson." Scolding will only keep your child from confiding in you in the future. You want to hear her out and then guide her. For example, eighteen-year-old Adriana lost her temper and yelled at a teacher who treated her unjustly. Although Adriana was correct about the unfairness of the situation, screaming was not useful or respectful. What her parents said to her was, "Well, it seems you were too upset and could not be assertive, is that correct?" To which Adriana said: "Absolutely. I know better now." Then they discussed methods for staying calm: breathing more deeply, counting to ten, and so on. It was a very useful conversation in which Adriana felt supported and which also guided her in how to change her behavior. If the parents had said, "I am sure it was your fault," or "You are always screaming at everyone," more than likely the conversation would have ended in an argument.

Furthering Independence and Autonomy with Love —Latino Style

Fighting the Lurking Demons: Alcohol, Drugs, and Cigarettes

A critical element in the furthering of independence in your adolescent is how to deal with alcohol, drugs, and cigarettes. I see this falling under the aegis of the new *respeto* because it relates to teaching your child self-respect. I do not recommend keeping your child at home or not letting her go to parties or out with friends whom you know. You may chaperone school dances, but try not to be at all the dances, because that sends a message of mistrust. Take turns with the other parents. It is a bit more difficult always to be with your older teen: she might want to go to a movie, bowling, or to a friend's house. If you have been following or if you apply the O.R.G.U.L.L.O. *consejos,* you will have a head start in protecting your child from the perils of drugs and alcohol because you have been stating very clearly your position on these issues.

In addition, these tactics are recommended:

- Be a role model—do not smoke marijuana or anything else. It is unrealistic to be a smoker yourself and to expect your child not to follow your example.
- Keep communication open by meeting your child's friends and their families.
- Be very clear in stating your values by informing yourself and sharing what you have learned with your adolescent. Being well in-

formed and having accurate information helps your child to make better decisions.

- Be very clear on the importance of not driving under the influence of alcohol and offer alternatives: for example, that someone should be the designated driver. Offer yourself to drive if your adolescent thinks he feels tipsy. You are not encouraging drinking by saying these things. The reality is that although there is a legal drinking age in most states, students can use fake IDs to get alcohol. This is why it is so important to have open communication with your child so that you can talk about how to handle these and other risky situations.
- Discuss with your daughter that women can get drunk on smaller quantities of alcohol than men.
- Stay up and wait for your child when she is out at a party.
- Remember that although the home cabinet full of liquor can be very seductive, parents can be the best role models by not abusing drugs or alcohol and by offering love and empathy to their children so that they do not need to cope by altering their minds.

The Transition to Sexual Maturity

Sexuality is a part of life. Very young children masturbate and feel great pleasure by doing so. Sexuality in adolescence takes a different and more intense turn, because the adolescent is awakened by hormones, and it poses new and significant risks.

It is crucial that you apply the O.R.G.U.L.L.O. *consejos* in this area, lest your adolescent not only be misinformed but take matters into her own hands and face possible deleterious consequences. Many parents and religious philosophies strongly advocate sexual abstinence. I will not focus on that, but rather on helping you to communicate with your adolescent about her sexuality.

Because your adolescent is undergoing profound biological hormonal changes that trigger powerful and aggressive needs, you need to change your approach. When your daughter was young, it was enough to say: "Good girls do not do those things," with regard not only to premature sex but to anything your child was exposed to that was not positive. Now that your little girl is an adolescent, it is not enough to say "I forbid you" or "I do not want you to have sex."

You must be very clear about your feelings, and be very careful not to swing to the extremes of too many limits or too much permissiveness. Perhaps the most important thing here is not to hide your head in the sand, because now your adolescent needs your guidance more than ever. Many of the Latina mothers interviewed for this book told me that although they find it very difficult to talk to their daughters about sexuality, they do make a point of establishing a dialogue. They tell me that usually what they tell their daughters is that they would prefer that they have sex when they are much older and that when they do they must be wise and protect themselves.

I told both of my sons that sexuality was in some ways similar to driving a car—it was a privilege that needed to be earned. We discussed that the earning was based on maturity, self-discipline, and using their common sense.

Consejo no. 4, Update your media awareness often, is of utmost importance here because parents need to have the most accurate information available on the dangers or risks their adolescent needs to know. These include the realities of genital warts, herpes, AIDS, syphilis, gonorrhea, and of course pregnancy. But parents must also follow O.R.G.U.L.L.O. *consejo* no. 1: Organize your feelings. Being in touch with their feelings is going to help parents to share this information in a factual, not frightening, manner. Sexuality is a normal and wonderful thing that at the appropriate time is a normal aspect for many adults.

This is not an easy topic for many parents. The key is not to compromise the adolescent's sense of herself, while also articulating and maintaining your own values. Many parents say to their daughters: "I do not want you to have sex until you are mature and, ideally, married. I would prefer that you wait, but when you make your decisions, be wise and careful."

The Open Door Policy and Other Privacy Issues

Privacy issues become a source of conflict in many Latino homes, when the young man or woman wants to close the door of his or her room to have some space, particularly when friends come to visit. Here you have to trust and verify. The reality is that you cannot expect to be able to protect your adolescent as completely as you did when he was very young and you fed him, held his hand when crossing the street, dressed him according to the weather, and so on. Now it is time for your adolescent to start taking care of himself. Forbidding him to close his bedroom door may ease your anxiety, but depriving him of much-needed privacy will be resented and cast you in the role of regulator, not teacher. You need to ask yourself what it is that you fear. Is it sex? Is it smoking cigarettes or using drugs? Is it that you feel left out and need to be involved in every aspect of your child's life? Are you treating your adolescent in an age-appropriate manner?

If you feel uncomfortable with your daughter closing the door of her room when a boy is visiting, have a good talk with your daughter and find out why she wants to have the door closed. It is possible but very unlikely that she is going to have sex right there in her room, in your house, when you are present. Sometimes, adolescents like to close the door of their rooms to feel special, to put some separation between them and their parents and to have their own space—not necessarily to do anything bad. (If they want to do something bad, they will not do it at home, when the parents are present; they are smarter than that.)

If you still feel unconvinced, consider doing what many Latino parents have done: compromise. They allow the door to be closed so that the adolescent can listen to music or talk in private, but they have an agreement that the parents can come and knock once in a while; the parents trust but need to verify. If this works for you, do it, but the teaching has to be instilled in your child, not imposed. When I came to this country, I was sixteen years old, and neither my mother nor I was aware of many of the customs in this country. When I turned eighteen and wanted to start dating, which is what my peers were doing, my mother had a very difficult time with this concept because in our country there was no such thing as dating. She was smart enough to talk with me and we agreed on rules. I had to be home by a certain time. I was not to drink or smoke, and she gave me good *consejos* on the risks of sex. One of the things that was most helpful for me was that my brother, who is nearly five years older than I, said to my mother, "If you have not taught her by now what is right and wrong, it is too late." I followed this way of thinking with my sons.

When Your Style and Your Children's Collide

Assuming you really want your adolescent to develop individuality and autonomy, what should you do if he is not showing signs of self-care? O.R.G.U.L.L.O. *consejo* no. 1, Organize your feelings, is clearly important here, because understanding how you feel about your child's unkempt appearance is very helpful. For example, is appearance very important to you because you believe that the way your son looks is a reflection on you? Do you feel that the way your child dresses must be in accordance with your taste? Is he malodorous and unkempt? In this case, you should consider the possibility that he might be depressed, something we will discuss in chapter 9. If your daughter is going through a phase of demonstrating her individuality by sporting a fashionable hairstyle that looks disheveled to you, you might want to leave that issue alone. Expressing your objections might only lead to more *rebellion*. On the other hand, if her style is too provocative sexually or is in very bad taste, a serious talk and exploration are essential. Similarly, when your child refuses to dress up for a special occasion, it is important to refer to *respeto,* which in this case has to do with respect for the guests, the hosts, or the occasion.

Redefining Gender Expectations

Another typical source of friction in the home sphere is the messy room and refusal to help around the house. These are behaviors that sometimes pose conflicts within the differing cultural expectations of *marianismo* and *machismo*. *Marianismo* is a gender-specific expectation that tends to cast girls as the caretakers. They are asked to do chores that are considered feminine or the duties of women. Are you asking your daughter to do things that you are not asking your son or your husband to do? In that case you are training your daughter to be overly compliant, to be the one who should do domestic chores alone. She will be submissive to these expectations of hers or quite angry and rebellious. She will not learn that she has rights to be helped by her mate later on. Your son may conclude that he should be taken care of. You could also be fostering unhealthy dependence in your son by having women take care of him and not requiring, for example, that he clean his room. If your husband has very clear and rigid *machismo* rules that certain things are not to be done by boys, your son may refuse to clean his room because this is considered your job as a woman. If this is the case and you allow it to continue, you are not helping your son to be a good partner in the future; you are teaching him to expect to be taken care of at home by women.

In summary, offering a loving and supportive home sphere is the best insurance for having your adolescent children want to be with you and follow your values Latino style. But remember the balance: trust but verify.

In parting, I want you to leave this chapter with my complete empathy and support. I see bringing up children as similar to gestation and giving birth—it is full of work, and at times full of pain (it is for good reason that it is called having labor *pains*). But the end result is beautiful. I wish you smooth sailing as you raise your adolescent Latino style in the United States.

CHAPTER 9

When the Latino Child Needs
Professional Help

Sana, sana colita de rana, sino sanas ahora, sanaras mañana.
(Get well, get well, little frog tail, if you don't get well now,
you will get well tomorrow.)

—nursery rhyme sung to Latino children when they are feeling sick
or have hurt themselves, from *Tortillas Para Mama* by M. C. Griego,
B. L. Bucks, S. S. Gilbert, and L. H. Kimberball (1981)

When I got sick as a child, my mother and grandmothers sang this rhyme to me. When my children Jaime and Miguel were growing up, my mother and I sang this rhyme to them. I remember feeling wonderful when this rhyme was sung to me; it felt as if indeed my mother and grandmothers had the power to heal me. When as a baby my younger son, Miguel, had an earache, he would point to his ear and would ask for this rhyme and to be taken to the doctor—then everything would be fine.

How wonderful it would be if we had the power to make our children well whenever needed. Unfortunately, in many situations we don't. Perhaps this can be best understood when it comes to emotional wellness by saying that children are born with their own temperament and genetic makeup, including the vulnerability for developing psychological problems. If your child needs psychological help, you should rely on the assistance of a *culturally competent* professional.

What Does "Culturally Competent" Mean?

A culturally competent mental health practitioner is someone who is trained to understand and take into account how culture and society influence people. The term applies both to professionals who share a patient's ethnicity and understand cultural differences and to those who have acquired skills in how to understand these differences when treating people from cultures other than their own.

There is no guarantee that a Latino mental health provider will be culturally competent—just as you as a Latino cannot assume that a non-Latino provider will not be culturally competent. It is not critical that your mental health professional be Latino, but it is imperative that she or he be culturally competent and be able to communicate in your own language, if required. Nowadays, many psychologists and other mental health practitioners in general are trained in cultural competence. Therefore, it is important for you to ask potential providers about their treatment philosophy, experience, and training.

Later in this chapter, I will be explaining much more about culturally competent mental health practices, as well as how to find the most effective support for your child's needs. First, I want to explore with you how to tell if your child may need professional help and what factors specific to Latinos will play a role in your decision to seek professional assistance.

How Do I Know What Is Normal and What Is Not?

In many cases, a sudden change in a child's behavior is in reaction to a change in the routine of the child or the household. Your child might just need your guidance via the O.R.G.U.L.L.O. *consejos.* But sometimes these difficulties persist and you need to consult a professional to determine a course of action.

Below is a series of questions that will help you decide if it is time to seek professional help for your child's problems. Answer them as impartially as you can, using the following categories: Always, Frequently, Sometimes, Rarely, Never.

Each question is followed by two blank spaces. Use the first line to rate intensity and the other frequency.

Do not allow yourself to be anxious or alarmed as you answer these questions. Imagine that you are talking with a trusted professional who is completely on your side and who is trying to determine what is going on with your child.

As you write down your answers, make note also of the length of time that your child has been experiencing these problems (weeks, months, years). Naturally, age appropriateness is essential to consider here. It might not be too alarming if your six-year-old cries when you leave him at school, but if you see this behavior in the later years, it may signal a problem and should be evaluated by an experienced professional. The last three questions refer to you, but affect your child.

Any of the following questions to which you answer "frequently" or "always," and which describe situations that have persisted for months without change, indicate a need for your child to be evaluated by a mental health professional. In some cases only a very brief intervention may be needed, while other problems might require a longer period of treatment, depending on the severity of the symptoms. If the answers include "sometimes" or "rarely," don't worry, just watch your child carefully to see if the behavior is transitory. If your child exhibits many of the behaviors below, then have your child evaluated by a professional.

- Does your child have difficulties going to sleep or staying asleep? _____ _____
- Is your child refusing to go to school? _____ _____
- Is your child reversing letters when she writes? _____ _____
- Does your child prefer always to be alone and never wants to play with his siblings and peers? _____ _____
- Is your child having difficulties relating to others her age? _____ _____
- Is your child frequently distraught or irritable? _____ _____
- Does your daughter have chronic problems with eating? _____ _____

- Is your child refusing to talk? _____ _____
- Does your child cry often, or say that he feels unloved by you or disliked by his peers—although this perception is unjustified? _____ _____
- Does your child talk about hurting herself or express to you that she wishes she were dead? _____ _____
- Is your child stealing or lying? _____ _____
- Is your child enraged with you and everyone else? _____ _____
- Is your child too physically aggressive, hitting other children, being a bully, arguing constantly? _____ _____
- Does your child have poor attention or concentration or very poor memory? _____ _____
- Does your child run away and skip school? _____ _____
- Is your child drinking or using drugs? _____ _____
- Does your child seem anxious, nervous, fearful, or afraid of leaving the house? _____ _____
- Is your adolescent interested in sexuality in a precocious manner? _____ _____
- Has your child been molested by a relative or a neighbor? _____ _____
- Are you constantly at the end of your rope, screaming at your children, excessively demanding absolute obedience? _____ _____
- Are you and your partner often arguing or screaming at each other? _____ _____
- Have you and your partner engaged in physical or excessive verbal abuse with each other? _____ _____

Do Not Blame It on Laziness

I have often seen that many traditional Latino parents mistakenly label their childrens' psychological or neurological problems as laziness, or as something transient—a stage that will pass. This is because there are times when it is very difficult for a parent to differentiate between what is a stage and what is not. It is also very difficult at times to differentiate between what is a psychological problem involving the emotions and the mind and what is a neurological problem involving the brain. Although both could manifest in similar behaviors and at times intertwine with each other, they can be quite different. Most important, understand that these problems are not the child's fault or yours.

The Connection Between Latino Values and Your Child's Psychological Problems

Throughout this book we have explored how traditional Latino child-rearing practices set rules for the child to behave in a certain manner according to cultural values. We have also included the development of language skills as part of this framework and how the traditional Latino parent and child in the United States can be faced with clashes between two languages and two cultures. Let's examine how these issues come into play in evaluating children for possible psychological problems.

Language Problems: What Are the Major Issues?

Traditional Latino parents seeking professional counseling for a child may have to contend with cultural issues that can be very important to the proper understanding of their child. For example, there have been cases where the child refuses to speak in the parents' language due to rebelliousness and as a way of exerting control. A child's lack of progress in school might be due to not having yet mastered English or to brain dysfunction, such as a learning disability. A professional needs to be aware of these special language-related issues in Latino children and must understand the psychological ramifications of language for both Latino parents and children who have immigrated to the United States.

Five-year-old Martina cries when her mother, Roberta, leaves for the hospital to give birth to a new baby and does not return for three days. When her mother returns, new baby in arms, she tries to hug Martina, who shoves her away. In the months that follow, Martina begins to throw tantrums and direct destructive behavior toward her mother, such as breaking her lipsticks and pulling clothing out of her drawers. When scolded, she rocks angrily on a rocker, pouting.

One year after her brother's birth, Martina is enrolled in kindergarten. Martina wails when she is dropped off in the morning and is still sobbing when Roberta comes to pick her up in the afternoon. Martina's teacher tells them that Martina is not speaking all day in school and the parents are aware that Martina is not talking to anyone outside of the home. When this behavior shows no sign of improvement, Martina's parents decide to seek professional help for their daughter.

By consulting a psychologist, these parents were able to help not only their daughter but themselves, as well. When the psychologist traces Martina's parents' own history, motivations, and behavior, Martina's behavior becomes clearer. Both Roberta and Manuel, Martina's father, were immigrants who arrived in New York City as adolescents. Manuel was enrolled in a public school, where he describes his first days as "nerve-wracking."

He describes himself a being painfully shy and unsure, struggling in the cafeteria, during recess, and in class, unable to speak a word of English. The stress was so extreme that he developed a stomach ulcer during that first year. He also recounts how he seemed to become a different person in the United States overnight—secure and outgoing in his own country but anxious and shy here. By recollecting his own story, he is able to see some similarities between his own and his daughter's behavior.

Martina received counseling, and her parents were also counseled to help them deal with their feelings of cultural isolation. They had kept themselves and Martina isolated because they feared rejection from non-Latino parents. They felt that their English was not on par with North Americans', and they did not understand many aspects of the North American culture. Martina was not allowed to participate in sports after school, play with other children, or go on play dates with other parents and their children. Martina's parents were helped to understand that it was unhealthy for Martina not to be allowed to participate in any sports and not to be with other children. They followed our advice and started inviting other parents and their children to their house for play dates, even if the families were non-Latino. They also began visiting these families with Martina.

Martina's parents were able to establish a trusting relationship with a therapist in their primary tongue and were helped to bridge cultures for the benefit of the entire family.

The Importance of Being Understood

I have seen Latino families in turmoil because their children refuse to speak Spanish. A professional who does not understand the ramifications of this situation might not be able to help you or your child sort out whether this stalemate is a temporary, age-appropriate phase—possibly due to your child's wanting to be like his peers—or whether it may indicate a more serious ethnic identity crisis.

There have been many times when a Spanish-speaking child in the process of learning English has been mistakenly termed learning disabled. A culturally competent professional will understand that there are common misdiagnoses in children due to cultural misunderstanding. Many Latino children have problems making the adjustment to school but function quite well at home and in their community. Helping professionals need to be aware of these unique issues in Latino families.

Different Ways to View Falta de Respeto

Falta de respeto can be a very serious matter in the traditional Latino culture. A child can be angry or sassy for many different reasons, including as the result of depression, anxiety, post-traumatic stress disorder (PTSD), learning problems, attention deficit hyperactivity disorder (ADHD), and other learning and emotional or psychological problems. How can parents tell when their child needs help?

Let me define the two common problems that bring parents to seek health care for their children and that are often seen as *falta de respeto*, or disrespect.

Learning Disabilities: A learning disability is a difficulty or a weakness in learning due to neurological or other problems in the brain. It can interfere with the proper learning of language, math, reading, or writing. A learning disability can also manifest in behavioral problems, disorganization, clumsiness, or poor memory.

Many people have weaknesses in some area of learning, but ultimately can read and write and learn if they focus on the task. But children with learning disabilities need special techniques in order to absorb and retain material learned in school. This help must be provided by both parents and teachers.

Not all learning difficulties stem from learning disabilities. Depression and other emotional or neurological problems can cause difficulty in school. A qualified mental health professional can help to determine what these problems are.

Attention Deficit/Hyperactivity Disorder (ADHD) is a neurological-based disorder believed to be a result of a neurochemical deficiency in certain specific areas of the brain. Approximately 3 to 5 percent of children in the United States suffer from ADHD. There are no statistics that refer specifically to Latino children with ADHD, but we know that the immigration experience coupled with what are called risk factors, such as psychological stressors and economic difficulties, can make ADHD more difficult to diagnose in Latino children. Cultural factors such as an expectation of absolute *respeto* and *obediencia* can make the management of ADHD more difficult for traditional Latino families, since the expectation of *obediencia* and *respeto* often cannot be met by children with these problems.

What Issues Within Familismo *Require Attention?*

In the traditional Latino family, anticipating what the child may want is seen as a way of giving love. Professionals counseling Latino families need a different understanding of the meaning of dependency lest they mistakenly confuse lack of opportunity to do certain tasks with a dependency or inability of a child to do things for himself.

Anticipating every need a child may have, within reason, may not be unhealthy and should be seen as one cultural view of rearing children. The traditional Latino family makes the child the center of their world. The only problem may be that the Latino child growing up in the United States may be faced with two contradictory sets of expectations—one at home and one in his larger world. The child's outside world needs to be taken into consideration; hence the importance of allowing age-appropriate independence.

Anger, too, needs to be understood in terms of *familismo*. Excessive anger in your child could at times be the result of stringent demands from family members, who may have very high expectations that are not age appropriate. Anger can be a sign of something else, as, for example, in those instances when a child loses a relative or witnesses violence or unpleasant acts. In such cases anger could be part of a reaction called post-traumatic stress disorder (PTSD). A child with PTSD may also be anxious, depressed, fearful, have night terrors, weepiness, and so on. Depression can manifest in excessive dependence on or withdrawal from other people important to the child, such as Grandma, Grandpa, an uncle, an aunt, the babysitter, a friend, or others.

In these situations, parents should use O.R.G.U.L.L.O. *consejos* to try to find out what is going on with their child. If the problem does not ease, consult a professional.

What Problems Within Simpatia Require Attention?

It is very important to understand that lack of *simpatia*, social withdrawal, or rudeness might be a symptom of a child's emotional difficulties. The ability to make and keep friends is an essential skill for all children. If a child is not socially adept or what we call *simpatico*, she is not going to be able to fit appropriately into her peers' society. If a child does not possess the appropriate skills to be part of a team, be a good sport, obey rules, play fair, help others, and so on, a professional should be consulted to help you to teach these skills to your child.

Shyness may be one of those behaviors that traditional Latino parents bring to therapy only when it is accompanied by other, more unpleasant things such as being disobedient or having bad grades. Although shyness may be outgrown, going through years of shyness without support can make your child feel very isolated, which can lead to other, more complicated problems. A professional can help parents guide the child through excessive shyness. Parents or well-intentioned relatives could put pressure on the child to socialize or to be *simpaticos*. These pressures only make the shy child feel worse.

You must help a child who is excessively shy by guiding her to outgrow her shyness, not by putting pressure on her. Excessive shyness should be remedied, because sometimes shyness is self-perpetuating and stays with the child throughout life, limiting many opportunities and achievements. Shyness is not your child's fault. It is a form of anxiety, a fear of social experiences that are new or unknown to the child. Studies indicate that children in the seventh and eighth grades seem to suffer from shyness the most, but shyness may be present from the very beginning of your child's life. You need not be alone in helping your child. There are many useful techniques for helping a child overcome shyness or social anxiety.

Dependence/Independence and Autonomy

As the child grows and peers become important, he will want to do things with them. Parents should understand that children should be given age-appropriate opportunities to be independent, even though it may entail certain risks.

It is much better if you offer your guidance but allow your child to handle problems with friends on her own. If these problems magnify, then professional help is needed.

When Is Desobediencia a Matter of Concern?

When your child is unable to follow certain requirements needed to help him to be part of the society he lives in, including at home, at school, and in the larger community, then there could be a problem. Learning problems may result in disobedience in cases where the child lacks the capacity to understand or remember what is expected of him or gets distracted too easily due to neurological problems.

I counseled a girl whose mother had grounded her for a year because she was not doing well in school, assuming she was being disobedient and lazy rather than finding out whether her daughter might have had learning problems. This girl had learning problems and was unable to comply with the demands of school, but her mother was expecting absolute *obediencia,* as it had been expected of her when she was growing up in her country of origin.

Another mother was having a great deal of problems with her son because she felt he was being disrespectful. The child was being taught in school to be assertive and speak his mind, but when he tried to do that at home, he was considered to be disobedient, labeled a bad boy, and told "Do as I say and don't argue." These mixed messages from his two worlds were very confusing for this child and needed to be tempered using the *consejos* of O.R.G.U.L.L.O.

Disobedience could also be the result of personality disorders, emotional problems such as depression or anxiety, or more serious mental problems that a professional can help you to understand. Neurological issues may coexist with depression, learning disabilities, attention deficit disorder, and other serious problems. When your child's anger escalates in spite of your trying every appropriate method, including following the *consejos* of O.R.G.U.L.L.O., a professional can help you find effective ways to deal with these problems. A professional will help you to set appropriate limits with a disobedient child that will work. You will be able to tell if you are asking too much of your child or are not applying the right techniques specific to your child's problem, even though you may have the best of intentions.

Do Not Do It Alone:
How to Choose the Best Professional Support

I want to emphasize that needing a mental health professional should not be seen as a failure on your part; you should view it in the same way as you would if your child needed to see an ophthalmologist, cardiologist, dermatologist, allergist, or other specialists. Problems in mental health, just as in physical health, require someone who is competent to treat them. In the case of Latino children, a culturally competent provider is ideal because language and cultural specifics can be very important in the assessment and treatment of your child. I have seen many traditional Latino parents attempt to treat their children without help when they are in need of a mental health professional, and they end up creating a lot of unnecessary grief for both the child and themselves. A competent professional will neither harm your child nor provide services that are not needed. Also remember that ethnicity per se does not define competency. A non-Latino professional is absolutely fine if this person is able to understand culture specifics, such as:

- If a Latino man calls his mother daily, he is not to be seen automatically as a "mama's boy."
- Latino parents who oppose the idea that their twelve-year-old be allowed to be dismissed from school without their being there to meet her need not be seen as overprotective.
- A Latina mother who insists on picking up her fifteen-year-old if he is out after ten o'clock, rather than allowing him to take the bus at night, might not be harming her child but being a good Latina mother. (These are only some examples.)

A culturally competent professional who understands how traditional Latino parents may choose to bring up their child Latino style should be able to:

- tell which behaviors are normal and functional in the Latino culture and which are not;
- understand the cultural origins of your parenting skills and not automatically see you as overinvolved or too intrusive;
- act as a cultural broker who will help you and your child maintain a balanced cultural position.

The Cultural Issues That Must Be Understood

Because the Latino population in the United States is very complex and diverse, a culturally competent professional also will be conversant with the following issues as they pertain specifically to the parent-child relationship:

- Awareness of the diversity and similarities among the subgroups that define the Latino culture in the United States.

- Respect for Latino cultural values and awareness of the essential concepts that define Latino culture, such as the ones we have discussed in this book.
- Respect for cultural and language differences and for the level of acculturation and English proficiency of the child and the family.
- Respect for family loyalty, or *familismo.*
- Respect for Latino reciprocity, in which children feel they must help their parents, who have sacrificed for them, and that they must therefore respect them at all costs.
- Understanding of how to provide the family with skills for maintaining a balance between the two cultures.
- Understanding of what problems might be due to the acculturation process or acculturation stress.
- Ability to provide a culturally sensitive diagnosis and treatment—but sensitivity is not the only issue to consider here; you also need someone who is trained to apply this cultural knowledge when conducting psychological examinations of your child.
- Understanding of beliefs that Latinos may have about mental illness, such as the belief in *brujeria* (witchcraft), and which beliefs are normal within the culture versus which are not.
- Familiarity with Latino relational behaviors; that is, misinterpreting or negatively labeling what might just be a different way of seeing the world.
- Conversance with the role of religion in Latino life and ability to view spirituality not necessarily as passivity but as a strength.
- Knowledge and understanding of the impact of immigration on the family and child, including issues such as poverty or being at a social status lower than they may have been in their country of origin.

If you suspect that your child is in need of professional help, you need to find a culturally competent professional who has training and experience in treating the type of problems your child is facing. Sometimes, a professional may refer you and your child to other specialists trained to conduct neuropsychological or pediatric neurological examination to determine whether your child has learning, behavioral, or neurological problems, or needs to be prescribed medication.

Many parents become very upset at the idea of giving medication to their child for psychological problems. It is beyond the scope of this chapter to talk about specific approaches, but suffice it to say that in many instances the improved quality of life of a child who needs medication and receives it, makes it worth trying. Please refer to the Recommended Resources section on this topic.

Putting Your Fears to Rest

Most traditional Latino parents don't hesitate to take their child to the pediatrician when necessary, but when it comes to seeking psychological counsel, everyone is an expert and wants to resolve things on their own. Many of these parents feel that raising children mostly requires common sense. It does, but there are problems that need more than that.

Traditional Latino parents often fear they will be blamed and seen as the cause of their children's problems. While there were theories in the past that blamed parents for being overinvolved and for causing some of their children's mental problems, these days no competent and responsible professional thinks this way. Taking your child to be evaluated by a culturally competent professional, when needed, should not be seen as something shameful but as an act of protection and caring for your child. Granted, it can be painful for parents when their child has a problem, but when this help is required, a competent mental health professional is your ally, not your enemy. Once you find someone who will view and understand a child's problems in a bilingual/bicultural context, this professional is not only an ally but similar to a *comadre* or *compadre*—someone who is there for you and your child.

The Competent Therapist as Culture Broker

A culturally competent provider is similar to a culture broker: someone with whom you and your child resolve specific psychological problems. This professional can also help you and your child learn to function within the two cultures or in your language, if needed; it is someone who understands and doesn't judge you because you relate differently to your family members than North Americans do to theirs. Otherwise, the real nature of whatever is going on with your child might be lost in a sea of confusion. Since your child is socializing within the North American culture, what you need is a balanced adaptation for you and your child within two cultures.

How to Go About Selecting a Culturally Competent Professional

The best way to find a culturally competent mental health professional is by word of mouth. Ask friends, your child's pediatrician, or other professionals you are in contact with to refer you to someone who fits your needs and who has experience working with Latino parents and their children. You can also contact your insurance company or local professional associations, which could be found on the Internet or in the telephone directory. By now you should have an idea of the most important points to keep in mind when speaking with the person you are considering for evaluation of your child.

You should copy the points listed in this chapter and discuss them with the provider over the telephone when you make your initial call or when you visit for the first time. A culturally competent provider will understand the importance of answering these questions and will gladly do so. If the provider refuses to answer these questions or says that they are not important, then you know that this is not the person you want to help you and your child.

Once you have found a culturally competent professional to help you and your child, then trust this person and remind yourself constantly that when your child needs help, it is not your fault. Remember that certain things are not in your control, as when your child needs glasses because her eyesight is poor. When your child needs help, find a professional ally and tell yourself the following affirmation: "I am the best parent I can be."

Hasta Luego (So Long)

This is the end of the chapter and the end of the book. I hope that the O.R.G.U.L.L.O. *consejos* I have given you will be taken in the spirit in which I intended—to be followed with *orgullo*: pride in our traditions, pride in our values, pride in who we are. The O.R.G.U.L.L.O. *consejos* are the product of my many years of experience both as a mother and as a culturally competent professional. I went through many of the experiences that I shared with you. These *consejos* have worked for me and for families I have worked with. They will work for you, as well.

Remember always that your Latino parenting values are worthy of the highest respect, and they are worth adjusting so that they can survive and enrich your child's life within North American culture. You can do it! Raise your wonderful child Latino style—but with the capacity to thrive in North America. *¡Hasta luego y buena suerte!* So long and good luck! I leave you to parent with pride.

References

The following list incorporates sources that I have consulted or that have guided me in the writing of this book. These are only a portion of the available references on these topics. My inclusion of these readings does not mean to exclude others that could be just as useful. It rather means that the listed resource was analyzed as part of my research for this book.

Chapter 1:
Parenting with Pride—Latino Style: The New O.R.G.U.L.L.O.

Aboud, F. "Ethnic Self-Identity." In *A Canadian Social Psychology of Ethnic Relations,* edited by R. C. Gardner and R. Kalin, 37–56. Toronto: Methuen, 1981.

Akhtar, S. *Immigration and Identity Turmoil, Treatment and Transformation.* Northvale, N.J.: Jason Aronson, 1999.

Badillo, S. B. *Understanding Puerto Rican Traditions,* 98–102. National Association of Social Workers, 1982.

Berry, J. W. "Acculturative Stress." In *Readings in Ethnic Psychology,* edited by P. B. Organista, Kevin M. Chun, and G. Marin, 117–22. New York: Routledge, 1998.

Berry, J. W., and R. C. Annis. "Acculturation Stress: The Role of Ecology, Culture and Differentiation." *Journal of Cross-Cultural Psychology* 5 (1974): 382–406.

Bhagat, R. S., and S. J. McQuaid. "Role of Subjective Culture in Organizations: A Review and Directions for Future Research." *Journal of Applied Psychology* 67(1982): 653–85.

Bronfenbrenner, U. *Two Worlds of Childhood.* New York: Russell Sage Foundation, 1979.

Capsi, A. "Continuities and Consequence of Interactional Styles Across the Life Course." *Journal of Personality* 57 (1989): 375–406.

Conyers, J. T. Kappel, and J. Rooney. "How Technology Can Transform a School." *Educational Leadership* 56 (1999):82–85.

Diaz-Guerrero, R. "Transference of Psychological Knowledge and Its Impact on Mexico." *International Journal of Psychology* 19(1984):123–34.

Dicochea, P., and J. Mata. "Hispanic: What's in the Name?" Hispanic Graduate Student Association of Arizona State University newsletter, October–November 1997.

Gil, R. M., and C. I. Vazquez. *The Maria Paradox: How Latinas Can Merge Old World Traditions with New World Self-Esteem.* New York: Perigee, 1996.

Gopnik, A., A. Meltzoff, and P. K. Kuhl. *The Scientist in the Crib: What Early Learning Tells Us About the Mind.* New York: Perennial, 1999.

Henriquez, U. P. *Historia de la cultura en la America Hispanica* [History of the Culture in Hispanic America]. Buenos Aires: Coleccion Popular, 1964.

Hubert, J. M., and J. G. Kempen. "Moving Cultures: The Perilous Problems of Cultural Dichotomies in a Globalizing Society." *American Psychologist* 53, no. 10 (1998):1111–20.

LaFrambroise, T., L. K. Coleman, and J. Gerton. "Psychological Impact of Biculturalism: Evidence and Theory." In *Readings in Ethnic Psychology,* edited by P. B. Organista, Kevin M. Chun, and G. Marin. 123–55. New York: Routledge, 1998.

Novas, H. *Everything You Need to Know About Latino History.* New York: Penguin, 1991.

Oetting, E. R., R. C. Swaim, and M. C. Chiarella. "Factor Structure and Invariance of the Orthogonal Cultural Identification Scale Among American Indian and Mexican American Youth." *Hispanic Journal of Behavioral Sciences* 20, no. 2 (1998):131–54.

Padilla, A., ed. *Hispanic Psychology: Critical Issues in Theory and Research.* Thousand Oaks, Calif.: Sage, 1995.

Phinney, J. S. "When We Talk About American Ethnic Groups, What Do We Mean?" *American Psychologist* 51, no. 9 (1996):918–27.

Phinney, J. S. "Ethnic Identity in Adolescents and Adults—Review of Research." In *Readings in Ethnic Psychology,* edited by P. B. Organista, Kevin M. Chun, and G. Marin, 73–99. New York: Routledge, 1998.

Rodriguez, D. E. *Historia de Santo Domingo.* 3ra. edicion, nuevamente corregida y reformada por el autor con el consentimiento de don Emilio Rodriguez Demorizi. History of Sto. Domingo. 3rd edition, Newly Revised and Reformed by permission of don Emilio Rodriguez Demorizi, Sto. Domingo, Dominican Republic, 1969.

Rutter, M. "Pathways from Childhood to Adult Life." *Journal of Psychology and Psychiatry* 30 (1989):23–51.

Sabelli, H. C. "Becoming Hispanic, Becoming American: Latin American Immigrants' Journey to National Identity." In *Immigrant Experiences: Personal Narrative and Psychological Analysis,* edited by P. H. Elovitz and C. Kahn, 158–79. Cranfry, N.J.: Associated University Presses, 1997.

Sami, N. *La inmigracion explicada a mi hija* [Immigration Explained to My Daughter]. DeBolsillo, 2001.

Shorris, E. *Latinos, A Biography of the People.* New York: Avon Books, 1992.

Sodowsky, G. R., and others. "World Views of White, American, Mainland Chinese, Taiwanese, and African Students. An Investigation into Between-Group Differences." *Journal of Cross-Cultural Psychology* 25, no. 3 (1994): 309–24.

Storti, C. *The Art of Crossing Cultures.* Yarmouth, Maine. Intercultural Press, 1989.

Suarez, S. A., B. J. Fowers, and C. S. Greenwood. "Biculturalism, Differentness, Loneliness, and Alienation in Hispanic College Students." *Hispanic Journal of Behavioral Sciences* 19, no. 4 (1997): 489–505.

Schwartz, S. H., and L. Sagiv. "Identifying Culture-Specifics in the Content and Structure of Values." *Journal of Cross-Cultural Psychology* 26, no. 1 (1995): 92–116.

Triandis, H. C. "The Self and Social Behavior in Differing Cultural Contexts." *Psychological Review* 96 (1989):506–20.

Chapter 2:
Raising Children Is a Two-Way Street: The New **Respeto**

Briggs, D. *Your Child's Self-Esteem: The Key to His Life.* New York: Doubleday, 1970.

Diaz, R. *Respeto y dignidad: Dos temas centrales en la cultura Puertorriqueña* [Respect and Dignity: Two Central Themes in the Puerto Rican Culture]. Unpublished mimeograph.

Falicov, C. J. "Mexican Families." In *Ethnicity & Family Therapy,* edited by M. McGoldrick, J. K. Pearce, and J. Giordano, 134–163. New York: Guilford Press, 1982.

Flores, G., and others. "The Health of Latino Children: Urgent Priorities, Unanswered Questions, and a Research Agenda." *JAMA* 288(2002): 82–90.

Garcia, J. G., and M. C. Zea, eds. *Psychological Interventions and Research with Latino Populations.* Boston: Allyn and Bacon, 1997.

Lauria, A. "Respeto, Relajo and Interpersonal Relations in Puerto Rico." *Anthropological Quarterly* 37 no. 2(1964): 53–67.

M. McGoldrick, J. K. Pearce, and J. Giordano, eds. *Ethnicity and Family Therapy.* New York: Guilford Press, 1982.

Treviño, M. "Rising Numbers of Latina Teens Trying Suicide." *WE News,* 2002. www.womensenews.org. Webster's Ninth New Collegiate Dictionary.

Chapter 3:
Keeping the Peace: The New Familismo

Ainsworth, M. "Some Consideration Regarding Theory and Assessment Relevant to Attachments Beyond Infancy." In *Attachment in the Preschool Years,* edited by M. T. Greenberg, D. Cicchetti, and E. M. Cummings, 463–88. Chicago: Chicago Press, 1990.

Bernal, G. "Cuban Families." In *Ethnicity and Family Therapy,* edited by M. McGoldrick, J. K. Pearce, and J. Giordano, 187–207. New York: Guilford Press, 1982.

Cortes, D. E. "Variations in Familism in Two Generations of Puerto Ricans." *Hispanic Journal of Behavioral Sciences* 17, no. 2 (1995): 249–55.

Downey, G., and J. C. Coyne. "Children of Depressed Parents: An Integrative Review." *Psychological Bulletin* 108 (1990): 50–70.

Hamon, R., and R. Blieszner R. "Filial Responsibility Expectations Among Adult Child–Older Parent Pairs." *Journal of Gerontology* 45(1990): 110–12.

Holmes, J. *Attachment, Intimacy, Autonomy: Using Attachment Theory in Adult Psychotherapy.* Northvale, N.J.: Jason Aronson, 1996.

Kaelber, C.T., D. E. Moul, and M. E. Farmer. "Epidemiology of Depression." In *Handbook of Depression,* 2nd edition, edited by E. E. Beckham, and W. R. Leber, 3–35. New York: Guilford Press, 1995.

Kaplan, L. *Onenes and Separateness: From Infant to Individual.* New York: Simon and Schuster, 1978.

Kaslow, F. *Handbook of Relational Diagnosis and Dysfunctional Family Patterns.* New York: John Wiley and Sons, 1996.

La Roche, M., C. Turner, and M. S. Kalick. 1995. "Latina Mothers and Their Toddlers' Behavioral Difficulties." *Hispanic Journal of Behavioral Sciences* 17, no. 3(1995): 375–84.

Marin, G. "Influence of Acculturation on Familism and Self-Identification among Hispanics." In *Ethnic Identity Formation among Minorities,* edited by M. E. Bernal and G. P. Knights, 181–96. New York: New York State University of New York Press, 1993.

Menese, R., L. Feldman, and G. Chacon. "Estres, apoyo social y salud de la mujer con roles multiples." *Revista interamericana de psicologia / Interamerican Journal of Psychology* 199 33, no. 1(1999): 109–32.

"Mental Health of Women in Childbearing Years: A Hidden Problem?" *MHR News* (spring/summer 2002).

Minuchin, S., B. L. Rosman, and L. Baker. *Psychosomatic Families: Anorexia Nervosa in Context.* Cambridge, Mass.: Harvard University Press, 1978, 51–73.

Olmos, E. J., L. Ybarra, and M. Monterrey, eds. *Americanos: Latino Life in the United States / La Vida Latina En Los Estados Unidos.* New York: Little Brown, 1999.

Padilla, Y. C., and J. E. Glick. "Variations in the Economic Integration of Immigrant and U.S.-Born Mexicans." *Hispanic Journal of Behavioral Sciences* 22, no. 2 (2000).

Rodriguez, J. M., and K. Kosloski. "The Impact of Acculturation on Attitudinal Familism in a Community of Puerto Rican Americans." *Hispanic Journal of Behavioral Sciences* 20, no. 3 (1998) 375–390.

Rogler, L. H., and R. S. Cooney. "Puerto Rican Families in New York City: Intergenerational Processes" (monograph 11). Bronx, N.Y.: Hispanic Research Center, Fordham University, 1985.

Szapocznik, J., and W. M. Kurtines. "Family Psychology and Cultural Diversity: Opportunities for Theory, Research and Application" (invited article). *American Psychologist* 48, no. 4(1993):400–407.

Szapocznik, J., and others. "The Evolution of Structural Ecosystemic Theory for Working with Latino Families." In *Psychological Interventions and Research with Latino Populations,* edited by J. G. Garcia and M. C. Cea, 166–90. Boston: Allyn and Bacon, 1997.

Van Horn, K. R., and J. C. Marquees. *Social Skills and Social Support Relationships in Brazilian Adolescents.* Paper presented at the XXV Interamerican Congress of Psychology, San Juan, Puerto Rico, July 1995.

Van Horn, K. R., and others. "Cultural Attitudes and Everyday Activities in Brazilian and U.S. College Students." *Revista interamericana de psicologia Interamerican Journal of Psychology* 33, no. 1 (1999):173–90.

"Weighting the Grandma Factor," Science Times, *New York Times,* 5 November 2002.

Wheeler. T. C., ed. *The Immigrant Experience: The Anguish of Becoming American.* New York: Penguin Books, 1971.

Zayas, L. H., and J. Palleja. "Puerto Rican Familism: Considerations for Family Therapy." *Family Interventions. Family Relations* 37(1988):260–64.

Chapter 4:
How to Foster Simpatia *Within the* Nuevo Tradicionalismo

Berry, J. D., and others, eds. "Cultural Transmission and Development." In *Cross Cultural Psychology: Research and Implications,* 17–41. Cambridge, England: Cambridge University Press, 1992.

Comas-Diaz, L. "Mental Health Needs of Latinos with Professional Status." In *Psychological Interventions and Research with Latino Populations,* edited by J. G. Garcia and M. C. Zea, 142–65. Boston: Allyn and Bacon, 1997.

Gopnik, A., A. Meltzoff, and P. K. Kuhl. *The Scientist in the Crib: What Early Learning Tells Us About the Mind.* New York: Perennial, 1999.

Hakuta, K. *Mirror of Language: The Debate on Bilingualism.* New York: Basic Books, 1985.

Hakuta, K., and E. Garcia. "Bilingualism and Education." *American Psychologist* 44, no. 2(1989):374–79.

Ladrine, H. "Clinical Implications of Cultural Differences: The Referential Versus the Idexical Self." *Clinical Psychology Review* 12 (1992):401–15.

Marin, G., and B. V. Marin. *Research with Hispanic Populations.* Newburry Park, Calif.: Sage Publications, 1991.

Markus, H. R., and S. Kitayama. "The Cultural Construction of Self and Emotion: Implications for Social Behavior." In *Emotion and Culture Empirical Studies of Mutual Influence,* edited by S. Kitayama and R. Markus, 89–130. Washington D.C., American Psychological Association, 1994.

Rosenberg, M. *Conceiving the Self.* New York: Basic Books, 1979.

Rotheram, M. J., and J. S. Phinney. "Introduction: Definitions and Perspectives in the Study of Childrens' Ethnic Socialization." In *Children's Ethnic Socialization: Pluralism and Development,* edited by J. S. Phinney and M. J. Rotheran, 10–28. Newbury Park, Calif.: Sage Publications, 1986.

Saarni, C. *The Development of Emotional Competence.* New York: Guilford Press, 1999.

Triandis, H. C. "The Self and Social Behavior in Differing Cultural Contexts." *Psychological Review* 96(1989):506–20.

———. "*Simpatia* as a Cultural Script of Hispanic." *Journal of Personality and Social Psychology* 47(1984):1365–75.

Triandis, H. C., and others. "Allocentric versus Idiocentric Tendencies: Convergent and Discriminant Validation." *Journal of Research in Personality* 19 (1985):395–415.

Valsiner, J., and P. Hill. "Socialization of American Toddlers for Social Courtesy." In *Child Development in Cultural Context,* edited by J. Valsiner, 163–79.
Toronto: Hogrefe, 1989.

Zimbardo, P., and S. L. Radl. *The Shy Child: A Parent's Guide for Overcoming and
Preventing Shyness from Infancy to Adulthood.* New York: Doubleday, 1982.

Chapter 5:
Setting New Limits: Obediencia *Within* Nuevo Tradicionalismo

Aetna Life and Casualty Company. *Resolving Conflicts Through Mediation.* Hart-
ford, Conn.: 1982.

Albert, L. *Cooperative Discipline.* Circle Pines, Minn.: American Guidance Service, 1989.

Bluestein, J. *Twenty-First-Century Discipline.* Albuquerque, N.M.: Instructional
Support Services, 1998.

Bochner, S. "Cross-Cultural Differences in the Self-Concept: A Test of Hof-
stede's Individualism/Collectivism Distinction." *Journal of Cross-Cultural
Psychology* 25, no. 2 (June 1994):273–83.

Chamberlain, P., and G. R. Patterson. "Discipline and Child Compliance in
Parenting." In *Handbook of Parenting,* vol. 1, edited by M. H. Bornsein,
205–25. Mahwah, N.J.: Erlbaum, 1995.

Conti, A. "¿Que hago con estos salvajes? Manual de ayuda para padres desesper-
ados: como poner limites a los hijos." (What Should I Do with These Sav-
ages? Help Manual for Desperate Parents: How to Set Limits with Their
Children) Buenos Aires, Argentina: Perfil Libro, 2001.

Diaz-Guerrero, R. "Evolucion de la obediencia afiliativa." *Revista Latinoameri-
cana de psicologia* 32, no. 3 (2000):467–83.

Gordon, K. A. *The High School Assessment of Academic Self-Concept.* Stanford,
Calif.: Stanford University, School of Education, 1991.

———. "Resilient Hispanic Youths, Self-Concept and Motivational Patterns."
Hispanic Journal of Behavioral Sciences 18. no. 1 (1996):63–73.

Hoffman, M. L. "Parent Discipline and the Child's Consideration for Others."
Child Development 34 (1963):573–88.

Hyman, I. A. *The Case Against Spanking: How to Discipline Your Child Without Hitting.* San Francisco: Jossey-Bass, 1997.

Koenig, L. J. *Smart Discipline: Fast, Lasting Solutions for Your Peace of Mind and Your
Child's Self-Esteem.* New York: HarperResource, 2002.

Marsh, H. W., and I. M. Holmes. "Multi-Dimensional Self-Concept: Its Hierarchical Structure and Its Relation to Academic Achievement." *Journal of Educational Psychology* 80 (1990):366–80.

Staub, E. "Cultural-Societal Roots of Violence." *American Psychologist* 51, no. 2 (1996):117–32.

Chapter 6:
The World of the Preschooler: Instilling O.R.G.U.L.L.O.
from Day One

Anderson, S., and S. Messick. 1974. "Social Competency in Young Children," *Journal of Developmental Psychology* 10 (1974):282–93.

Archer, J. *The Behavioral Biology of Aggression.* Cambridge: Harvard University Press, 1988.

Azrin, N. H., and R. M. Foxx. "A Rapid Method of Toilet Training the Institutionalized Retarded." *Journal of Applied Behavior Analysis* 4 (1971):89–99.

Bayley, N. *Bayley Scales of Infant Development.* New York: Psychological Corporation, 1969.

Belsky, J. "Infant Day Care: A Cause for Concern." *Zero to Three,* 6 September 1986, 1–7.

Bemporad, J. R., ed. *Child Development in Normality and Psychopathology.* New York: Brunner/Mazel, 1980.

Borba, M. *Parents Do Make a Difference: How to Raise Kids with Solid Character, Strong Minds, and Caring Hearts.* San Francisco: Jossey-Bass, 1999.

Bryson, B. *The Mother Tongue: English and How It Got That Way.* New York: Morrow, 1990.

Buriel, R., and M. Hurtado-Ortiz. "Child Care Practices and Preferences of Native- and Foreign-Born Latina Mothers and Euro-American Mothers." *Hispanic Journal of Behavioral Sciences* 22, no. 3 (2000):314–31.

Buxbaum, E. "The Role of a Second Language in the Formation of Ego and Superego." *Psychoanalytic Quarterly* 18 (1949):279–289.

Cancelmo, J. A., and C. Bandini. *Child Care for Love or Money? A Guide to Navigating the Parent-Caregiver Relationship.* Northvale, N.J.: Jason Aronson, 1999.

Casement, P. J. "Samuel Beckett's Relationship to His Mother Tongue." *International Review of Psycho-Analysis* 9 (1982):35–44.

Fishman, J. A. *Language and Ethnicity in Minority Sociolinguistic Perspective.* Clevedon, England: Multilingual Matters, 1988.

Fox, R. C., and N. H. Azrin. "Toilet Training" In *Helping Parents Solve Their Children's Behavior Problems,* edited by C. E. Schaefer, and A. R. Eisen, Northvale, N.J.: Jason Aronson, 1998.

Frija, N. H. *The Emotions,* Cambridge, England: Cambridge University Press, 1996.

Gopaul-McNicol, S., and T. T. Presswood, eds. *Working with Linguistically and Culturally Different Children: Innovative and Educational Approaches.* Boston: Allyn and Bacon, 1998.

Greenson, R. R. "The Mother Tongue and the Mother." *International Journal of Psychoanalysis* 31 (1950):18–23.

Grosjean, F. *Life with Two Languages: An Introduction to Bilingualism.* Cambridge, Mass.: Harvard University Press, 1982.

Hakuta, K. *Mirror of Language.The Debate on Bilingualism.* New York: Basic Books, 1985.

Hakuta, K., and E. Garcia. "Bilingualism and Education" *American Psychologist* 44, no. 2 (1989):374–79.

La Roche, M. J.,T. Castellano, and M. S. Kalik. "Latina Mothers and Their Toddlers' Behavioral Difficulties." *Hispanic Journal of Behavioral Sciences* 17, no. 3 (1995):375–84.

Miller,W. I. *Humiliation.* Ithaca, N.Y.: Cornell University Press, 1983.

Piontelli, A. "Infant Observation from Before Birth." *International Journal of Psycho-Analysis* 68 (1987):453–63.

Powell, D. R. *Strengthening Parental Contributions to School Readiness and Early School Learning.* Prepared for the U.S. Department of Education, Office of Educational Research and Improvement, 1991.

Schaefer, C. E., and A. R. Eisen, eds. *Helping Parents Solve Their Children's Behavior Problems.* Northvale, N.J.: Jason Aronson, 1998.

Stern, D. N. *The Interpersonal World of the Infant.* New York: Basic Books, 1985.

Valsiner, J. *Culture and the Development of Children's Action.* New York: John Wiley and Sons, 1987.

Wierzbicka, A. "Does Language Reflect Culture? Evidence from Australian English." *Language in Society* 5(1986):349–74.

Winnicott, D. W. "The Theory of Parent-Infant Relationship." In *The Maturational Process and the Facilitating Environment,* 37–55. New York: International Universities Press, 1965.

Chapter 7:
An Integration of Cultures: The World from Kindergarten Through Junior High School

Baumrind, D. "Current Patterns of Parental Authority." *Developmental Psychology Monographs* 4, no. 1, pt. 2 (1971).

Berger, E. *Raising Children with Character—Parents, Trust, and the Development of Personal Integrity.* Northvale, N.J.: Jason Aronson, 1999.

Brooks R., and S. Goldstein. *Raising Resilient Children.* Lincolnwood, Ill.: Contemporary Books, 2001.

Covey, S. *Seven Habits of Highly Successful People.* New York: Simon and Schuster, 1989.

Gopnik, A., A. Meltzoff, and P. K. Kuhl. *The Scientist in the Crib: What Early Learning Tells Us About the Mind.* New York: Perennial, 1999.

Knight, G. P., M. K. Cota, and M. E. Bernal. "The Socialization of Cooperative, Competitive, and Individualistic Preferences Among Mexican American Children: The Mediating Role of Ethnic Identity." *Hispanic Journal of Behavioral Sciences* 15, no. 3 (1993):291–309.

Rutter, M. "School Influence on Children's Behavior and Development." *Pediatrics* 65 (1980):216.

Chapter 8:
The Culturally Diverse Adolescent: Turn the Stormy Years into Smooth Sailing

Barkley, B. H., and E. Salazar Mosher. 1995. "Sexuality and Hispanic Culture: Counseling with Children and Their Parents." *Journal of Sex Education and Therapy* 21 (1995):255–67.

Benson, E. "The Perils of Going Solo." *Monitor of Psychology* (November 2002): 25–27.

Bernal, M. and G. P. Knight. "Ethnic Identity of Latino Children." In *Psychological Interventions and Research with Latino Populations,* edited by J. G. Garcia and M. C. Zea, 15–38. Boston: Allyn and Bacon, 1997.

Best, D., and others. "Parent Interactions in France, Germany and Italy: The Effects of Gender and Culture." *Journal of Cross-Cultural Psychology* 25, no. 2 (1994):181–93.

Brown, B. B. "Peer Groups and Peer Cultures." In *At the Threshold: The Developing Adolescent,* edited by S. S. Feldman and G. R. Elliott, 171–96. Cambridge, Mass.: Harvard University Press, 1990.

Coleman, J. S. *The Adolescent Society: The Social Life of the Teenager and Its Impact on Education.* New York: Free Press, 1961.

Connell, J. P., and J. G. Wellborn. "Competence, Autonomy, and Relatedness: A Motivational Analysis of Self-System Processes." In *Self Processes and Development,* vol. 23, edited by M. R. Gunnar and L. A. Srouge, 43–77. Hillsdale, N.J.: Lawrence Erlbaum, 1991.

Marsh, H. W. "The Effects of Participation in Sport During the Last Two Years of High School." *Sociology of Sport Journal* 10 (1993): 18–43.

Martinez, I. Z. "¿Quien Soy? Who Am I? Identity Issues for Puerto Rican Adolescents." In *Race, Ethnicity, and Self: Identity in Multicultural Perspective,* edited by E. P. Salett and D. R. Koslow, 89–116. Washington, D.C.: National Multi-Cultural Institute, 1994.

Mehta, P. "The Emergency, Conflicts, and Integration of the Bicultural Self: Psychoanalysis of an Adolescent Daughter of South-Asian Immigrant Parents." In *The Colors of Childhood: Separation-Individuation Across Cultural, Racial and Ethnic Differences,* edited by S. Akhtar and S. Kramer. 129–68. Northvale, N.J.: Jason Aronson, 1998.

Okagaki, L., and D. K. Ethnic Moore. 2000. "Identity Beliefs of Young Adults and Their Parents in Families of Mexican Descent." *Hispanic Journal of Behavioral Science* 22, no. 2 (2000):139–62.

Phinney, J. S. "Ethnic Identity in Adolescents and Adults: Review of Research." In *Readings in Ethnic Psychology,* edited by P. B. Organista, K. M. Chun, and G. Marin, 73–99. New York: Routledge, 1998.

Phinney, J. S., B. T. Lochner, and R. Murphy. "Ethnic Identity Development and Psychological Adjustment in Adolescence." In *Ethnic Issues of Adolescent Mental Health,* edited by A. R. Stiffman and L. E. Davis, 53–73. Newbury Park, Calif.: Sage, 1991.

Shulman, S. "Close Relationships and Coping Behavior in Adolescence." *Journal of Adolescence* 16 (1993):267–83.

Chapter 9:
When the Latino Child Needs Professional Help

"Assuring Cultural Competence in Health Care: Recommendations for National Standards and an Outcomes-Focused Research Agency." *Federal Register* 65, no. 247 (22 December 2000): 80865–79. Available online at www.OMHRC.gov/CLAS.

Ben-Amos, B. "Depression and Conduct Disorders in Children and Adolescents: A Review of the Literature." *Bulletin of the Menninger Clinic* 56 (1992):188–208.

Benson, L. T., and T. E. Deeter. "Moderators of the Relation Between Stress and Depression in Adolescents." *The School Counselor* 39 (1992):189–94.

Blechman, E. A., and S. E. Culhane. "Aggressive, Depressive, and Prosocial Coping with Affective Challenges in Early Adolescence." *Journal of Early Adolescence* 13, no. 4 (1993):361–82.

Calderone, M. "Adolescent Sexuality: Elements and Genesis." *Pediatrics* 76(1985):699–703.

Cultural Competence Standards in Managed Care for Four Undeserved/Underrepresented Racial/Ethnic Groups. Final report from Working Groups on Cultural Competence in Managed Mental Health Care. Rockville, Md.: Center for Mental Health Services, 2000.

Dana, R. H. "Understanding Cultural Identity in Intervention and Assessment: Cultural Care for Multicultural Populations." In *Multicultural Aspects of Counseling Series,* vol. 9, 35–62. Thousand Oaks, Calif.: Sage Publications, 1998.

Ginorio, A. B., and others. "Psychological Issues for Latinas." In *Bringing Cultural Diversity to Feminist Psychology,* edited by H. Landrine. Washington, D.C.: American Psychological Association, 1995.

Griego, M. C., B. L. Bucks, S. S. Gilbert, and L. H. Kimberball. *Tortillitas para Mama and Other Nursery Rhymes Spanish and English.* Marso 7 C. Grieco, Betsy L. Bucks. New York: Henry Holt, 1981. Illustrated by Barbara Cooney.

Haffner, D. W. *Facing Facts: Sexual Health for America's Adolescents.* SIECUS report, 1995.

Jackson, V. H., and L. Suar and S. Gilbert and Laurel H. Kimball, Lopez, eds. *Cultural Competency in Managed Behavioral Healthcare.* Providence, R.I.: Manisses Communications Group, 2001.

Johnson-Powell, G., and J. Yamamoto, eds. *Transcultural Child Development.* New York: John Wiley and Sons, 1997.

Jouriles, E. N., L. J. Pfiffner, and K. D. O'Leary. "Marital Conflict, Parenting, and Toddler Conduct Problems." *Journal of Abnormal Child Psychology* 17 (1988):513–25.

Koss-Chioino, J. D. "Depression Among Puerto Rican Women: Culture, Etiology, and Diagnosis." *Hispanic Journal of Behavioral Sciences* 21, no. 3 (1999): 330–50.

Koss-Chioino, J. D., and L. A. Vargas, eds. *Working with Latino Youth (Culture, Development, and Context).* San Francisco: Jossey-Bass, 1999.

Leaper, C., and D. Valin. "Predictors of Mexican American Mothers' and Fathers' Attitudes Toward Gender Equality." *Hispanic Journal of Behavioral Sciences* 18, no. 3 (1996):343–55.

Luepnitz, D. B. *The Family Interpreted: Feminist Theory in Clinical Practice.* New York: Basic Books, 1988.

Maldonado-Duran, J. M., ed. *Infant and Toddler Mental Health: Models of Clinical*

Intervention with Infants and Their Families. Washington, D.C.: American Psychiatric Association, 2002.

Martinez, K. J. "Cultural Sensitivity in Family Therapy Gone Awry." *Hispanic Journal of Behavioral Sciences* 16, no 1 (1994):75–89.

Mental Health: Culture, Race, and Ethnicity Executive Summary. A Supplement to Mental Health: A Report of the Surgeon General. Washington, D.C.: Department of Health and Human Services, U.S. Health Service, 1999.

Portes, P. R., and M. F. Zady. "Self-Esteem in the Adaptation of Spanish-Speaking Adolescents: The Role of Immigration, Family Conflict and Depression." *Hispanic Journal of Behavioral Sciences* 24, no. 3 (2002):296–318.

Prout Thompson, H., and D. T. Brown, eds. *Counseling and Psychotherapy with Children and Adolescents: Theory and Practice for School and Clinical Settings,* 3rd edition. New York: John Wiley and Sons, 1999.

Saldaña, D. *Cultural Competency: A Practical Guide for Mental Health Service Providers.* Austin, Tex.: Hogg Foundation for Mental Health, the University of Texas at Austin, 2001.

Silver, L. B. *Attention-Deficit / Hyperactivity Disorder: A Clinical Guide to Diagnosis and Treatment for Health and Mental Health Professionals.* Washington, D.C.: American Psychiatric Press, 1999.

Schmitz, M. F., and M. Velez. "Latino Cultural Differences in Maternal Assessment of Attention Deficit/Hyperactivity Symptoms in Children." *Hispanic Journal of Behavioral Sciences* 25, no. 1 (2003):110–22.

Spreen, O., and E. Strauss. *A Compendium of Neuropsychological Tests: Administration, Norms and Commentary,* 2nd edition. New York: Oxford University Press, 1998.

Suzuki, L. A., P. J. Meller, and J. G. Pontertto, eds. *Handbook of Multicultural Assessment Clinical, Psychological, and Educational Applications.* San Francisco: Jossey-Bass, 1996.

Sue, D. W. "Multidimensional Facts of Cultural Competence." *Counseling Psychologists* 29, no. 6 (2001):790–821.

U.S. Department of Health and Human Services. *Mental Health: A Report of the Surgeon General–Executive Summary.* Rockville, Md.: National Institute of Health, 1999.

Vargas, L. A., and J. D. Koss-Chioino, eds. *Working with Culture: Psychotherapeutic Interventions with Ethnic Minority Children and Adolescents.* San Francisco: Jossey-Bass, 1992.

Vazquez, C. I. *Assessing Children Exposed to Lead in a Diverse Context.* King of Prussia, Pa.: Mealey Publications, 2002.

Vazquez, C. I., and L. Myers. "The Case of Alicia." *Journal of Infant, Child and Adolescent Psychotherapy* 2, no. 3 (2002): 121–30. New York: Other Press, 2002.

Velazquez, C., E. Saez Santiago, and J. Rosello. 1991. "Coping Strategies and Depression in Puerto Rican Adolescents: An Exploratory Study." *Cultural Diversity and Ethnic Minority Psychology* 6 (1999): 65–75.

Recommended Resources

Charles Kuralt's America, by Charles Kuralt. New York: Putnam, 1995. This is a fun book and useful for becoming familiar with some aspects of U.S. culture. Reading it feels similar to a visit to or a vacation in the United States.

Fiesta Femenina: Celebrating Women in Mexican Folktale, by Mary-Joan Gerson and Maya Christina Gonzalez. Barefoot Books, New York, 2001. A tribute to women in the Mexican culture.

Helping Parents, Youth, and Teachers Understand Medications for Behavioral and Emotional Problems, edited by Mina K. Dulcan and Claudia Lizaralde. A Resource Book of Medication Information Handouts Second Edition: APA Washington, D.C.: 2003. This is a very practical guide providing medication information for parents, youngsters, and teachers.

How to Lose All Your Friends, by Nancy Carlson. New York: Penguin, 1994. A humorous book that clearly points out what should not be done in order to keep your friends.

Las vacunas de mi bebe (My Baby's Immunization Book), produced by the National Alliance for Hispanic Health, Washington, D.C., 2003. This is a bilingual guide on immunization needs during baby's first year.

The Maria Paradox: How Latinas Can Merge Old World Traditions with New World Self-Esteem, by Rosa Maria Gil and Carmen Inoa Vazquez. New York: Penguin Putnam, 2001. This is a book that helps Latinos understand aspects of their culture that can create low self-esteem and acculturation stress. It tells the reader how to remedy these problems and how not to perpetuate them. This book has been translated into Spanish under the title *La paradoja de Maria.* New York: Random House en Español, 2002.

More Than Manners! Raising Today's Kids to Have Kind Manners and Good Hearts, by Letitia Baldrige, New York: Rawson Associates, 1997. A useful guide to teach good manners and compassion skills to your child.

National Hispanic Family Health Helpline, 1-866-783-2645/1-866-SU-FAMILIA (toll free). This is a resource center with information offered in English and Spanish into linkages where the family could be helped with their general health needs nationwide.

The New Latins, Fateful Change in South and Central America, by Georgie Anne Geyer. New York: Doubleday, 1970. A broad historical presentation of cultural changes in Latin America.

Picture Tales from Mexico, by Dan Storm and Mark Storm. Gulf Publishing, Houston 1995. Cultural stories easily understood.

The Shy Child: A Parent's Guide for Overcoming and Preventing Shyness from Infancy to Adulthood, by: Phillip Zimbardo and Shirley L. Radl. New York: Doubleday, 1982. A good guide to help children conquer shyness in its early stages.

Teaching Your Child the Language of Social Success, by Marshall P. Duke, Stephen Nowicki Jr., and Elisabeth A. Martin Atlanta, Ga.: Peachtree, 1996. This is a great book to help parents to teach nonverbal social skills to their children.

Together, by George Ella Lyon. New York: Orchard Books, 1989. This children's book illustrates the value of teamwork.

What to Do . . . When Kids Are Mean to Your Child, by Elin McCoy. Pleasantville, N.Y.: Reader's Digest Books, 1997. This book presents a series of useful tactics to help your child deal with bullies.

Bilingual Books for Children

The Bakery Lady (La señora de la panaderia), by Pat Mora and Pablo Torrecila. Houston, Tex.: Arte Público Press: Houston University Press, 2001.

Cinderella / Cenicienta, by Francesca Boada, et al. Chronicle, San Francisco, 2001.

Cucu: un cuento folkfloriko mexicano (Cuckoo: A Mexican Folktale) by Lois Ehlert and Gloria De Aragon Andujar. Harcourt, New York 2000.

Cuentos, an Anthology of Short Stories from Puerto Rico, edited and with a preface by Kal Wagenheim. New York: Schocken Books, 1978.

Goldilocks and the Three Bears (Ricitos de oro y los tres osos), by Marta, et al, Chronicle: San Francisco, 1998.

La llorona (The Weeping Woman), by Joe Hayes et al. Cinco Puntos, Texas, 1987.

Legend of Food Mountain (La montaña del alimento), by Harriet Rohmer and Rosalma Zubizarreta. Children Books Press, San Francisco, 1987.

Little Gold Star: A Spanish American Cinderella Tale, by Roberto D. San Souci and Sergio Martinez. New York: HarperCollins, 2000.

Momentos magicos (Magic Moments), by Olga Loya and Carmen Lizardi-Rivera. Little Rock: August House, 2001.

Puerto Rican Tales, Legends of Spanish Colonial Times, by Cayeano Coll y Toste. Translated and adapted by Jose Ramirez Rivera. Mayaguez, Puerto Rico, Ediciones Libero, 1977.

Tortillitas para Mama and Other Nursery Rhymes Spanish and English, selected and translated by Margot C. Griego, Besy L. Bucks, Sharon S. Gilbert, and Laurel H. Kimball. New York: Henry Holt, 1981. Nursery rhymes and lullabies from all over Latin America that have been passed on from generation to generation. Good for the preservation of culture and language.

In Spanish Only

Coleccion de estudios Puertorriqueños. San Juan, Puerto Rico: Industrias Grafica Pareja Barcelona, 1977.

Cuentos favoritos de Puerto Rico, by cuentos por David Garcia and Gus Anivitate. San Juan Puerto Rico Almanacs, 1992.

Cuentos Folkloricos de Puerto Rico, Quinta Edision recogidos y editados por Ricardo E. Alegria, 1977.

Juegos infantiles de Puerto Rico, by Calixta Velez Adorno. San Juan: Editorial de la universidad de Puerto Rico, 1991.

La noche que se cayo la luna: Mito Maya, by Pat Mora and Domi. Toronto: Groundwood Books, 2002.

Web Sites for Parents

www.SpanishToys.com

This site sells educational software in English and Spanish for ages 0 to adolescence.

www.caseyfamilyservices.org

This is a site with valuable information for parents, children of all ages, and professionals working with them. Parents can get help with foster care, adoption, and family issues. Children can learn how to play and get to know other children. Technical assistance is provided in how to find resources, and news that are relevant to Latino families.

www.saddonline.com/pdf/openinglines_print.pdf
> This brochure is designed to help parents talk to their adolescents about life decisions, peer pressure, and destructive behavior.

www.aacap.org/info_families/index.htm
> Facts for families from the American Academy of Child and Adolescent Psychiatry.

www.aboutourkids.org/mh/resources/index.html
> For parents seeking general and educational resources on child and adolescent mental health. Affiliated with the New York University Child Study Center.

FirstGov en Español

www.espanol.gov
> The government's new Spanish-language information web portal links visitors to the entire spectrum of Spanish-language Web sites and web pages available from federal and state governments.

education.indiana.edu/cas/adol/mental.html
> A collection of online resources for parents, educators, researchers, health practitioners, and teens regarding mental health risk factors for adolescents.

www.personal.psu.edu/faculty/n/x/nxd10/adolesce.htm
> An extensive guide for parents on adolescent developmental changes, transitions, and family relations. Includes a large subsection on psychosocial problems experienced by adolescents.

www.kidsource.com/LDA/adhd.html
> A guide for parents about attention deficit hyperactivity disorder (ADHD).

www.futureofchildren.org/usr_doc/vol9no2Art4done.pdf
> Guide to successful parenting in high-risk neighborhoods.

www.athealth.com/Consumer/newsletter/FPN_7_8.html
> Teens and mental health.

www.kidsource.com/kidsource/content4/fail.school.what.2.do.html
> Includes Anne S. Robertson's article "If an Adolescent Begins to Fail in School, What Can Parents and Teachers Do?"

parentingteens.miningco.com/blchat.htm
> Online chat room and support for parents of adolescents.

www.bpkids.org/community/supportgroups/local/
  Child and Adolescent Bipolar Foundation directory of local support groups for parents.

www.strugglingteens.com/cgi-bin/ultimatebb.cgi
  Online support group for parents with struggling teenagers.

www.strugglingteens.com/lr/New_York/
  New York resources.

www.parentsinc.org/support.html
  Very extensive database for parenting support and resources.

www.rcs.k12.va.us/csjh/parent.htm
  General database of links for parenting resources.

www.parentsoup.com/

www.parentsplace.com/
  Parenting resources and online articles.

Web Sites for Children

These Web sites offer resources and can be entertaining and educational. They are free.

www.brainpop.com

pbskids.org

www.monroe.lib.in.us/childrens/ninos.html
  This one is in Spanish.

www.nickjr.com

www.nick.com

www.disney.com

www.nationalgeographic.com/kids

www.sesameworkshop.org/

www.kidswb.com

www.yahooligans.com

www.ajkids.com/

school.discovery.com/students/index.html

Resources for Clinicians / Health Care Providers:

www.ama-assn.org/ama/pub/category/1981.html
American Medical Association Adolescent Health Resources.

www.casbrant.ca/family%20support%20services.htm
Parent Adolescent Conflict support group (PAC). Could serve as a useful resource/guide/model for group work.

www.crosshealth.com
Center for Cross-Cultural Health. This is a clearinghouse for information on training and research relating to the relevance of culture to health.

www.xculture.org
Cross-Cultural Health-Care Program. A national program that provides training on to the relevance of culture and language health care.

www.cooperativediscipline.com

Index